A book about British cultural identities raises a number of questions; Whose Britain? Whose culture? Whose identity? Do a majority of people in the UK think of themselves as being British anyway? This book analyses contemporary British 'cultural identity' in terms of the various and changing ways in which people who live in Britain position themselves and are positioned by their culture today. It has core chapters on seven intersecting areas: place and environment; education, work and leisure; gender, sex and the family; youth culture and age; class and politics; ethnicity and language; religion and heritage.

British Cultural Identities will be of particular use to overseas students of English language and culture. Each chapter is clearly structured around key themes, has a timeline of important dates, a list of recent British cultural examples – books, films, television programmes – recommended reading and a section of questions and exercises, carefully chosen by experienced teachers. It is illustrated with photographs and tables throughout.

Mike Storry is Senior Lecturer in English at Liverpool John Moores University. **Peter Childs** is Senior Lecturer in Literary Studies at Liverpool John Moores University.

ROUTLEDGE

LONDON AND NEW YORK

British Cultural Identities

- Edited by Mike Storry and
  Peter Childs

First published in 1997
by Routledge
11 New Fetter Lane,
London EC4P 4EE

Simultaneously published in the USA
and Canada
by Routledge
29 West 35th Street, New York
NY 10001

Typeset in Sabon and Futura by
Florencetype Ltd, Stoodleigh, Devon

Printed and bound in Great Britain by
Redwood Books,
Trowbridge, Wiltshire

*British Library Cataloguing in
Publication Data*
A catalogue record for this book is
available from the British Library

*Library of Congress Cataloging in
Publication Data*
British cultural identities / edited by
Mike Storry and Peter Childs.
    p.   cm.
Includes index.
    1. Great Britain – Social life and
customs – 20th century. 2. Popular
culture – Great Britain – History –
20th century. 3. Great Britain –
Civilization – 20th century.
4. National characteristics, British.
I. Storry, Mike, 1943– .
II. Childs, Peter. 1962– .
DA589.4.B74   1996   96-22720
941.082–dc20

ISBN 0–415–13698–9 (hbk)

ISBN 0–415–13699–7 (pbk)

To Anne and Helen

Contents

1 Place and environment: nation and region 43

2 Education, work and leisure 83

Conclusion: present and future Britain

Illustrations

Tables

Contributors

Peter Childs is Senior Lecturer in Literary Studies at Liverpool John Moores University. He is currently editing, with Mike Storry, *The Routledge Encyclopaedia of Contemporary British Culture*.

Jo Croft, is Lecturer in Literary Studies at Liverpool John Moores University.

Edmund Cusick is Lecturer in Imaginative Writing at Liverpool John Moores University.

Ross Dawson is Lecturer in British and American Studies at Liverpool John Moores University.

Roberta Garrett is Lecturer in Literature and Cultural Studies at the University of East London.

Frank McDonough is Senior Lecturer in Modern Political History at Liverpool John Moores University.

Gerry Smyth is Lecturer in Cultural History at Liverpool John Moores University.

Mike Storry is Senior Lecturer in English at Liverpool John Moores University. He has taught widely in Britain and abroad in North and South America and in the Middle East. He has published fiction and poetry and is currently editing, with Peter Childs, *The Routledge Encyclopaedia of Contemporary British Culture*.

Preface

A book about British cultural identities immediately raises a number of questions: Whose Britain? Whose culture? Whose identity? Do a majority of people in the UK still think of themselves in terms of being British anyway?

British Cultural Identities is aimed at people who are interested in these questions. It approaches the idea of British identities through contemporary practices and activities: not through institutions or economics, but through culture. The book is written in a clear, accessible style, making it especially useful to the student or visitor who wishes to be introduced to the variety of British experiences at the millennium. A different kind of book about the contemporary UK, one which looks at Britain in not sociological or historical but cultural terms, it will be of particular use to overseas students of English language and British culture. Each chapter is clearly structured around key themes, has a timeline of important dates, a list of recent cultural examples, and a section of questions and exercises. The book is illustrated throughout with photographs and tables.

All the contributors to this collection outline the plurality of identities found across the UK at the end of the twentieth century.

The essays start from the belief that identities are the names we give to the different ways we all are placed by, and place ourselves within, our culture. The contributors have been asked to think of culture as the practices and beliefs which people encounter and share – events, ideas and images that shape their lives everywhere and every day. The introductory chapter deals with tradition: the cultural baggage that the term 'British' brings with it. Where appropriate it pinpoints moments in which recent culture has changed direction, but you will find most information about contemporary British identities in the chapters that follow. These cover seven intersecting areas: gender, sex and the family; religion and heritage; place and environment; youth culture and age; class and politics; language and ethnicity, and education, work and leisure.

The chapters are structured in the following way. At the beginning of each you will find a timeline, usually of the most significant dates in the chapter's discussion. There follows a structured discussion of ways in which that area can be understood in different ways and at different levels. The conclusions drawn by each chapter are open because all the contributors believe there are many Britains and many British cultural identities. You will find many opinions expressed, but all the writers aim to outline debates, key moments and speculative questions rather than to supply definitive answers. Consequently, our collective aim is to explore the face of British culture today, while at the same time suggesting that it will have changed tomorrow.

At the end of each chapter you will find some questions and exercises, preliminary answers to most of which will be contained in the text. However, the questions are designed to stimulate your thoughts and to encourage you to go to libraries where necessary to conduct research or to test our suggestions by looking at the numerous cultural products that supply a way into an understanding of cultural identity in contemporary Britain. The further reading shows you where to go next for more detailed study. Some of the books suggested will also have been chosen because they cover aspects which the chapter itself has not been able to treat at length. In an introductory text such as this we cannot cover the minutiae of all social, ethnic or even regional groupings; however, we intend to sensitise readers, particularly those outside the UK, to Britain's cultural diversity. Finally, we have also listed at the end of each chapter some recent cultural examples which we feel will give you an insight into concerns, anxieties and tensions within contemporary British culture. These novels, films and television programmes are of great importance because they provide specific British cultural representations relevant to the issues under discussion. We have chosen to select books, films and programmes which are either both current and particularly helpful or widely available in print or on video.

Acknowledgements

The photographs in *British Cultural Identities* were reproduced by kind permission of Peter Childs, Helen Cooke, Edmund Cusick, Lisa McRory and Mike Storry. Figure 0.5 is reproduced by courtesy of the *Guardian*, Figure 4.2 by courtesy of Giles Andreae, Figure 4.3 by courtesy of *Just Seventeen*, Figure 6.1 by courtesy of Routledge and Figure 6.3 by courtesy of Routledge.

FIGURE 0.1 Shopping day in Chester: a contemporary scene amid Tudor-style buildings

Introduction: the ghost of Britain past

■ Mike Storry and
Peter Childs

1

Timeline

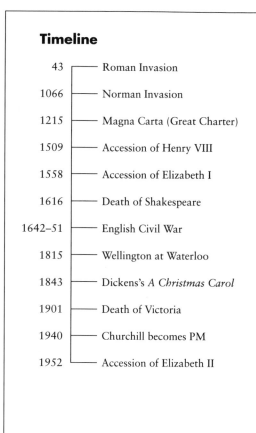

43	Roman Invasion
1066	Norman Invasion
1215	Magna Carta (Great Charter)
1509	Accession of Henry VIII
1558	Accession of Elizabeth I
1616	Death of Shakespeare
1642–51	English Civil War
1815	Wellington at Waterloo
1843	Dickens's *A Christmas Carol*
1901	Death of Victoria
1940	Churchill becomes PM
1952	Accession of Elizabeth II

Introduction

THIS IS A BOOK ABOUT CONTEMPORARY Britain and British people. On the one hand, Britain is a country with defined boundaries, a recognisable landscape, a long and contentious history, and a position in the various international economic, social and political league tables. On the other hand, British people are much harder to describe. To begin with, some British people do not live in Britain. Furthermore, many people living in Britain do not think of themselves as British. Nationality is a matter of allegiance and cultural affiliation. Some people say that your nationality is indicated by where you choose to live or by the team you support at sports events; others say that it is a question of whom you would fight for. It has also been argued that nationality is no longer a powerful force in Britain, that it is simply a matter of circumstance, and that today it is far less significant than local or global identities: relatives, friends and communities are more important to us and so is transnational culture, such that notions of national identity are both less persuasive and more contentious than they used to be. Above all, nationality is a question of identity and so is crossed by other kinds of identity, such as ethnicity, gender, sexuality, religion, age and occupation.

This book aims to outline some of the kinds of identity found at those intersections in Britain at the end of the twentieth century. As such, it will implicitly question the difference between British cultural identities and cultural identities in Britain. Forty-five years ago, T.S. Eliot famously said that 'culture' was something which included 'all the characteristic activities and interests of a people'. He thought that this meant for England: 'Derby Day, Henley Regatta, Cowes, the twelfth of August, a cup final, the dog races, the pin table, the dart board, Wensleydale cheese, boiled cabbage cut into sections, beetroot in vinegar, nineteenth-century Gothic churches, and the music of Elgar.' Forty-five years on, conceptions of English and British identity have changed enormously; for example, few people would attribute any significance to 'the twelfth of August', the opening day of the grouse-shooting season.

Contemporary British culture is a mixture of all the cultures of the past that people are influenced by – but certain figures, symbols and narratives exercise particularly strong control over the ways we imagine ourselves to be and to have been. In Dickens's *A Christmas Carol*, Scrooge is shown pleasant and unpleasant edited highlights of his life by 'The Ghost of Christmas Past'. Scrooge recognises the person he has been and understands how events have made him the way he is now, but, after seeing different glimpses of the present and the possible future, he rejoices in the fact that the life to come is only strongly influenced, not determined, by history. Dickens's ghost story, itself a potent narrative in British mythology, is a fable about self-knowledge; it concerns the importance of understanding the individual's responsibility within society and the significance of history in shaping identity. The figures and images which have shaped ideas of a British identity are the subject of this introductory chapter.

At sporting occasions like the Football Association Cup Final, annual events like the Last Night of the Proms, commemorations like the fiftieth anniversary of Victory in Europe (VE) day and public celebrations like a royal wedding, there are signs of a traditional grass-roots national culture, often accompanied by patriotic singing and flag-waving. But, in common with much of the world, Britain's major unifying influence today is the mass media (not all of which is British), and a connection between all of the above events is that they will be shown on television, broadcast on the radio and reported in the press. A popular magazine like *Hello!*, a peak-time television show like *Blind Date* and a competition like the National Lottery lead to much discussion throughout the country. A recent book on Britain has claimed that 'Television is clearly the basic component of the national culture', but, at Eliot's time of writing, it was not even a part of

TABLE 0.1 Subjects of conversation between friends and family (1991)

Subject	Percentage of people who ever talk about subject
Advertising	2
Big business	2
Bringing up children	26
Clothes and fashion	19
Cost of living	43
Education	20
Gardening	16
Law and order	16
Neighbours or workmates	21
Politicians	8
Religion	6
Sport	25
Television programmes	48
The government	19
Trade unions	1
Newspaper articles	19
Health and welfare services	18
Unemployment	16
Personal health	21
None of above/don't know	3

Source: TOM Attitudes to Advertising Survey

any local culture. According to a 'TOM Attitudes to Advertising Survey', the topics of conversation which people say they have are listed in Table 0.1 revealing that television, the cost of living, children and sport are arguably the most important subjects to most people.

Regional and local identities are extremely strong in Britain and the diversity of beliefs, practices, loyalties and accents is immense. In George Bernard Shaw's 1913 play, *Pygmalion*, the language specialist Professor Higgins believes he can, just by the sound of an accent, pinpoint any Londoner's place of birth to within two or three streets. Shaw's play was written at the start of the twentieth century when people were far less likely to move from one area to another, and yet distinct local identities continue to be easily discernible in the 1990s. The UK of the 1990s is enhanced by diversity and difference, and for this reason we must use the plural form and talk of 'identities'; throughout the remainder of this book you will find the multiplicity of British identities emphasised more than traditional single images.

What is the connection between national culture and identity? While culture may be seen as 'lived experience', shared by a community of people who relate to one another through common interests and influences, identity is concerned with how people see themselves, or are seen, in relation to others: as northerners or southerners, football or rugby enthusiasts, opera or blues fans and so on. In short, identity is perhaps two things: who people take themselves to be, and who others take them to be. As the debate in Britain over whether or not to issue national identity cards has shown, questions of national and personal identity are highly complex and contentious.

At one end of the scale, identity is partly prescribed by what the state considers to be important about people: their physical characteristics, place of birth and area of employment; for example, these details are usually included on passports. At the other end of the scale, many people might consider the most important aspects of their identity to be their emotional life, their aspirations, their sporting or intellectual achievements and so on. So we are also inevitably left with *versions* of identity rather than a single definitive identity for each individual. In May 1995, mocking the official view that 'identity' can be contained on a card, a *Guardian* columnist, Armando Iannucci suggested that children, who have developing personalities, will have to swap identity cards in the playground as they change week by week! This kind of identity expressed on an official form, similar to a gas bill or a birth certificate, is actually understood not as someone's identity but as their 'i.d.' – a kind of statistical identification far removed from any individual's notion of who they are. The lead character in a cult British television series of the 1960s, *The Prisoner*, famously used to say every week, 'I am not a number, I am a free man'. The British response to 'identity cards' has been similar.

We also have to consider individuals within their community and country. Collective identity and action can supply a focus for pride in a society and enable people to improve their material conditions; however, from another perspective, both patriotism and nationalism are uneasy notions in today's post-colonial world. As long ago as the eighteenth century, patriotism was described by Dr Johnson, compiler of the first authoritative English dictionary, as 'the last refuge of a scoundrel'. Similarly, nationalism, which has been linked so closely to imperialism and the resistance to it over the last two centuries, has unhealthy implications for those who define themselves as 'British'. Since the Second World War, most countries within the British Empire have, through revolt or reform, gained independence. Over the last few decades, perceptions of British expansion overseas have also undergone many changes as the traditional and dominant paternalist attitude adopted by Britain towards its colonies has been reviewed as not benevolence but condescension overlaying economic greed. Comparisons between European fascism and imperialism, reflections on England's hold on Ireland, the only European country to have both an early and a late colonial experience, and disapproval of the blustering patriotism associated with the Falklands War of 1981, have all added to a British reappraisal of its empire.

A famous English novel, *The Go-Between* by L.P. Hartley, begins with the sentence, 'The past is a foreign country: they do things differently there.' No matter what view is held of the past, history provides many indications of how a country such as Britain has traditionally been perceived and the extent to which its people, often accused of living in the past, used to do things differently. In the remainder of this chapter we will look at how British history can serve as a starting point for the idea of a national cultural identity, partly framed by the perception of Britain as seen from overseas. In the next section we will consider past images of England and the UK, and in subsequent sections we will look at the icons and representatives which have portrayed or stood for this traditional Britain.

Traditional Britain

A simple overview of Britain might show the country as passing through a number of historical periods. It might identify them as 'rural', 'industrial', 'imperial', 'suburban', 'tourist', 'multicultural', and these would follow one another in time. In fact, phases such as these are not just in sequence but overlap, though many people like to see Britain as still stuck in one of these stages.

Below there is some historical background information to contrast with the contemporary pictures drawn in the chapters which follow. We will look at those formations of national identity that have held sway and attempted to define and delimit British culture. As we do so, we would like you to remember that 'Britishness' was never a straightforward, uncomplicated term: it is and long has been a diverse, highly contested and varied label. For example, while the monarchy has provided the most famous icons of national identity, for the last millennium English monarchs have usually been foreign. England's figureheads have been Normans (Plantagenets), Welsh (Tudors), Scots (Stuarts), Dutch (House of Orange) and German (Hanoverians).

The British Isles were invaded by the Romans in the first century AD and settled by Germanic tribes, the Jutes, Angles and Saxons, in the fifth century. (Some of the days of the week are still named after their gods: Tiw, god of War (Tuesday), Woden

(Wednesday), Thor (Thursday), Frig, wife of Woden (Friday).) These tribes drove the native Celts to the western parts of Scotland, and to Cornwall, Ireland and Wales.

Life was precarious and, littered throughout the British countryside, there continue to be preserved places of refuge where early Britons could go when being attacked by neighbouring tribes and invaders. This accounts for the large number of Iron Age forts, medieval castles, Piel towers and fortified manor houses which still exist in Britain today. Britain's last invasion from overseas was in 1066, when it was conquered by Normans, Viking settlers from northern France. There followed many centuries of European rivalry and imperial expansion.

The most widely taught period of history in British schools is that of the Tudors (1485–1603). This is often taken to be the start of modern England because it included the revival of classical learning, the discovery of the Americas, the introduction of the printing press, the beginnings of the Church of England and notable military successes such as the defeat of the Spanish Armada. Its figureheads are Henry VIII, Elizabeth I, Walter Raleigh and Shakespeare: four figures who to this day appear at the head of a schoolchild's list of important Britons. Thomas Carlyle, perhaps the greatest influence on British cultural thought in the nineteenth century, referred to the Elizabethan era as 'that strange outbudding of our whole English existence' in his influential book *On Heroes, Hero-Worship and the Heroic in History*. The continued prevalence of this view can be seen in the enormously successful recent comedy television series *Blackadder*, which focused on one character's exploits in four stages of Britain's history: medieval Britain, the reign of Elizabeth I, the period of revolutions and Romanticism at the threshold of the nineteenth century and the First World War. Between the Middle Ages and the nineteenth century only the Tudor period was represented, omitting such key events as the English Civil War, the Glorious Revolution of 1688 and the American War of Independence. Literature courses at most levels taught across the country similarly devote little study to the period between Shakespeare and the Romantic poets. This ties in with popular notions of what it means to be 'British' and 'English', conceptions of a national identity which are often rooted in Tudor times but which are more recent in their articulation: products of the eighteenth and particularly the nineteenth centuries. Nationalism is a comparatively new invention, issuing from the formation of modern nation states since such eighteenth-century social upheavals as the French Revolution, and developing from, but often not superseding, identities based on such ideas as tribe, region, religion and class or 'blood'.

Broadly speaking, Britain has a historical heritage of whose gross features everyone is aware: colonised by the Romans; last invaded in 1066; a rural country up until the eighteenth century; unprecedented industrial growth in the nineteenth century; the largest empire the world has known; postwar decolonisation, and economic decline. Its features have left a notion of Britishness, and more particularly Englishness, that remains today for many people and is prevalent in sections of the media: an island people 'unconquered' for centuries; a largely rural community but the first industrial nation; an imperial leader; a land divided between north and south or London and the rest of the country, and a class-ridden society, from the monarchy through the aristocracy and the middle classes to the working classes. Consequently, in the rest of this section we will look at three traditional ways of understanding Britishness and Englishness, beginning with an examination of the English countryside, followed by consideration of the national character, and then of the British as an island race.

The English countryside

With the growth of London and the Industrial Revolution of the early nineteenth century, experience for many people in Britain became *urban* as the country entered its accelerated phase of trade and manufacturing. Factories and mills created areas of dense population such as Manchester, Newcastle, Leeds and Sheffield, as people migrated there to work in the textiles, steel and shipbuilding industries. This was the time in which Britain saw itself as 'the workshop of the world', and the stamp 'Made in England' became famous across the globe. (Its supposed mark of authenticity and quality is still found, for example, in Elton John's record of the same name in 1995.) However, throughout the Industrial Revolution the underlying idea of Britain didn't change in many respects: it was still thought to be essentially a rural place even for those in the towns and cities, and the wealthiest would build houses away from the metropolitan centres. A 'countryside' outlook can still be found in the 1930s (when rambling and Sunday walks became national occupations). For example, J.B. Priestley in his famous *English Journey* dealt with three types of community: the metropolitan, the urban and the rural. He said England was at heart a rural country which had a countryside ethos. The implication of his model was that the cities, at a time of mass unemployment, financial crisis and widespread poverty, should become more like the rest of Britain. If cities were unsavoury places it was because they had lost touch with the innocence of their agricultural roots.

One can argue that Britain still has the self-image of the rural society (evident in magazines such as *Ideal Home* and *Country Life*). This belief lies behind immensely popular television series like the crime-solving *Inspector Morse* (set in Oxford) or, similarly, *Bergerac* (set in the Channel Islands, which are crown dependencies off Normandy) in which the city or island community must be restored week by week to a 'rightful' tranquillity. Many of the novels of Agatha Christie, Britain's most famous crime writer, are also principally about this restoration of a natural and lawful order of countryside innocence, and many of the most popular novels in British libraries, by writers such as Catherine Cookson, indulge in a supposedly simpler past before the fast-paced and largely irreligious city living of the twentieth century.

A further example of the persisting non-metropolitan idea of Britain is the number of bookmaker's shops, principally for betting on horse races, of which there are many thousands in Britain – a retail industry unknown for example in Germany. Here the country world comes to every British high street. Horse racing, a countryside pastime known as 'the sport of kings', enters the urban environment and links the 'rural' aristocracy and monarchy with the 'urban' working class. So, in many ways, contemporary Britain harks back to a localised and harmonious but essentially feudal way of life.

In city pubs people drink the beer of the countryside. You can sit in London's Leicester Square and drink a bottle of Black Sheep ale or a pint of Shepherd Neame bitter and eat a shepherd's pie or a ploughman's lunch (a recent invention containing bread, cheese, pickles and salad). Why not a coal-miner's pie or a fireman's lunch? Because these industrial or urban professions do not hold the appeal of the jobs of the rural past and they cannot be romanticised in the same way. Such attitudes are by no means recent. There is a long tradition in Britain of 'pastoral' poetry, where sophisticated court dwellers pretended to be simple country folk and wrote one another charming poems of seduction – such as Christopher Marlowe's *The Passionate Shepherd to his Love* ('Come live with me and be my love'). A similar Elizabethan nostalgia for a golden Arcadia is found in Shakespeare's *As You Like It* and *A Midsummer Night's Dream*.

A final indication of the appeal of the concept of rural England is that when builders sell houses which they have erected on agricultural land, the new roads are frequently named after what they have just destroyed (for example, Four Acre Coppice, Oak Tree Farm Crescent). Former habitats of birds are commemorated as Wild Herons Way or Tern Crescent. As we will see in Chapter 1, many people want the difficult combination of urban society and jobs with rural peace and beauty.

Character and accent

Perhaps the most enduring of all the tokens of a dominant traditional Britishness is the 'English character' itself, which is often easily encapsulated and parodied in terms of its accent(s).

Both accent and dialect are very important in British life and the public acceptability of regional accents has changed with a shift of focus from the capital to the regions. The English upper-class accent, as spoken by the Queen or announcers on the BBC

World Service, was accepted until twenty years ago as the guide to correct pronunciation for Britain as a whole. Those with regional accents from the industrialised areas of the Midlands and north, let alone Northern Ireland, were not encouraged to apply for jobs as announcers on radio or TV. At one time it was thought that one of the effects of a national radio network would be to eradicate regional accents. This hasn't happened. Instead, regional accents have persisted and in areas of the media there is currently a move to employ more broadcasters and performers with northern or Scottish accents. On television, Terry Christian, host of recent late night cult show *The Word*, has an aggressively Mancunian accent, while the 1960s pop singer turned presenter Cilla Black has steadily broadened her Liverpudlian accent during her appearances over the last thirty years.

There are wide variations in the use of dialect or slang across Britain. In terms of actual vocabulary, there are words throughout the UK whose use is purely local. For example, the word 'bleb', meaning blemish, though listed in dictionaries is only widely known in the north-east. There are regional variations in the words which children use when playing games at school. In the playground chase of 'tick' or 'tag', when children are 'safe' (for example, by standing on a stone), on Merseyside they will shout 'barley', while in London they will say 'home'. Because of greater mass communications and some increased mobility, regional variations are more commonly understood throughout Britain than they were in previously 'closed' communities.

Accents and expressions are diverse; but what about the myth of the British 'character'? British people are often considered to be withdrawn and reserved. Stereotypically, they are supposed to undertake their tasks out of duty, without thought of personal gain. Their aims are understated. They are meant to display characteristic if often deceptive British reserve, as in the stylised images of Hugh Grant or Diana, Princess of Wales (or if not, then an ostentatious class consciousness, as in the flamboyant manners of Noel Coward or the aggressive campaigning of miners' leader Arthur Scargill). Such reserve is not considered to be confined to well-bred members of the upper classes. A typical story is that when the British soldiers, called 'Tommies' after a music-hall character, finally met the Russian counterparts with whom they had been fighting against the Germans in the First World War, they approached them and shook hands. In a moment of national elation, this would appear to be a very understated action and is taken to indicate two things: first, at that time people practised British reserve, and second, it was displayed not just by those with stiff upper lips, (the upper classes), but equally by working people.

Across all classes, few people shake hands. Handshaking on meeting is today a more widespread practice in much of the rest of the world than it is in the UK. British people do shake hands, not routinely on meeting one another, but usually when they are introduced to a stranger, whether at home or at work. While it is still often taken as a sign of reserve, such behaviour is equally part of a rejection and dislike of formality. This image of reserve also contrasts with that other enduring stereotype of British behaviour: eccentricity. This supposedly denotes a kind of outrageousness that has spanned upper-class eccentrics, the Masons, 1960s fashions, punk rock, and the contemporary artist Damien Hirst or violinist Nigel Kennedy. Such images are most often reproduced in today's consumer culture as part of an idiosyncratic Britishness that can be successfully marketed and sold abroad. On the one hand, Rowan Atkinson's TV mime character 'Mr Bean' exemplifies this kind of awkward, inquisitive but repressed and easily embarrassed national stereotype. On the other hand, Richard O'Brien's camp reworking of the Gothic Frankenstein story in *The Rocky Horror Show* illustrates well the idea of British peculiarities and closeted sexual flamboyance.

An island race

> The Germans live in Germany;
> The Romans live in Rome;
> The Turkeys live in Turkey;
> But the English live at home.
>
> (J.H. Goring, The Ballad of Lake Laloo
and other Rhymes, 1909)

Britain has been described as 'a tight little right little island'. In the early nineteenth century, the poet Byron wrote of 'the bitter effects of staying at home with all the narrow prejudices of an islander'. Later in the century, critics of Victorian overseas expansion were known as 'Little Englanders', but the term has since come to mean isolationists who believe in the concept 'my country right or wrong'. Winston Churchill, Britain's Prime Minister during the Second World War, used the title 'The Island Race' at the start of his history of the English-speaking people. He also recalls in his memoirs the time he was scheduled in his early career to meet Hitler, until the latter discovered that Churchill had written articles condemning his Jewish policy. The Germans quietly cancelled the meeting and Churchill's conclusion was: 'Thus Hitler missed the only chance he ever had of meeting me.'

A story which further illustrates British insularity refers to a news announcement which said, 'There has been a persistent fog at London airport during the weekend, and the Continent has been cut off for twenty-four hours.' That this parochialism is still common in the UK despite increased air travel and the Channel Tunnel is illustrated by the politician Norman Lamont who described a united Europe as 'yesterday's idea', and by the fact that according to a recent MORI survey 48 per cent of Britons do not see themselves as Europeans but as having more in common with Americans.

The British have been considered as an island race partly because of their imperialism, cultural isolation and international policies. Some of this attitude can be explained historically, and it has been argued that, compared with most European countries, Britain's ethnic mix did not greatly change between the eleventh and the twentieth centuries, although there were, for example, some 20,000 Africans working in London in the mid-1700s and many Jewish settlers arrived at the end of the nineteenth century, while the oldest Chinese community in Europe was established in Liverpool as early as the eighteenth century. There have also been considerable influences from overseas, particularly from the exploitations of empire, the architectural signs of which are still visible everywhere. For instance, Liverpool, one of England's largest ports, and at one time Europe's major slave port, has sheaves of corn moulded into cornices over the entrances to several of its buildings and the heads of African elephants and slaves carved in the stone of its town hall, while London has a Great Pagoda at Kew Gardens and Moorish designs incorporated into many of its theatres and museums. Up until the early twentieth century there were Egyptian halls in Piccadilly, while Bolton in Lancashire has Indian motifs cast into the stalls in its market-place and the oriental style of Brighton's Royal Pavilion makes it the town's most famous building. In addition, Britain's language and food reflect its colonial history in India ('verandah' and 'bungalow', tea and pepper), while its Regency furniture adopted Egyptian designs, and Chinese Willow Patterns on its crockery have long been popular.

Today, Britain has sizeable populations from, for instance, Australia, Bangladesh, Poland, Vietnam and West Africa. Particularly in the 1950s there was substantial immigration to Britain from the Caribbean. The other notable influx in the 1950s and 1960s was from both India and Pakistan (and later from Uganda, when Asians were expelled by Idi Amin). Both of these waves were encouraged by the British authorities and by employers such as London Transport, who set up recruitment offices in Jamaica and elsewhere.

Although quite small in relation to Britain's population as a whole (about 4 per cent), these communities form the majority of certain areas of towns like Bradford and Leicester. The cultural tension for children in these communities is often greater than for their parents, who came to Britain with more positive expectations and often did not intend to settle. The second generation in these communities has had a profound effect on British culture but has also been faced with divided loyalties and opposing cultural pulls. Many young people have adopted (and modified) British pop music and clothes and, particularly in the case of Asian communities, have developed more casual attitudes than their parents towards the opposite sex (a lesser but similar observation of the generation gap could also be made of white British people).

In 1992, a British Social Attitudes survey suggested that for the first time people in Britain were more optimistic than pessimistic about race relations. Facets of the island outlook of the majority population remain, however. Statistics also show that black people are still discriminated against at immigration control, in the courts, by the police, at work and on the streets. Unlike the American 'melting pot' approach, where minority ethnicities have been encouraged to blend into and become assimilated by the local culture, migrants to Britain have often not sought, nor been encouraged, to integrate into British society. In many respects this means that they have been excluded from the dominant culture. Moreover, if ethnic groups do not have a high profile on TV, the major national cultural arena, they are also marginalised in social and political debates. This awareness is behind Welsh-speakers, claims of the importance to their cultural survival of the TV channel S4C and also partly behind other communities' insistence on better and greater representation on television. The remit of Channel 4, the most recent national television station, was framed explicitly to address such issues and is perceived by some to only show 'minority' programmes while others feel it does not have enough cultural variety and still caters for an ethnic mainstream.

The political Left has tended to welcome the influx of other nationals. For the Right, immigration remains a heated subject, hedged around by xenophobic myths and racist fears, based on the idea of 'our' beautiful island filling up with foreign nationals. For example, the Conservative MP Winston Churchill said in a speech at Bolton in May 1993 that 'Immigration has to be halted to defend the British way of life'. Contrary to the belief of many, it is a fact that more individuals have left Britain each year since 1964 than have entered. Furthermore, white immigration from countries such as Canada, New Zealand and Australia far outnumbers that from countries such as India, Bangladesh, Ceylon and Jamaica.

Recent debates have added extra significance to the versions of Britishness outlined in this section. On the one hand, some influential critics such as Stuart Hall have begun to explore seriously the possibility of 'New ethnicities' that are black and British – thus redefining old notions of British identity. On the other hand, social commentators such as John Solomos have warned that a new right-wing conception of England as 'the island race', separate from Europe and distinct from minority ethnicities within the UK, is emerging once more.

National identities

Throughout this book we look at practices, artefacts, rituals, languages, customs and environments – shaping forces of *cultural* identity. However, national identity is often also embodied in public figures. The British image has been described repeatedly in terms of certain strong individuals who stand for single aspects of Britain. This doesn't just apply to stock Shakespearean characters like Falstaff, or Henry Fielding's Parson Adams, or Dickens's Mr Pickwick or Sarah Gamp. It applies to single strong figures who somehow stand for or represent the nation as it has been seen at particular moments. British stereotypes have been created or reinforced by figures with whom you may be familiar from history, politics, sport or films. For example, the following is a list of symbolic individuals who have all been thought to be quintessentially British: Florence Nightingale and the Queen Mother (sturdy, supportive English womanhood), Winston Churchill and Lord Kitchener ('boys of the bulldog breed', from a popular Victorian music-hall song called 'Sons of the Sea, All British Born'), W.G. Grace and Bobby Charlton (gentlemanly sportsmen) and David Niven, Joyce Grenfell or Margot Fonteyn (the well-mannered, charming English performer). Particularly in fiction there are numerous strong characters in whom British readers are invited to invest their hopes and values. These are figures entrusted with fighting for the country (Biggles), or unravelling a mystery (Miss Marple or Sherlock Holmes), exploring the world (Allan Quartermaine in *King Solomon's Mines*), unmasking spies (Richard Hannay in *The Thirty-nine Steps*), redressing social and financial injustice (Robin Hood) or saving

Britain, if not the world, from an evil mastermind (James Bond). These are idealised figures who express strong patriotic beliefs but, unlike the icons we will be looking at in this section, do not *personify* the country.

In the section that follows, we will look at a number of figures who offer alternative representative forms of British identity: Britannia, Albion, John Bull, and the heroes of Arthurian mythology and other folk stories. These are foils against which we would like you to try your own views about Britain and the British: we hope you will register the obvious disparity between appearance and reality, and that these images are not just part of history. They are powerful ideological images which are routinely used to exercise power in contemporary Britain.

Britannia or Albion

An important cultural and symbolic figure is Britannia, a personification of the country with the name by which the Romans called the area of the islands they controlled – roughly equivalent to modern England and Wales (the islands were only named 'Britannia' because Claudius Caesar wrongly thought that the Britanni, a Gaulish tribe from near Boulogne in northern France, had colonised them). Britannia was a mythical figure who came to represent Britain, and she appears throughout the imperial period in engravings and paintings as the woman, often seated in a Roman chariot and accompanied by a lion, spear and shield, to whom colonised peoples make their offerings and show their subservience. A current use of Britannia herself as an offering to represent all-conquering achievement is given to winners of the annual Brit awards or 'Brits'. These are the 'Oscars' of the British music industry, and the trophy is a small Britannia figure complete with helmet, trident and shield. There are numerous other cultural reminders of this heritage, such as the many 'Britannia' inns and the Britannia bridge that spans the Menai straits (between the island of Anglesey and the Welsh mainland). The royal yacht is called Britannia, as is Britain's foremost holiday airline, while the oldest and largest English language encyclopaedia, first produced

ISLE COLLEGE
RESOURCES CENTRE

in Scotland but now with a heavy American slant, is called the *Encyclopaedia Britannica*, and is still widely advertised and sold at shopping complexes throughout the country. From the UK's Roman heritage, Britannia has therefore come to be associated to various degrees with learning, royalty, seafaring and the figure of the woman warrior. The importance of the first three is perhaps easy to understand from British history, but what of the last?

This idea of the strong, noble queen is easily invoked in Britain. Ancient familiar images are those of the warrior Boadicea who led the Iceni tribe against the Romans, the Celtic Fairy Queen Mab, and Cathleen, the personification of Ireland. Queen Elizabeth I and Queen Victoria have both repeatedly been represented as such a defiant queen, leader of a warlike nation, for purposes of imperial rule as well as national pride. Margaret Thatcher's success and charisma were arguably associated with this symbolism which is encapsulated in the song 'Rule, Britannia':

> When Britain first, at heaven's command,
> Arose from out the azure main,
> This was the charter of the land,
> And guardian angels sung this strain:
> 'Rule, Britannia, rule the waves;
> Britons never will be slaves'.
> (Alfred: A Masque (1740),
James Thomson)

These words were put to music by Dr Thomas Arne and became a focus for patriotism when sung annually at the Last Night of the Proms summer concert at the Royal Albert Hall. Today, alongside 'Rule, Britannia', will be sung William Blake's famous extract from *Milton* which envisages a new *Jerusalem* in 'England's green and pleasant land' (significantly, when Enoch Powell appealed to the British people in his argument against immigration he used this phrase). The other key song is Arthur Benson's imperial anthem 'Land of Hope and Glory':

FIGURE 0.2 The Britannia Building Society showing the figure of Britannia (top left)

Land of Hope and Glory, Mother of the Free,
How shall we extol thee, who are born of thee?
Wider still and wider shall thy bounds be set;
God who made thee mighty, make thee mightier yet.
                    ('Song' from *Pomp and Circumstance*,
                                        Edward Elgar)

These songs are an expression of group identity and display an element lying beneath the surface of some British attitudes. The noble, seafaring, essentially pastoral island is still the nostalgic

FIGURE 0.3   Morris dancers

image of Britain retained by some sections of the national press. It is also part of a traditional view which equates British identity with rural pastimes such as morris dancing, clay pigeon shooting, beagling, fox-hunting and other country sports (Figure 0.3). Additionally, it is tied up with the idea of Britain as a strong military and naval power: the conquering island race we considered earlier.

In his 1941 essay, 'England, Your England', George Orwell wrote that the diversity of British identity was illustrated 'by the fact that we call our islands by no less than six different names, England, Britain, Great Britain, the British Isles, the United Kingdom and, in very exalted moments, Albion'. Particularly since the French revolution, Britain has been seen from abroad as *Albion perfide*, 'treacherous Albion'. The name Albion, or Albany, may have been the Celtic name for Britain, but the term itself probably comes from the imposing white (Latin: *albus*) cliffs of Dover, facing France.

In Britain, Albion is associated with English aspirations and high sentiment. Thus, in 1579, Sir Francis Drake intended that California would be called 'New Albion' when he annexed it. Two hundred years later, however, at the time of the French Revolution, William Blake, always critical of the English establishment, wrote 'Visions of the Daughters of Albion'. This poem of 1793 speaks out for the rights of women and against contemporary injustices such as slavery. It begins: 'Enslav'd the Daughters of Albion weep: a trembling lamentation.'

Together, the images of Britannia and Albion provide us with contrasting representations of Britain. Opposed to the image of the free imperial island and the strong female leader are Blake's less patriotic but more historically accurate references to Britain's involvement in the slave trade and its restriction of women's rights.

John Bull

A third image of cultural and symbolic significance is that of John Bull: a stubborn, kindly and affable but blustering farmer. In his 'Notes on the English Character' of 1920, the novelist E.M. Forster agreed with the Blakean view of Britain as Albion and thought that the British national characteristic was hypocrisy (followed by caution, integrity, solidity, efficiency and lack of imagination). He also thought the English were 'essentially middle class' and afraid to have an emotional life:

> The national figure of England is Mr Bull with his top hat, his comfortable clothes, his substantial stomach, and his substantial balance at the bank. Saint George may caper on banners and in the speeches of Parliament, but it is John Bull who delivers the goods.

John Bull is the commercial, roast-beef eating, imperialist Englishman. He is like a bulldog in appearance and temperament. He was established (though not invented) in 1712 by Dr John Arbuthnot and appears in numerous cartoons as the ebullient, well-fed, matter-of-fact, robust Englishman, dressed in a gaudy waistcoat and a jaunty hat. He is invoked at times of national crisis, especially war, and incorporates the England which attracts hostility abroad. He is the narrowly patriotic Englishman who robustly defends his country's 'rights'. A figure from the mid-eighteenth century who resembles John Bull in many ways is the original Toby Jug decoration, the famous drinking-pot celebrating the traditional British male social space, the pub.

The Irish dramatist George Bernard Shaw wrote his play *John Bull's Other Island* in 1904 at the request of W.B. Yeats, for the Irish Literary Theatre. An historical allegory, it depicts the gradual takeover of an Irishman's life by an honest but ambitious Englishman. Two years later, the name John Bull was adopted as the title for a staunch British weekly, and so we can say that the enduring name is associated with Britain's belief in its world purpose and its paternalistic attitude towards its empire. In the 1950s the word 'jumble' was a mocking contraction of 'John Bull' used by West Africans to describe a white English person. The figure is rarely seen today but the idea of a strong, free and independent country remains a dominant if outdated image of Britain and its role in the world; it surfaces in such assertions of national importance and identity as accompanied the Falklands War in 1981, when Prime Minister Thatcher asserted that Britain was still the country which had built an Empire and that its people still had the same 'sterling qualities'.

Arthur and mythology

In this third section, we will look at one further example of Britishness in modern popular mythology: Arthurian Britain. For many people, England is the land of St George and King Alfred, of Avalon, the Knights of the Round Table and King Arthur at Camelot. Historically, Arthur is a shadowy figure, a Dark Age chieftain possibly created in the Middle Ages by the Welsh historian Geoffrey of Monmouth but enshrined in literary history by Sir Thomas Malory in the fifteenth century in his *Morte D'Arthur*. The legend of Excalibur, the 'sword in the stone' that Walt Disney turned into a cartoon film, is famous here: 'Whoso pulleth out this sword of this stone and anvil is rightwise king born of all England' (*Morte D'Arthur*, Book 1, Chapter 4). It is possible to think of such stories of the past as remote but, while they exert less direct influence than, for example, television programmes they in fact touch British lives every day. For example, the company running Britain's national lottery, which sells many millions of tickets every week, is called Camelot – to suggest a fundamental Britishness, a traditional identity and a sense of equality and fairness. Its three lottery machines are called Lancelot, Guinevere and Arthur.

In Victorian times the idea of Arthur's Britain was fostered by many romantic painters such as James Archer, and by writers such as Lord Tennyson, whose sequence of Arthurian poems 'Idylls of the King' was a bestseller. During a period when Britain was heavily industrialising, this invented nostalgia enabled people to hark back to a mythical England of chivalry and romance. Even today, areas like Glastonbury, where Arthur and Guinevere's bones were supposedly found in the twelfth century, are places of pilgrimage for those who seek an Arthurian version of Britain. Mythology and paganism still have a strong hold on the public imagination: the standing stones at Stonehenge on Salisbury Plain (where Thomas Hardy's *Tess of the D'Urbevilles* ends) have been recently roped off because they were a site of congregation for thousands of people on midsummer's night and other occasions.

National representatives

As we have seen from the examples above, cultural identity is in many ways about representation. This should be understood in two ways. On the one hand there is representation as portrayal, and in this section we will look briefly at some figures, or 'heroes', who have come to represent Britishness (and who are honoured in pub names across the country, from the 'Duke of Wellington' to 'The Nelson' (Figure 0.4). On the other hand, there is political and constitutional representation, where an individual or group

FIGURE 0.4 Lord Nelson, hero of the Battle of Trafalgar, honoured in a pub name

'stands in' or speaks for the whole country. So, before looking at some national heroes, we will begin this section by considering two groups of people who 'represent' Britain in both these ways – the monarchy and statespeople: those who act as figureheads, but who also wield constitutional power in the name of the nation.

Royalty

Perhaps the most enduring stereotypical version of Britain is that which revolves around the idea of monarchy. As an institution, the British monarchy has been both popular and deeply unpopular at different times in its history. It has often survived because of its links outside the country, though most tourists would think of it as quintessentially British. The idea that the Royal Family should be an ideal British family, associated with morals rather than power, only really stems from Victoria and Albert, whose 'family values' of a close, loving relationship and a harmonious household have been held up by the press as a standard by which the current royals are found wanting.

Earlier in this chapter, we mentioned the traditions of the countryside persisting into the present. The monarchy also stresses its rural and regional base. An example would be the ceremonial investiture in Caernarfon Castle of Prince Charles as Prince of Wales – a traditional and not a legal title of the sovereign's eldest son. This might be seen as a move to consolidate and symbolise the power of the monarchy in Wales, but a less obvious and more revealing indicator of the rural basis of monarchy is supplied by the widespread locations of the royal estates of Balmoral, Sandringham and Blenheim. Further, individual members of the Royal Family are officially known by their titles, such as the Duke of Edinburgh, Duchess of York and Duke of Gloucester, to indicate their regional responsibilities. At national sporting occasions, such as Wimbledon or the FA Cup Final, royalty are still invited to present the trophies in the way that barons and earls presided at jousts or tournaments in medieval times, where they would honour the knight-champion. Today, in Britain as elsewhere, this

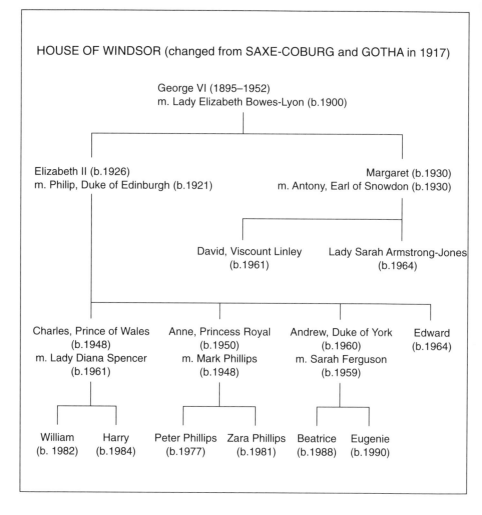

HOUSE OF WINDSOR (changed from SAXE-COBURG and GOTHA in 1917)

George VI (1895–1952)
m. Lady Elizabeth Bowes-Lyon (b.1900)

Elizabeth II (b.1926)
m. Philip, Duke of Edinburgh (b.1921)

Margaret (b.1930)
m. Antony, Earl of Snowdon (b.1930)

David, Viscount Linley
(b.1961)

Lady Sarah Armstrong-Jones
(b.1964)

Charles, Prince of Wales
(b.1948)
m. Lady Diana Spencer
(b.1961)

Anne, Princess Royal
(b.1950)
m. Mark Phillips
(b.1948)

Andrew, Duke of York
(b.1960)
m. Sarah Ferguson
(b.1959)

Edward
(b.1964)

William
(b. 1982)

Harry
(b.1984)

Peter Phillips
(b.1977)

Zara Phillips
(b.1981)

Beatrice
(b.1988)

Eugenie
(b.1990)

function has been copied and localised, so, while the Queen or Diana, Princess of Wales will still bless ships and officially inaugurate important public buildings, local television and sports stars will 'open' supermarkets and fêtes.

This awe and respect for monarchy sits alongside a disapproval of the Royal Family's social privilege and national income, particularly with regard to those members who are 'paid for' by the public but who are not in the Queen's immediate family. In the early 1970s, the American magazine *Time* described Captain Mark Phillips, Princess Anne's then future husband, as a 'semi-articulate dragoon' at a time when few English people, let alone the media, would use such insulting language about someone who was about to marry into the Royal Family. Nowadays, even quality newspapers in Britain are openly critical of the behaviour of younger members of the Royal Family and there is no doubt that in some quarters the popularity of the whole family has been eroded despite the fact that the Queen herself is one of those monarchs like Henry VIII, Elizabeth I and Victoria, who have enjoyed broad popular support. However, as a focus for media fascination, the Royal Family remains unequalled: both the tabloids and the broadsheets regularly feature them in their main items, and there are several royal documentaries made for television each year. Many of these are celebrations or exposés, but others raise the perennial question of whether the monarchy, through tourism, brings in more money to the country than it spends. The ancient view that the state of the nation is embodied in the monarchy persists today in a weaker version that requires both propriety and profit as well as manners from its figureheads.

Politicians

The second group of people who both wielded power and 'stood for' Britain are those politicians who have governed the nation at times of great success or crisis, such as William Pitt, Gladstone and Churchill. The traditional portrayal of these people in the UK has been as natural political leaders dedicated to public service. Because of Britain's strong class system, which we will be examining in Chapter 5, it is easy to see this misplaced faith in *noblesse oblige* as veneration for the aristocracy, based on the principle that only the rich can be relied upon to perform public service because they are beyond the reach of corruption. Partly for the same reason, the right-wing Conservative Party, traditionally the party of the aristocracy and commercial enterprise, has been portrayed as the 'natural' party of government. Elements of the idea that running the country was a part-time job, almost akin to running an estate, persisted until the mid-nineteenth century, when Britain had its first 'professional' prime minister, Disraeli. Hitherto the office had been a part-time duty rather than a full-time occupation. It was not formally recognised as a government position until the twentieth century.

The emphasis on 'great statespeople' signalled a British distrust of professionalism and ambition. In the past, what had been wanted in Britain was 'effortless superiority' (the motto of a college of Oxford University). The 'gifted amateur', someone who struggled against all the odds but who was content to be placed second, supposedly appealed more to the British public, who traditionally favoured the underdog at sporting events and were told by the aristocracy that 'playing' was more important than winning: the public school ethos.

However, that tradition may have been largely broken by the advent of Thatcherism. A grocer's daughter, who rose to political prominence through determination and ambition, Margaret Thatcher's assertiveness and qualities of leadership gained her an international reputation such that she now spends much of her time on the lecture circuit, particularly in the United States where her championing of market forces, com-mercial materialism and self-help philosophies sells well. Though against the image of a reserved Britishness, Thatcherism has become synonymous with a revived kind of proud but narrow British 'island race' nationalism centred on the individual – Thatcher once said that there is 'no such thing as society'. By contrast, Tony Blair's 'New' Labour Party promotes a 'stakeholder' society in which everyone is supposed to be involved, benefited and committed.

Heroes

In addition to monarchy and certain politicians, a number of enduring cultural figures – or heroes – have been dominant in British society as role models and objects for national pride. Bertolt Brecht once said: 'Pity the land which has no heroes. No! Pity the land that has need of heroes.' It is perhaps to be regretted therefore that Britain's cultural commentators for at least the last two centuries seem to have felt a need to promote hero-worship. We will refer here to a number of representative heroes from Britain's past whose influence is still found in politicians' speeches, advertising, the media, classrooms and the tourist trade.

Shakespeare is Britain's most famous writer. However, in many ways, 'Shakespeare' is not so much an individual dramatist as a commercial enterprise that generates T-shirts, playing cards, tea-cloths and pints of beer as well as plays and poetry. Also, despite the populism of the original Globe Theatre in London, his work has come to represent élite cultural values. The role of organisations such as the British Council is to bring this type of high art to the rest of the world, perpetuating the image of present-day Britain as in many ways a version of its past. The individual in the street in Britain may have no relation to the culture of this manufactured Shakespearean England, but the Shakespeare industry, as it now is, forms part of a cluster of 'heritage tours': to Anne Hathaway's cottage in Stratford-upon-Avon, to Wordsworth's Dove Cottage in Grasmere, to the Brontës' parsonage in Haworth.

Other figures who have long stood at the centre of groups or fan clubs but around whom there is now a newly minted heritage industry are Dickens in London, Grace Darling on the Farne Islands, Francis Drake in Plymouth and Jane Austen at Bath. The representation of many of these figures stresses the island or nautical aspect of Britain and such insularity has been credited with forming the warlike character of British imperialists from Walter Raleigh to Winston Churchill. British political and military history provides many other cult figures. For example, the Duke of Wellington's defeat of Napoleon in Belgium in 1815

has been engrained in the public consciousness (the equal presence of Belgian, Dutch and German forces is not widely known
in Britain) and the expression 'met his Waterloo' has entered into
the British vocabulary along with the saying that 'the battle of
Waterloo was won on the playing fields of Eton' – a reference to
the importance of public school sports in developing discipline,
strategic thinking and a competitive spirit. The list of figures
who are celebrated through stamps, banknotes, statues and
speeches is too long for us to mention more than a few of
the most prominent: Clive of India, Lord Kitchener, Lawrence of
Arabia, Lord Mountbatten, Montgomery of Alamein and Admiral
Nelson. In almost every case, these explorers and military
men will be referred to as part of some appeal to national
responsibility, destiny or identity (against them, figures from an
alternative pantheon, such as the women's rights campaigners
Mary Wollstonecraft and Emmeline Pankhurst, will be promoted
by others).

Lacking a contemporary mythical personification as strong
as Uncle Sam, old-fashioned British rhetoric is liable to turn to
these historical figures when rallying people in the name of the
nation. Most of them, of course, will alienate or offend many of
today's British population, who do not feel they have a positive
association with such people – consequently, more sensitive politicians will avoid celebrating such figures. Virginia Woolf said in
1938 that women were excluded from Britishness, and many
others, from gay, youth or black communities feel the same way
today. It is ironic that the only English person whose name is
given to a much-loved national annual event is a would-be regi-
cide or king-killer: Guy Fawkes, who tried to blow up the Palace
of Westminster in 1605. Across the country on 5 November, there
are public and private bonfire nights when fireworks are lit and
a life-sized effigy or 'Guy' is thrown on to a pyre. Children will
be seen for weeks beforehand, accompanied by figures made from
stuffed shirts and trousers, asking passers by for a 'penny for the
guy' so that they can buy fireworks.

Such festivities and figures as bonfire night and Guy Fawkes,
as well as the other people and events we have discussed in this

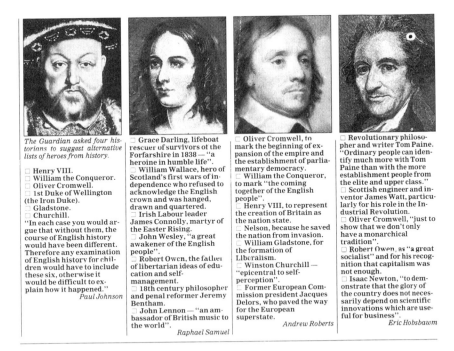

The Guardian asked four historians to suggest alternative lists of heroes from history.

☐ Henry VIII.
☐ William the Conqueror.
☐ Oliver Cromwell.
☐ 1st Duke of Wellington (the Iron Duke).
☐ Gladstone.
☐ Churchill.
"In each case you would argue that without them, the course of English history would have been different. Therefore any examination of English history for children would have to include these six, otherwise it would be difficult to explain how it happened."
Paul Johnson

☐ Grace Darling, lifeboat rescuer of survivors of the Forfarshire in 1838 — "a heroine in humble life".
☐ William Wallace, hero of Scotland's first wars of independence who refused to acknowledge the English crown and was hanged, drawn and quartered.
☐ Irish Labour leader James Connolly, martyr of the Easter Rising.
☐ John Wesley, "a great awakener of the English people".
☐ Robert Owen, the father of libertarian ideas of education and self-management.
☐ 18th century philosopher and penal reformer Jeremy Bentham.
☐ John Lennon — "an ambassador of British music to the world".
Raphael Samuel

☐ Oliver Cromwell, to mark the beginning of expansion of the empire and the establishment of parliamentary democracy.
☐ William the Conqueror, to mark "the coming together of the English people".
☐ Henry VIII, to represent the creation of Britain as the nation state.
☐ Nelson, because he saved the nation from invasion.
☐ William Gladstone, for the formation of Liberalism.
☐ Winston Churchill — "epicentral to self-perception".
☐ Former European Commission president Jacques Delors, who paved the way for the European superstate.
Andrew Roberts

☐ Revolutionary philosopher and writer Tom Paine. "Ordinary people can identify much more with Tom Paine than with the more establishment people from the elite and upper class."
☐ Scottish engineer and inventor James Watt, particularly for his role in the Industrial Revolution.
☐ Oliver Cromwell, "just to show that we don't only have a monarchical tradition".
☐ Robert Owen, as "a great socialist" and for his recognition that capitalism was not enough.
☐ Isaac Newton, "to demonstrate that the glory of the country does not necessarily depend on scientific innovations which are useful for business".
Eric Hobsbawm

FIGURE 0.5 The 'kings and dates' sense of history under attack *(Reproduced by permission of the* Guardian*)*

chapter, form the popular mythology of Britishness, the ghost of Britain past that many would prefer to exorcise, or cast out, but which still haunts many other people's notions of British identity. In 1995 there was a call, by government ministers and others, for British heroes to be systematically taught in history classes at school, precisely to instil a sense of national cultural identity. We reproduce an article about this here (Figure 0.5), but in the remainder of this book, we will be concentrating not on these national representatives but on the ways in which a wide spectrum of different British people see themselves and on the importance they attach to the cultural influences by which *they* have been moulded.

Conclusion

Obviously the above is not an exhaustive list of characters and characteristics in the formation of a dominant national cultural identity, but it gives an idea of the way in which Britain has traditionally been seen. Today, these aspects do not carry anywhere near as much weight as they did only fifty years ago, and there is much current debate about the kind of Britain that will emerge in the twenty-first century, and the problems attendant upon putting forward any coherent notion of 'Britishness' given the variety of people who now live in the United Kingdom. Even within organisations such as the National Trust there is discussion about whether to preserve in aspic the many British stately homes and gardens, or whether it would be better to modernise and update 'our heritage' by preserving elements across the range of British culture, including mines, textile mills and wartime bunkers. Others see British culture (rather than heritage) as being in a constant process of evolution and being far more about the present than the past.

Many tourists, for example, are attracted to Britain for alternatives to its traditional culture of castles, cathedrals and village greens, described elsewhere as 'Theme Park Britain'. Those alternatives include such events as the Reading Music Festival, the Notting Hill Carnival and the Edinburgh Festival Fringe – events which serve as magnets for tourists and also as a focus for local counter-culture.

In the remainder of this book, we will be exploring some of the legacies of and the alternatives to traditional conceptions of Britain. It will be important to keep in focus the historical images of Britain outlined in this introduction, because they do continue to impinge upon the present, but they should be continually questioned by an awareness of contemporary people, alternative cultural practices and other versions of history. Whereas in the United States society is constituted by ethnic and cultural diversity, in the United Kingdom, many argue, there continues to be a desire for 'monoculturalism': an attempt to ignore difference in favour of a dominant idea of 'Britishness'.

At bottom, the aim of this book is therefore to broaden out notions of British identity from a narrow base to a mixture of cultural plurality and multiple identities.

EXERCISES

1   How important do you think mythology and folklore are to a 'sense of identity'? From the descriptions in this chapter, and from your own knowledge, what common images of England and of Britain have you noticed, and what characteristics do you think they represent?

2   In Chapter 1, you will find it suggested that the British, and the English in particular, are being presented in a certain way in Hollywood in the 1990s. Before you read this however, we would like you to consider the following question.

   ■   Thinking of the American films you have seen, how many English actors can you remember? Have they usually played English characters? How have the English been stereotyped by Hollywood in the past?

   ■   In terms of recent Hollywood films, James Bond is perhaps the most famous English character (first played by Sean Connery, a Scot). What other similar larger-than-life images of British people has Hollywood produced? How many of these originated in British novels?

   ■   Does Hollywood portray British women differently from British men (you might think of Deborah Kerr, Joan Collins, Glenda Jackson, Julie Andrews, Emma Thompson, or even the Americans Katherine Hepburn in *The African Queen* and Bette Davis in *The Virgin Queen*)?

3   How important do you think wider geographical perspectives, such as those offered by Europe or the Commonwealth, are to understanding British identity? How is national culture altered by these larger communities? Can you name fifteen countries that are in the Commonwealth, and can you list them by (a) size of population? (b) year of Independence?

4   British daily national newspapers are extremely varied, from the tabloid press to the broadsheets, and so are their readerships. A long-standing characterisation of newspapers categorises them in terms of the people who buy them. Listed below are the newspapers and the descriptions of their readers: can you match the one with the other?

■   *The Times*; *Daily Mail*; *Sun*; *Financial Times*; *Guardian*; *Daily Telegraph*; *Daily Mirror*; *Morning Star*
■   Read by the people who own the country.
      Read by the people who think they run the country.
      Read by the people who think they ought to run the country.
      Read by the people who do run the country.
      Read by the wives of the men who run the country.
      Read by people who don't care who runs the country.
      Read by those who think the country should be run by another country.
      Read by those who think the country is being run by another country.

5   In this chapter we have looked at traditional British identities. What do you know of the following people and characters who have become important or comic

cultural figures to the British: Lady Godiva, Henry VIII, Queen Guinevere, Dickens's Mr Podsnap, Shakespeare's Falstaff, Biggles, Bulldog Drummond, Robert the Bruce, Lord Nelson, Lawrence of Arabia, Clive of India, and Bunyan's Christian? What are the problems with continuing to advance these characters as icons of Britishness?

6   How important do you think it is to consider language when describing other people? For example, the word 'immigrant' has not been used in this chapter but you will come across it elsewhere in this book because it is the common term used by most British people to describe others who have come to settle in the UK. By contrast, the British abroad are almost never regarded (by the British) as 'immigrants' in other communities or even as 'emigrants' from Britain. They are more often called 'expats' (short for expatriates). Why do you think this is?

READING

Gascoigne, Bamber. *Encyclopedia of Britain*, revised edition, Macmillan, 1994.
Impressive reference work, meticulously researched, which contains an A to Z guide to almost every aspect of British culture, from pre-Roman times to the present.

Porter, Roy. *Myths of the English*, Blackwell, 1993.
Careful analysis of aspects of Britishness from cricket to the British 'bobby'.

Room, Adrian. *An A to Z of British Life*, OUP, 1992.
Handbook containing a lot of information on background

detail to British culture, history, idiosyncrasies and 'institutions' such as Ascot, Henley and Glyndebourne.

Samuel, Raphael. (ed.) *Patriotism*, 3 vols, Routledge, 1989. Detailed examination of kinds of British identity in terms of history, gender, race, politics, cultural icons and much more.

CULTURAL EXAMPLES

■ *Films*

Brief Encounter (1945) dir. David Lean
Mid-twentieth century. Noel Coward's play about repressed middle-class English passion.

Chariots of Fire (1981) dir. Hugh Hudson
Early twentieth century. Famous Oscar-winning film about a Scottish missionary and a Jewish undergraduate at Cambridge running in the 1924 Olympics. Films of E.M. Forster's novels are other examples: *Maurice*, *Howards End*, *A Room With A View*, *Where Angels Fear to Tread* and *A Passage to India*.

Henry V (1989) dir. Kenneth Branagh
Tudor England. Latest film of Shakespeare's most pro-English play, with comic relief and small roles set aside for the Welsh, Scottish, Irish and French.

Sense and Sensibility (1996) dir. Ang Lee
Regency England. Most successful recent award-winning film of a Jane Austen novel to hit the screens. Adapted by Emma Thompson.

Tess (1979) dir. Roman Polanski
Nineteenth century. Loving evocation of the English rural way of life and countryside, filmed in France with a German playing Hardy's heroine. (It is worth comparing this with earlier versions of nineteenth-century classics, such as *Far From the Madding Crowd*, *Jane Eyre*, *Great Expectations*, *Oliver Twist* and *Wuthering Heights*)

■ *Books*

Henry Fielding, *Tom Jones* (1749)
One of the first highly praised English novels, this is a comic story of an orphan's adventures and travels across the English countryside and aristocracy.

Elizabeth Gaskell, *North and South* (1855)
Class conflict and labour relations in industrial Manchester.

George Orwell, *The Road to Wigan Pier* (1937)
An ex-Eton boy travels up north to report on the working classes for the Left Book Club.

H.G. Wells, *Tono-Bungay* (1909)
Analysis of the 'condition of England' through country houses, patent medicines, romance, business enterprises, sea adventures and London's urban sprawl.

■ *Television programmes*

Antiques Roadshow
Experts tour Britain's old cities and towns so that the middle classes can empty their attics of heirlooms and be amazed at the price they would fetch at auction.

The Jewel in the Crown
The British being terribly 'English' in India between 1942 and 1947. Drama of colonial relations under the Raj interspersed with clips from wartime newsreels.

Middlemarch
The BBC's version of George Eliot's text: the book most often cited as the greatest English novel.

Poldark
Repeated in 1996 on cable and satellite station UK Gold, this serial from the 1970s was voted the programme viewers most wished to see broadcast again. From Winston Graham's novels, it is a story of love and betrayal in an eighteenth-century Cornish mining community centring on the passion between Ross Poldark and the strong-willed, flame-haired Demelza.

Pride and Prejudice
Yet another extremely popular Jane Austen blockbuster in 1995.

FIGURE 1.1 Map of the British Isles showing location of counties, cities, towns and village discussed in this chapter

Chapter 1

Place and environment: nation and region

■ Peter Childs

Timeline

1536	England and Wales joined
1707	Act of Union for England and Scotland
1801	Ireland incorporated
1922	Independence of Southern Ireland
1931	Commonwealth officially formed
1972	Direct rule imposed on Northern Ireland
1973	UK joins EEC
1974/5	Redrawing of county boundaries
1979	Devolution referenda
1994	Eurotunnel opened

Introduction

G REAT BRITAIN, BY WHICH PEOPLE usually mean the United Kingdom, comprises the countries England, Wales, Scotland and Northern Ireland. On the one hand, these four countries have become part of one nation over the last five hundred years: Wales was linked with England in 1536; an Act of Union joined the crowns of England and Scotland in 1707; Ireland was incorporated in a Union lasting from 1801 to 1921, when all but Northern Ireland gained independence (taking effect in 1922). On the other hand, as European history repeatedly demonstrates, political union is not cultural union, and it has often been maintained that Scotland and Wales should have devolution, a transfer of power from the government in Westminster to a regional assembly. However, when a referendum was held in March 1979, the vast majority of Welsh voters did not want devolution and while a little over half of the Scottish did, only one-third of the eligible population voted. By contrast, Northern Ireland had self-rule in most governmental areas except foreign affairs and defence prior to 1972, at which date direct rule from London was reintroduced following increased sectarian violence.

When situating British identity in terms of place, we should both turn to smaller geographical units, such as the ancient counties whose boundaries were contentiously redrawn in 1974, and look to the larger outside world. In recent years Britishness has often been defined in relation to the Continent as European political and physical links have become stronger: in 1973 the UK joined the European Community (now European Union) and in 1994 the Channel Tunnel was opened, providing a rail connection from England to France. From another perspective, their eventful history means that British people have ties throughout the world, particularly with those fifty-one countries who in 1994

TABLE 1.1   Resident populations of UK countries
(1981 and 1994)

	1981 ('000s)	1994 ('000s)
England	46,821	48,707
Scotland	5,180	5,132
Wales	2,813	2,913
Northern Ireland	1,538	1,642
Total UK population (rounded)	56,352	58,395

Sources: OPCS and General Register Offices

were still members of the Commonwealth of Nations, a loose association of independent countries formerly of the British Empire. In between all these geographical and political groupings there has arisen not just a few but a multitude of British cultures and identities.

To give an initial outline of the UK in terms of place, we can begin by looking at three aspects: size, population and people. The United Kingdom, roughly the same size as Romania, Laos or Oregon, has a land area of just over 93 m^3 (241,000 km^3), a little over half of which is in England. This is one reason why England is sometimes mistaken abroad for Britain, but a stronger factor is the relatively large size of England's population – an imbalance that allows it to dominate the union by, for example, beaming its television programmes to the rest of the nation. In 1994, the fairly stable UK population stood at nearly 58.5 million people.

In terms of culture, the figures in Table 1.1 can be misleading. On the one hand, strength of cultural identity does not increase with size of population – indeed, many would argue that the opposite is more likely to be the case. It is therefore not surprising that to confuse Britain with England is akin to treachery in Wales, Scotland and Northern Ireland. History provides ancient reasons for this vehemence of feeling: England is named after the Angles, a tribe which invaded Britain's south-east coast from northern Europe in the fifth century and, with other conquering tribes such as the Saxons, drove the older inhabitants, the Celts, to the west. Celtic influence is still present in Ireland, Scotland, Wales and Cornwall, and this ethnic difference remains one basis on which England, of the UK's four countries, is sometimes considered to have the least in common with the others. On the other hand, the breakdown into English, Welsh, Scottish and Irish histories can also be misleading when it comes to contemporary cultural identity. The domestic histories of these four countries do not adequately represent the people of the UK today because Britain now has a richer mix of ethnicities than those associated with the ancient Anglo-Saxon or Celt. Over the last century and before, the Empire has led to the arrival in Britain of many people from the Caribbean, the Indian subcontinent and Africa, such that, for example, the number of British people of Asian descent is now greater than the population of Northern Ireland. Similarly, refugees from Bangladesh and Uganda, as well as communities uprooted from Cyprus, Vietnam and China, have added to the different cultural identities found in Britain. In 1991, the number of people who classified themselves as members of an ethnic minority stood at roughly 3 million – about half of whom were born in Britain. Again, while this book deals with people within the UK, there are strong British identities to be found in, for example, Hong Kong, a British crown colony up to 1997, the Falkland Islands, over which Britain fought with Argentina in 1982, and the vast Commonwealth of Nations. Thus, while this chapter will focus on places within the UK, the cultural life of British people is both always in flux and much wider than these geographical boundaries suggest.

Nation

The British mainland, separated from the European continent by the English channel, is the eighth largest island in the world. Its inhabitants are an island people, and their attitude towards the rest of the world is sometimes said to reflect this.

While the Commonwealth offers many indications of the cultural and ethnic influences on modern Britain, and is at the same time a sign of the UK's international links and imperial past, it is Europe's economic policies, legal dictates and bureaucracy that are increasingly forcing the British to reconsider their identity. For some people, 'Brussels' has become a major opponent, in the face of whose recommendations and legislation they are trying to assert a national culture that they feel is coming under attack. Alongside genuine fears such as a loss of local languages, there has also arisen a mythology of European Union policies: rumours maintaining that traditional British foods, such as dairy milk chocolate, crisps, fish and chips and Cornish ice-cream are under serious threat because of EU standardisation. Through appeals to such recognisable staples of national heritage, a powerful resistance to the EU has been built up, but other voices maintain that Britain's political, economic and legislative future has to lie within a united Europe. Consequently, the split over the EU within the Conservative Party has constituted the government's major policy stumbling-block for the last decade. While the majority of British people are happy in principle to participate in an economic union they are also defensive of their distinctive traditions and their cultural separation from other European countries: in other words, of their identity.

An article in the *Sunday Times* on 5 February 1995 was entitled 'Disunited We Stand'. It maintained that while each of Britain's four countries has a strong identity and inspires patriotic loyalties, there is no 'British' identity as such. The article noted that a 1994 survey revealed that 75 per cent of people 'north of the border' would call themselves Scottish and not British. Furthermore, the large national and private organisations, such as British Rail, British Telecom, British Petroleum and the British Broadcasting Corporation, all known by their initials, are either decentralising, breaking up for privatisation or turning into multinationals. The 'British' element is redundant, the article argued, and the United Kingdom is only England with other countries attached in the same way that the Soviet Union now appears to much of the outside world to have been just Russia with other communities uneasily tied to it. Such a view has made British studies courses often turn to a 'four nations' approach.

Country

To illustrate some traditional ways in which the countries of the British Isles have developed separate cultural identities, we can begin with examples of their various images and emblems. England's patron saint is the probably fictional St George, a knight who slew a fire-breathing dragon in medieval English mythology. St George's Cross is the name of the English flag, which depicts a red cross on a white background – and English teams still play rugby and football predominantly in white. The English emblem has been the rose since the War of the Roses in the fifteenth century, when the House of Lancaster, whose symbol is a red rose, fought for the English Crown against the House of York, whose symbol is a white rose. More recently, as a symbol of both tradition and socialism, the red rose has been adopted as its emblem by the Labour Party. Red is also the colour of Wales, whose mascot since 1801 has, interestingly, been the red Welsh dragon, which is the central figure on the country's flag. The patron saint of Wales is a sixth-century monk called St David, and his day, 1 March, is regarded as the country's unofficial public holiday. Wales's twin emblems are the leek and the daffodil.

Intranational rivalry is suggested by two other adopted animals: the warring lion (England) and the unicorn (Scotland). Since James VI of Scotland became James I of England in 1603, these animals have featured on the Royal Arms holding the monarch's shield. The lion has become a symbol of the strength of the crown and Britain in general, while the Scottish unicorn represents purity. Scotland's patron saint is one of the twelve apostles, St Andrew, and its emblem is the thistle, a symbol of defence. St Andrew's cross forms a part of the British flag, the Union Jack, together with the crosses of St George and St Patrick, the patron saint of Ireland. A fifth-century ex-slave, St Patrick made the base for his gospel preaching in Armagh and from there led the successful resurgence of Christianity against chieftains on the British mainland. His feast day, 17 March, is an official holiday in Northern Ireland and his cross is the country's flag (it is not that of the Republic of Ireland). Ireland's emblem is the sham-rock, whose three-in-one leaf was supposedly used by St Patrick to demonstrate the Holy Trinity, but on the British coat of arms Ireland is represented by a harp, now most widely recognised as the logo for Guinness, the famous Irish stout. The majority of these symbols have become signs of a collective heritage and the degree to which people align themselves with such images today is negligible, but on the saints' days a few individuals do wear badges with their country's emblem in their lapels. In terms of popular culture, the Union Jack had already become simply a minor fashion design in the 1970s, appearing on watch faces and T-shirts. It was also taken up in the 1980s by football fans, who since then have visited Europe with the flag daubed on their faces (reminiscent of the Ancient Britons who with a substance called woad would paint their faces blue to frighten their enemies). In the 1990s individuals are more likely to turn to television person-alities, film and pop stars or sports players for their country's heroes and icons.

Ireland is the second largest of the British Isles. However, unlike smaller islands which are wholly British, such as the Isle of Wight and the Shetlands, Ireland is officially partitioned. In 1921, when an agreement was signed giving the rest of the country independence, six of the nine Irish counties which constituted the ancient province of Ulster remained part of the United Kingdom – these were the predominantly Protestant north-eastern counties. Northern Ireland therefore has national and official links with the rest of Britain but its people share deep roots with histories and traditions south of the border, and since the Anglo-Irish agree-ment of 1985 the Republic of Ireland has participated in its political and legal matters. Ireland is officially divided, but in several respects it is culturally united for many people, not least because the Irish have retained a national distinctiveness despite the globalising and American influences that are so evident in England. In the 1960s, traditional Irish music saw a resurgence which has continued into the 1990s; government policy has been to revive the Irish language; indigenous sports such as hurling and Gaelic football have remained popular, and Irish literature is flourishing. For example, in Seamus Heaney, the Irish have arguably produced the finest poet writing in the English language since W.B. Yeats – who was also Irish. Also, in 1993, Roddy Doyle won the most well-known literary award in Britain, the Booker Prize, with his comic novel *Paddy Clarke, Ha Ha Ha*, a popular and distinctively Irish story about a young boy growing up in Dublin.

In 1994, the Booker Prize was won by James Kelman, a Scot, with his novel *How Late it Was, How Late*. This is a story written in Glaswegian slang, and its part-abusive, part-aggressive patter is peculiar to that city such that its idioms are not always intelligible in much of Scotland outside of Glasgow, let alone in the rest of Britain. In addition to a unique vocabulary, the Scots have their own legal and educational systems, a stronger Calvinist tradition than the English, and a history which has forged closer links with the French and Irish than the English. When the Scots move abroad, it is said that their national identity emigrates with them, which is significant when approximately four times as many Scots live outside of Scotland as within. It is important to remember that such feelings of belonging do not cease at the border and, in England for example, there is a strong sense of Scottish identity – as any night on 25 January spent at thousands of English pubs will demonstrate. This is Burns' night, when the birth of Scotland's national poet, Robert Burns, is celebrated with drink, song and dance in a way that Shakespeare's very seldom is. Scotland is also different from England politically: in recent national government elections, less than one in four Scottish people voted for the winning Conservative Party, and this has repeatedly raised the question of devolution – a major rallying-point for those keen to assert a distinctive Scottish identity.

Officially, the most closely tied countries in the UK are England and Wales, which includes the large Island of Anglesey across the narrow Menai Strait. Often mentioned as one unit for purposes of surveys, censuses and polls, England and Wales are joined administratively as well as politically and economically. However, many of the arguments for devolution rest upon the view that Wales, as well as Scotland, is readily distinguishable from England in terms of language, culture and history. For example, a traditional cultural event which identifies Wales separately from the rest of Britain but which is held in many forms is the Eisteddfod, a bardic competition from pre-Christian times. The name, meaning 'chairing' or 'session', derives from the ceremonial seating of the bard or poet whose work has been awarded the first prize. The Royal National Eisteddfod, conducted entirely in Welsh, is held annually in different locations throughout the country. It involves music, drama and other arts, as well as poetry. The Eisteddfod is announced over a year in advance at a harp ceremony conducted by the Gorsedd, or Court, encircled by specially laid stones. The festival is associated with a nationalistic Welsh identity and *Plaid Cymru*, 'the party for Wales', was founded in a hotel room in Pwllheli during the Eisteddfod in 1925. As a cultural event the Eisteddfod remains identifiably Welsh, even though there are English language spin-offs, just as Highland reels and sword dancing are Scottish. In terms of place, it is country (England, Scotland, Wales, Northern Ireland) rather than nation that remains the major cultural, though not necessarily political, grouping with which people identify.

Representations of the British are not only generated from within Britain however. In terms of culture, Hollywood remains a dominant influence. In the 1940s and 1950s, English actors commonly played the roles of well-mannered, upper-class socialites. At present, there is an identifiable trend in which male English actors take the roles of 'bad guys': killers, psychopaths or terrorists. In the late 1980s and early 1990s there has been a run of such films in which the villain, though not English, is played by an Englishman: *Schindler's List* (Ralph Fiennes), *JFK* (Gary Oldman), *Die Hard* (Alan Rickman) and *Reversal of Fortune* (Jeremy Irons). An actor such as Anthony Hopkins, who played the part of Hannibal Lecter in *The Silence of the Lambs*, is likely to be included in this group because the Welsh, unlike the Scottish and Irish who have large populations in the US, do not yet appear to have a strong cultural identity in Hollywood (and Hopkins plays the title role of Tricky Dicky in the 1996 film *Nixon*). A Scottish actor such as Sean Connery and a Northern Irish actor such as Liam Neeson have, by contrast, often played the roles of heroes. Arguably, Celtic sympathy in the USA, combined with an increased awareness of colonialism, has meant that, post-cold war, the English are temporarily becoming one of the latest kinds of enemy in tinsel town.

Region

It is important to remember that culture varies for Welsh, Scottish or English people depending on which region of their country they come from. In Wales, three-quarters of the population live in the valleys and coal regions of the south, which instil a different sense of Welsh identity from the mountains and seaside towns of the more militantly anti-English north; while in England it is the heavily populated metropolitan areas that have created several of its strongest regional identities. People from these different areas are associated with specific names and local characteristics, though it is their dialect that most obviously distinguishes them. For example, those from Newcastle and Tyneside in the north-east of England are called Geordies, after a mining lamp designed by George Stephenson, while people from Liverpool are known as Scousers, after a sailor's stew of meat and potatoes called lobscouse, and anyone brought up in the vicinity of London's Cheapside is known as a Cockney, originally the name for a spoilt city child. Each of these has a strong, singular identity which is reflected in television series devoted to personalities from the major cities: *Auf Wiedersehen Pet* and *The Likely Lads* about canny, tough-minded Geordies, *Brookside* and *Boys from the Blackstuff* about long-suffering but brave-faced Scousers, and *Minder* and *Only Fools and Horses* about wily, enterprising east-Londoners 'on the make'. The importance of regional identity can also be understood from any phone-in radio programme where presenters will almost invariably cite the area that callers are from, as though in some significant way this influenced their viewpoint, determined their record request or mattered to the show's listeners.

England is often talked about in terms of a north–south divide which is cultural, economic and political (the Labour Party has far more support in the north and the Conservative Party in the south). This was accentuated in the 1980s by differences in unemployment levels, crime rates, house prices and standards of living, all of which were worse in the north. The divide does not occur in the middle of the country however, and southerners some-times refer to a cold, industrial region that is everywhere 'north of Watford', a town not particularly far from London. In turn, some northerners caricature many southerners as 'Yuppies', an American slang word short for young 'urban professional' or 'upwardly mobile' people. This is because people from the south-east are seen as fast living, career-minded, and sometimes unfriendly, but the stereotype has little applicability away from London. Differences between north and south have evolved over the last two centuries and are more cultural than simply indus-trial or economic (during certain periods of the nineteenth century the north was more prosperous than the south). The largest number of 'enterprise zones' and development areas, assisted by government funding and incentives for industry, are in regions such as the Midlands, the north-east, east central Scotland and south Wales – but this economic difference from the south of England is frequently exaggerated. That a southern English region such as south-west Cornwall is also a development area is often ignored because it is distant from London and the financially dominant south-east.

Other regional differences are evident in sport, food and housing: the north has rugby league, the south rugby union; the north has butties, barmcakes and baps (all breadcakes) while the south has sandwiches and rolls; terraced housing is more common in the north, detached houses and bungalows in the south. Between these two regions lies the Midlands, a band of counties such as Staffordshire and Nottinghamshire across central England which,

FIGURE 1.2 In Wales it is usual to see signs written in Welsh first, then in English

caught between two cultures, often seems to be regarded as the north by people in the south and vice versa. However, a strong regional identity associated with the dales, hills and moors is felt by people in the Midlands, and the countryside of a county such as Derbyshire is often considered to be the most beautiful in England (for example, by Jane Austen in *Pride and Prejudice*). A distinct personality also attaches to Birmingham, the UK's second largest city, and the distinctive 'Brummie' accent is as recognisable as a Scottish or Welsh one.

Language, accent, vocabulary and idioms of speech form important regional differences. For example, Welsh, a version of which was spoken in Britain when the Romans invaded in 55 BC, is one of the oldest languages in the British Isles. Tens of thousands of people still speak Welsh, adult educational institutions run language courses, and since 1970 education in Wales, or

Cymru, has been bilingual. About a quarter of the Welsh population speak both languages, and because Welsh and English are both officially supported it is usual to see signs written in the two languages (see Figure 1.2). Irish is still spoken in Ireland, while Gaelic, another variant of the ancient Celtic languages, is still spoken in Scotland and, to a lesser extent, the Isle of Man. Accent and idiom vary enormously throughout Britain, although in the 1990s there has been concern expressed over the spread of 'estuary English': an outer-London accent and dialect characterised by features of pronunciation such as lisped 'r's and by words such as 'basically' (it is thought by some to be reducing speech variations). In England there are still great differences in regional accent but the clearest boundary is that between north and south. No English person is likely to mistake the long, soft vowels of a west-Londoner who could rhyme 'garage' with 'large' for the short, hard vowels of a Lancastrian who could rhyme 'garage' with 'ridge'. As for local vocabulary and idioms, if we take Scotland as an example, some words have become national expressions and most British people will understand 'ken' (know) or 'wee bairn' (small baby). However, an English person would be unlikely to know the meaning of such words as 'wabbit' (tired and weak), 'toom' (empty) or 'reidh' (smooth).

Scottish words come from different languages that lie either side of an ancient regional divide. The majority of Scots are Lowlanders and have an ancestry that is part Teutonic and part Celtic. In the past, they were considered to be different from the traditionally more aggressive, independent, Gaelic-speaking Highlanders, who were a minority but supplied the national symbols of the tartan, bagpipes, kilt and sporran (like the Highland Games, these are largely produced for tourists nowadays). However, except in the crofting (loosely, farming) communities of the west, this division is historical more than contemporary, and religious denomination, football team allegiance and city of birth are more likely to form points of cultural identity, especially for Lowlanders. Today, Gaelic is the principal language only in the Outer Hebrides and a few other mainly island communities.

TABLE 1.2 Resident populations of largest urban districts (1994)

	Thousands of people	Percentage of UK population
Greater London	6,969	11.9
West Midlands (including Birmingham)	2,628	4.5
Greater Manchester	2,578	4.4
West Yorkshire (including Leeds and Bradford)	2,194	3.6
Central Clydeside (including Glasgow)	1,621	2.8
Merseyside (including Liverpool)	1,434	2.5
South Yorkshire (including Sheffield)	1,305	2.2
Tyne and Wear (including Newcastle and Sunderland)	1,134	1.9

Sources: OPCS and General Register Office for Scotland

While it is a comparatively small country, Britain still has regional television companies which, as well as making and carrying the nationally transmitted programmes, provide localised information to such areas as Granada in the north-west of England and Central in the Midlands. In the 1980s and 1990s, regional accents have been allowed on to the airwaves of the BBC which were previously saturated by announcers with the clipped, southern tones of Received Pronunciation, an upper-class accent used by public schools to standardise speech in the nineteenth century. Today there are also local radio broadcasts in Welsh, and since 1982 there has been a Welsh-language television channel called *Sianel Pedwar Cymru*, which means Channel 4 Wales and is abbreviated to S4C. However, national stations are more culturally influential for most people, and satellite stations for some. While there are regional weekly and even daily papers, a similar picture is true of newspapers: even locally, national media are frequently more popular than regional. Region is an imprecise term and one which is used differently in weather reports, television broadcasts, and expressions of loyalty or identity at a level between the national and the local. In many ways, regions can be identified by the points of the compass, and if a person is described as coming from the south-east or the north-west, most British people will find this at least as meaningful as the mention of a person's religion or job. Table 1.2 lists the most heavily populated areas of Britain – some denoted by their county (e.g. West Yorkshire), others by a city (e.g. Manchester) and some by their region (e.g. West Midlands).

County

After region, the largest area with which the British identify themselves is their county, a geographical fusion of landscape, culture and administration most likely to affect people in terms of its natural scenery and historic landmarks. County boundaries partitioned Ancient Britain and three counties in the south – Sussex, Kent and Essex – were Anglo-Saxon kingdoms. Although modified in 1975 and currently under review, counties still form the basis of local government in England and Wales. In terms of county types, the most famous grouping is the 'home counties', a nineteenth-century phrase referring to the counties around London, such as Kent, Surrey, Berkshire, Middlesex and Essex. Some counties are known for their countryside: Cumbria's Lake District (made famous in Wordsworth's poetry) and Hampshire's New Forest (a royal hunting ground for William the Conqueror); others for their industry: Lancashire's factories and mills (described in novels by Dickens and Gaskell) and Nottinghamshire's mines (think of D.H. Lawrence's *Sons and Lovers*).

Northern Ireland is sometimes known simply as 'the six counties'. Local government there now operates on the basis of small district and borough councils, but ancient county identities are stronger. To take one example: Antrim, which derives its name from the fifth-century monastery of Aentrebh, occupies the north-east corner of Ireland. A county of moorlands and wooded glens, it is bordered on three sides by the sea. On the north coast is the famous Giant's Causeway. This is a promontory of vertical basalt columns formed by a volcanic rift which stretches under the sea to the Hebrides Islands off the west coast of Scotland. However, Irish legend holds that a giant built this as a walkway from Ireland to a cave on the Hebridean island of Staffa, so that he could attack the legendary Scottish hero Fingal. The roof of Fingal's Cave is also formed of straight six-sided rock columns which the two giants supposedly threw at each other. Celtic mythology adds a magical dimension to local identities and has been used in Ireland in attempts to forge a national consciousness, but even English Romantic poets such as Keats, Wordsworth and Tennyson have written about Fingal's Cave.

Most of England's thirty-nine counties have a recognisable identity and will be said to have their own particular character-istics and distinctive inhabitants. Counties have given their names to famous stretches of countryside (for example, Surrey hills or Devon moors), to types of people (unsophisticated socialites are 'Essex girls' and those with determination have 'Yorkshire grit'), to food (Cumberland sausage and Cornish pasty) and even to breeds of animal (Staffordshire bull terrier and Berkshire pig). However, one of the strongest ways in which county loyalties are continued is through sport. For example, one of the seventeen county cricket clubs, Yorkshire, refused up until 1992 to allow anyone not born in the county to play for the team. Despite this, Yorkshire has won the County Championship more often than any other team.

Of course, geographical features are also significant. Yorkshire is separated from its historic rival Lancashire by the Pennines, a range of limestone hills popular with walkers and sometimes described as the backbone of England. Yorkshire is famous abroad for the moors on which the Brontë sisters used to live, but the county is also well-known in Britain for a section of the Pennines, the Yorkshire Dales, which was designated a National Park in 1954. These parks are areas of significant natural beauty in England and Wales protected under an act of 1949. The act prohibits building or development in such areas as Dartmoor and the New Forest in England, Snowdonia and the Pembrokeshire coast in Wales. Similar protection applies to 'listed buildings', usually those dating back to before 1840, throughout the country. Such measures preserve the past for the heritage and tourism industries and, partly in consequence, listed buildings and national parks are sometimes put forward as representative of an authentic Britishness that is at threat from the architecture, pollution and city-oriented life of the present.

Yorkshire is particularly famous for having a strong identity, but this is actually true of most counties. For example, in 1995 inhabitants of Britain's smallest ex-county, Rutland, which was merged with Leicestershire in 1974, were trying to have the county officially recognised again, by raising funds through a 'Rutland' credit card. In the 1970s, this sense of local county identity was satirised in a television series called *Rutland Weekend Television*, a spin-off from *Monty Python's Flying Circus* that had nothing to do with the county – it just pretended to be run on a low budget by a small community of amateur enthusiasts.

In 1975, the Welsh counties were rearranged with others to reduce their number from thirteen to eight. Powys, in mid-Wales, covers the old counties of Montgomeryshire, Radnorshire and most of Breconshire, but the name itself is that of an ancient province dating from about the fifth century. Like all British counties, it is steeped in history and contains Powis and Montgomery castles, the Dan-y-Ogof Caves, Brecon Cathedral and Gregynog Hall, but its most famous landmark is the Brecon Beacons (*Bannau Brycheiniog* in Welsh). These are a collection of mainly red sandstone mountains, created a national park in 1957, that run for forty miles away from the English border. Along and between the mountains are standing stones from 5000 to 6000 years ago, ancient castles and cairns (hill markers made from piles of stones). The forests, mountains and reservoirs of the Beacons provide excellent grounds for outdoor activities which, because of increased leisure time, have become increasingly popular since the Second World War: angling, gliding, riding, boating, trekking and cycling.

Since the local government reorganisations of 1974/5, Scotland has been divided into nine large administrative regions and three island areas, instead of thirty-three counties. Fife was the only county not to be renamed as a region and it now covers roughly the same area as it did before. The administrators of the Local Government Act had intended that the county be split in two but the people of Fife protested so vehemently that the plans were dropped. It is also economically and politically significant that off the coast of Fife are the drilling ships and rigs that have been exploring for oil and gas in the North Sea since the 1970s. Some of the arguments put forward for devolution by the Scottish National Party, which has seats at Westminster and campaigns for an independent Scottish Parliament, turn on the standpoint that North Sea gas and oil are Scottish and would enable the country, free from England, to run a prosperous economy well into the next century.

City

In all, the United Kingdom has fifty-eight cities, a title many British people wrongly think is given to a town with a cathedral. City is actually a title of dignity conferred on towns of religious, commercial or industrial importance by statute, royal charter or tradition (for example, Coventry, Exeter and Norwich are mentioned as cities in William the Conqueror's eleventh-century *Domesday Book* of landholdings). Britain's cities vary enormously, from the industrial giants Manchester and Newcastle in the north to the southern ports such as Southampton and Bristol. There are also the cities noted chiefly for their cathedrals, such as Hereford and Ely, and the heritage cities such as the Roman town of Chester, whose entire medieval surrounding wall has survived, or Winchester, a small city of only 30,000 people which was the capital of England in Anglo-Saxon times.

Of course, the most famous city in England is London, within which there is a 'square mile' of offices and banks that encompasses the original walled area also sometimes referred to simply

as 'the City' and the financial hub of Britain's business activities. At over 6.5 million, London has the largest population of any city in Europe although people have been steadily moving away to the outer suburbs and commuter zones since the Second World War. Britain's capital is one of the best-known cities in the world but in many ways it is different from the rest of the UK. Forging an identity from Carnaby Street and the King's Road in the swinging sixties, heavy metal and punk styles in the glam seventies and American consumerism in the materialistic eighties, London in the postmodern nineties is less easily labelled. London fashions are likely to sample different clothes and styles of the past, specialist shops sell anything from military armour to body jewellery, and musical styles are eclectic, forming such hybrids as Bungle, a mixture of Bhangra and Jungle music, or Gujarati Rock, a fusion of Western guitars with Indian sitars and tablas. Such meetings illustrate the blended histories London now represents because its 'conglomerate nature', as Salman Rushdie records in his controversial 1988 novel *The Satanic Verses*, now echoes the cultural diversity of the old empire.

Britain's high culture is famously represented everywhere in London from the National Gallery in Trafalgar Square and the Royal Academy of Arts in Piccadilly to the Royal Opera House in Covent Garden and the National Theatre on the South Bank. Museums in central London are around every corner from the Museum of the Moving Image (MOMI), which celebrates film and television, to the vast British Museum which was the world's first public museum and is currently Britain's second greatest tourist attraction. As much as anything in London, the British Museum serves as a reminder of Britain's imperial history, and yet it is only one of around a hundred major museums in the capital. These, from the Museum of the Jewish East End and the Museum of Eton Life to the Sherlock Holmes Museum and the Florence Nightingale Museum, represent the variety of Britain's lucrative cultural heritage industry.

Tradition is still celebrated all year round, from the Lord Mayor of Westminster's New Year's Parade through to the Lord Mayor's Show in November. However, in a modern consumer culture such as Britain's, the past is often used for commercial profit or for charity: 'punks' are quite likely to be art students looking to supplement their grants by simulating a Britishness for photographers; pearly kings and queens, who were originally arbitrators in arguments between traders, are now usually on show, with their coats covered in mother of pearl buttons, to raise money for local causes.

To many people outside the capital, the word 'London' conjures up a collection of buildings, landmarks and monuments such as Buckingham Palace, St Paul's Cathedral, the Tower of London, Westminster Abbey, Big Ben and Piccadilly Circus. However, London is best seen as not one city but a patchwork of cities stitched together: the cockney East End, the Docklands development, the Parliament at Westminster, the administration at Whitehall, the parks and the Thameside areas, the museums, theatres, shops and galleries of the West End, the residential areas such as Hampstead and Belgravia, the City, the exhibition area around Earls Court, and the famous suburbs from Richmond in the west to Greenwich in the east. Despite this diversity, it is the tourist attractions that survive in the popular imagination as representative of London: a fascination with Britain's past which was illustrated in the 1960s when London Bridge was bought by wealthy Americans who had it taken apart and rebuilt in Arizona.

A further less well-publicised characteristic of London and other British cities in the 1990s is the rise in the number of homeless people sleeping on the streets, which now exceeds 2000, and a parallel increase in begging, which is common in the central metropolitan areas. In London and elsewhere, inner-city areas are generally less well off than the suburbs, to which the more affluent sections of society have moved (a small counter-trend has brought the middle classes into the renovated dockland areas of London and other cities). Lifestyles are different too: in the inner cities the neighbourhood and street in which people live impinge more on their sense of identity than they do in the suburbs, where people's homes and gardens are major preoccupations and sources of pleasure. Inner-city regeneration has become a central policy for successive governments since the Second World War, and more especially since the 'riots' that broke out in the 1980s in the inner cities of London, Liverpool, Bristol and Birmingham, and which led to violent clashes between police and protesters against the government's race, housing and employment policies.

Sadly, the capital city of Northern Ireland is most famous throughout the world for its violence. Since 1968, Belfast has chiefly made the front pages of British newspapers for its sectarian killings, although statistically it has been a safer place to live than many American cities. Separated as they are by the fortified wall of the 'Peace Line', the Falls Road (Catholic) and the Shankhill Road (Protestant) have become notorious throughout Britain, and 'the troubles', as they are locally known, have contributed to Belfast's population of around 300,000 having one of the highest unemployment levels in Britain. Following the tentative peace negotiations in 1995, the Northern Ireland Tourist Board is actively trying to attract visitors back to the country through a publicity campaign including newspaper and television advertisements. A largely rural country without the crowded motorways or the fast-paced life of England, Ireland's difference from the rest of Britain is illustrated by the fact that Belfast is the country's only industrial city.

The capital of Scotland is Edinburgh, cut across by the famous Royal Mile – central streets that run through the old town marking the area walked or ridden by numerous kings and queens. Although it is Scotland's first city, Edinburgh is far smaller than Glasgow whose population of three-quarters of a million is about 300,000 greater. Culturally, Edinburgh is probably most famous for its annual Summer Festival, which has grown since the war into a series of different festivals devoted to drama, film, literature, music and dance. The festival takes over a million pounds in receipts and sells tickets to hundreds of thousands of visitors. On New Year's Eve, which is known as Hogmanay in Scotland, people gather round Tron Church in Edinburgh, just as they do in Trafalgar Square in London, to celebrate the coming year and to sing 'Auld Lang Syne'.

Cardiff (Caerdydd in Welsh), in the county of South Glamorgan, is the capital of Wales and its largest city with a population of just under 300,000. Developed on a site originally built on by the Romans in the first century, the city stands alongside the River Taff (though the common nickname for the Welsh, 'Taffy', does not come from this but derives from the pronunciation of the Welsh equivalent of David, 'Dafydd'). In the nineteenth century, Cardiff became a major port when it provided an outlet for the coal mined in local valleys such as the Rhondda. In more recent decades, as the coal industry has declined so have the Cardiff docks, which used to export more coal than any other port in the world. However, in the last few years Cardiff's docklands, like London's, have been greatly renovated and the extensive redevelopment has meant that the entire waterfront has been restructured. Cardiff is also home to two fierce Welsh amateur passions: rugby union and singing. Cardiff Arms Park is the centre of Welsh rugby football and stages internationals as well as local matches. Since 1946, Cardiff has also been the base for the Welsh National Opera, which started from amateur roots and is the oldest of Britain's regional opera companies (the others are Scottish Opera and Opera North). A new opera house is being commissioned as the centrepiece for the docklands area development.

Town

On the one hand, many people regret a creeping sameness in British cities and towns – for example, in most high streets you will see more or less the same shops, such as Boots, Marks & Spencer, Next, Mothercare, Debenhams, John Menzies, Burton, Woolworth and W.H. Smith (see Figure 1.3(a) and (b)). On the other hand, British towns are still enormously varied, from the seaside towns, market towns, country towns, tourist towns, and industrial towns, to the postwar 'new' towns or satellite towns as they are called in the United States. Some coastal towns such as Blackpool and Bournemouth are chiefly known as seaside resorts and are extremely popular with British holiday-makers, although overseas tourists are more likely to visit historic towns

FIGURE 1.3 (a) A British high street often features the same shops. Here in Wigan are Debenhams, Marks & Spencer, Mothercare, Burton and John Menzies

such as Roman Colchester or Shakespeare's Stratford-upon-Avon. Other popular spots, famous since the seventeenth century for their 'healing waters', are spa towns such as Harrogate and Buxton. Many northern towns like Wigan and Huddersfield retain, for southerners, the unfair image of industrial decline gained between the wars, while market towns in the Midlands such as Melton Mowbray in Leicestershire still suggest the traditions of the English countryside. Towns do not have the large cultural life of cities or the close-knit community feel of small villages, but they combine aspects of each, providing a balance that many people feel is preferable to the bustle of the urban areas or the relative isolation of the countryside. Each county also has a 'county town' which traditionally, but in many cases no longer, was the seat of county government. County towns can often be

FIGURE 1.3 (b) Manchester City Centre (the site of an IRA bombing in June 1996)

inferred from their names, such as Lancaster in Lancashire and Shrewsbury in Shropshire.

Traditional English towns retain many of the architectural signs of the nineteenth century. Victorian, iron-framed, glass-roofed, covered markets remain in the centres of Bolton and Halifax, for example. Many towns still have magnificent municipal buildings from their heyday over a hundred years ago and grand public houses from the turn of the century. Impressive corn exchanges, where samples were auctioned or sold, still stand in many country towns like Bury St Edmunds and Bishop's Stortford, while imposing workplaces like the Bliss Valley Tweed Mill at Chipping Norton in the Cotswolds and the Clocktower Mill in Burnley stand out as reminders of the industrial revolution in mill towns. Every sizeable British town has a central park such as Jephson Park in Leamington Spa or Avenham Park in Preston, and while each town is different its development of terraced housing, shops, factories and schools around church, railway station, market, town hall and square will be familiar.

Many modern towns have arisen because of the New Towns Act of 1946. These include Harlow and Stevenage near London, East Kilbride near Glasgow and Cwmbran in south Wales. However, of the total of thirty new towns the most well-known and recent example is Milton Keynes in north Buckinghamshire. The new towns were designed to enable a redistribution of the metropolitan populations and they had to cope with the preferences indicated by commuter life: a traditional English liking for the countryside wedded to a practical need to be able to reach the city. The intention was always to plan towns for modern living in every aspect by blending industrial and residential areas with full leisure facilities, and by separating traffic from pedestrians through a network of underpasses and walkways. However, Milton Keynes was not built up from nothing: it was designed to unite thirteen existing villages which are now enclosed by sweeping 'bypass' roads. Britain's largest new town in terms of area and population, Milton Keynes covers 50 square miles and has about 180,000 inhabitants. Despite its image of cleanliness and hi-tech living, much of the large town is still underdeveloped and underused, and yet its diverse range of amenities and accommodation, from solar-powered to timber-framed houses, make it a more ambitious town project than any other since the war.

Most British towns have their own distinctive characteristics or annual events that promote a local cultural identity. For example, two Welsh towns in the county of Powys are Hay and Brecon. Hay-on-Wye is a small town which has become the book trade capital of Britain. Almost every shop in the town is an antiquarian or second-hand bookseller, and people drive great distances to spend a whole day searching the shelves; club, university and school trips are sometimes especially arranged to come and browse through what has become the largest collection of second-hand books in the world. The nearby town of Brecon is the site of a distinctly Welsh community-based jazz festival each August which attracts some 30,000 people and takes place throughout the town in the Cathedral, halls, pubs and streets.

Jazz is enjoyed by its fans for its musical anarchism, flair and improvisation; consequently its appropriation by the Welsh at such festivals can be seen as an assertion of their independence from English culture.

However, against this individuality, we must also note that the look of larger modern British towns has been greatly influenced by the United States. British planners, in the light of a general cultural imitation of American trends, are adopting stateside practices such as the 'doughnut effect', where town centres become abandoned by shoppers for malls on the outer ring. A largely consumer culture has been imported across the Atlantic and modern buildings reflect this: shopping malls, multiplex cinemas, theme parks, out-of-town supermarkets, Disney stores and fast-food restaurants, some of them drive-ins. The result is a sameness that is convenient and reassuring but also, on a national scale, numbing. Most cities and towns in Britain can be expected to have a number of fast-food outlets such as Burger King, a range of clothes shops like The Gap, a Safeway or similar shopping centre away from the town, a Super Bowl, Laserquest or ten-screen cinema complex, leisure centres with computerised workout gyms, and hoardings that advertise the American Dream along with their cigarettes. Milton Keynes is a prime example of this cultural saturation. It has imitation sheep and cows, acres of Astroturf, a grid road network, huge parking lots, a Milton Keynes Bowl for rock concerts, and 'California Collection' houses. The planners' aim has been to emulate the values and facilities of the ideal American town: efficiency, convenience, easy access, cleanliness, even air-conditioning, together with such un-British aspects as indoor gardens, straight roads and parking for thousands of cars. In this, the city's designers have probably succeeded, but Milton Keynes more than any other town remains the butt of numerous contemporary jokes for the many British who unfairly caricature it as a place lacking culture, history or interest.

Village

By stark contrast, very little American influence will be found in Britain's villages, some of which can still be described as rows of thatched cottages nestling in fields between hedgerows and small streams. Since the war, people have moved back to rural areas, reversing the trend started by the industrial revolution. In recent decades, the number of people living in villages has increased by several million to comprise around 25 per cent of the total population in the 1980s. Villages in Britain are traditionally associated with a close-knit society centred on a hall, which serves as a kind of community centre, a market, parish church, pub and 'green', an area for fairs, fêtes, cricket matches and other sporting events or public gatherings. Most villages therefore promote a strong blend of social identity, because people usually have a number of roles within the community, and personal identity, associated with land ownership and family history. A village's focus is likely to be on continuity and community life, and it is often said that everyone will know everyone else's business.

FIGURE 1.4 Unmechanised ploughing, a traditional rural scene

FIGURE 1.5   A rural cottage, often an attractive home to city commuters

However, village life is changing. A modern phenomenon is the commuter village. These are hamlets or villages which have sufficiently good transport links for office workers to travel by road or rail to the major cities, such as London and Birmingham, sometimes on journeys that take hours. Many city business people live in villages for the peace and quiet, the clean air, scenery and wildlife – but they probably have little involvement in the life of the village unless they also have children whom they want to bring up locally in the comparatively friendly, unpolluted and safe environment of the country. Similarly, second homes in villages throughout, for example, the Yorkshire Dales, are not unusual. City workers visit them at weekends or just in the summer for holidays (in 1995, the pop group Blur's number one song 'Country House' satirised this very phenomenon). Such people are sometimes resented by the local villagers because they may force up property prices and they also pose a threat to the continuity of village life. In the 1980s, 'holiday homes' in Wales were occasionally targets for arsonists resentful of this intrusion by outsiders, particularly from southern England. The increase in village populations since the Second World War has also occurred because more and more people, who are also living longer, are retiring to the countryside from the city. Historically, village work has been based around a farming community, but since the war the agricultural workforce has decreased year by year. Britain now has nine counties that are classed as rural and, to give an indication of how they are still in some ways isolated from city life, about a quarter of the villages in these areas still have no food shop, post-office or doctor's surgery.

Oddly, Britain's most talked about village is fictional. Ambridge is the setting for *The Archers*, the world's longest running radio serial. Begun by the BBC in 1950, the programme is broadcast during the week for fifteen minutes twice a day, and by radio's standards it has a large, devoted following. In the serial, Ambridge is close to the market town of Borset in the fictional county of Borsetshire (shire is a term for the central English counties whose names have that suffix – *The Archers* was initially broadcast only in the Midlands). The ongoing saga revolves around the Archer family at Brookfield Farm and portrays a close-knit village community in which everyone interacts with everyone else. Episodes are full of domestic incident and minor moral dilemmas but there are fewer exaggerated, intense emotional scenes and revelations than in the television soaps. The programme has always aimed to reflect realistically and unsensationally the concerns and interests of a village community and it has a farming correspondent who ensures the serial's treatment of agricultural issues is factual and accurate. Ambridge's counterpart in reality is Hanbury in Worcestershire, where some outside location scenes have been recorded and the programme also has a tradition of including real people, the most noted of whom was the Queen's sister, Princess Margaret, in 1984. In 1989, the Post Office issued a set of commemorative stamps to mark the 10,000th episode. A similar stalwart of BBC Radio 4 has been *Gardeners' Question Time*, which has taken a panel of experts around the country from village hall to village hall since 1947. Like much of Radio 4's broadcasting, the programme thrives on consistency and from 1951 to 1980 the trio of gardening authorities remained the same, but in 1994 an entirely new panel was introduced. Such changes, seemingly trivial, are extremely contentious for the station's loyal and conservative following.

Conclusion

In this concluding section, as well as summing up we will look at four thematic aspects to British culture that are linked to place but are shared by everyone throughout the UK: the country and the city; travel; the weather, and the environment.

Apart from political borders, one of the strongest kinds of geographical division in Britain is that between those who look for the natural tranquillity of the countryside and those who prefer the amenities at hand in the city. This is a long-standing difference of taste and in the eighteenth century, the poet William Cowper, in his poem *The Task*, wrote the famous line 'God made the country and man made the town'. Today, culture in cities tends to be diverse, reflecting the highly concentrated rich mix of different peoples with varied lifestyles: life is mostly anonymous, formal and based around groups with specialised interests. Country life by contrast is generally associated with tradition, custom, community, cultural unity and 'the outdoor life' (in Britain, camping, caravanning, walking, mountain biking, riding and boating are all very popular and there are mile-long traffic queues of day-trippers in such places as the Peak District on Sunday afternoons).

It is often maintained that rural and urban people have different attitudes to the traditions of British life; for example, one cultural pursuit that many feel marks a division between people in cities and villages is fox-hunting. It is a frequent generalisation that city people want what they call 'blood sports' banned; and it is just as common to hear from those in favour of what they call 'field sports' that anti-hunting campaigners do not understand, as villagers do, the need for control of the population of predatory animals in the wild. For reasons such as this, the kind of cultural division in England between north and south is also sometimes found throughout the country between 'townies' and 'yokels'.

Finally, before moving on to consider the travel and the weather, we must note that in addition to the country and the city, there is a third place of escape for people from either of these communities: the coast. Because all Britons live on an 'island' there is a strong coastal culture incorporating trawler fishing, watersports, ports and docks, shipping, yachting, and, for visitors, the British tradition of seaside holidays, with its staple ingredients of piers, buckets and spades, postcards, amusement arcades, deckchairs, donkey rides and promenading. Again, there are also dozens of smaller islands off the British mainland, and the largest of these, the Isle of Wight below the south coast of England, is a county in its own right.

These areas are of course linked by travel on road, rail, air, river or sea. On average, across the nation, about 70 per cent of British households today own at least one car. In the 1930s, more miles of road in Britain were covered by bicycle than by car, but in the 1990s it is mainly those conscious of their health and the environment who choose two wheels over four. Commuting by train, on the main network or the London Underground, is a daily activity for millions of Britons, many of whom will complain that the rail services are far worse than on the Continent. In response to this constant criticism, a charter was introduced in the early 1990s to compensate people for delays, cancellations, and poor reliability. London's main airport, Heathrow, is the busiest in the world, although only 20 per cent of its 40 million customers take domestic flights. In addition, though they were superseded by the railways as a mode of transport in the nineteenth century, Britain is carved across by hundreds of streams and rivers, some with houseboats, and over 4000 miles of canals and waterways. Furthermore, in the 1990s trams have been reintroduced in cities such as Manchester, a light railway links the city area in London with Docklands, and a monorail has been built for the streets in the centre of Sheffield.

An influence that on another level links city, country and coast is a shared climate. In the eighteenth century, Samuel Johnson, who we mentioned in the introductory chapter, said that 'When two Englishmen meet, their first talk is of the weather.' Throughout Britain today the weather is still a frequent topic of conversation, and not usually for agricultural reasons but simply because it is so changeable. Many British people will be only too willing to offer a forecast of likely shifts in the weather. On top of experience and barometers, several other, often proverbial methods of prediction are sworn by. For example, a herd of cows sitting in a field indicates rain, as do twitching bunions and rheumatic attacks. Similarly, the old saying, 'Red sky at night, shepherds' delight; red sky in the morning, shepherds' warning' is passed down from generation to generation as a sure method of anticipating fair or foul weather throughout the country. The national hobby of predicting rain, sunshine, hail, thunder, snow or sleet is nicely summed up by the annual bets on whether there will be a white Christmas. Perhaps because of their obsessive interest in the weather, the British are generally sceptical of official forecasts. While this scepticism is distinctly unfair, it was bolstered in October 1987 by a freak hurricane which a BBC television weather forecaster famously asserted would pass Britain by. The storm blew over fences and light buildings, brought down telegraph wires and poles, put television stations out of action, resulted in eighteen deaths, and left many cars crushed by fallen trees.

Britain in fact has a moderate climate in terms of its temperature, which has never been recorded as high as 100°F (38°C) or as low as −18°F (−26°C). Generally, it is between 35 and 65°F, and the climate is milder in England and Wales than in Scotland. The weather remains a constant talking point in Britain because of its local variations and seasonal oddities: for example, though winter runs from December to February, a cricket match has been 'snowed-off' in June in Buxton, Derbyshire. August, in high summer, is one of the wettest months of the year and many Britons will swear that May and September are usually sunnier months. Rainfall differs greatly between regions and average annual levels vary from 500 mm in East Anglia in southern England to 5000 mm in the Scottish Highlands.

Finally, a country is frequently discussed in terms of its environment. For different reasons, the human maintenance and manipulation of the environment is of particular interest to two groups of people: environmentalists and the disabled. While they lagged behind other Europeans, the British became increasingly sensitive to ecological concerns in the late 1980s, as the following examples indicate. The British Green Party, founded in 1973 as the Ecology Party, polled 15 per cent of the European Parliament votes in 1989. Most large cities are now circled by a 'green belt' on which little building is allowed. The Forestry Commission, which has its headquarters in Edinburgh, was set up in 1919 because of the timber shortage that became apparent in the First World War. By the 1980s, through grants and government administration, it had already reached its target for the year 2000 of nearly 5 million acres of forest land. Recycling centres have also been stationed at shopping centres and other public places, for people to bring along their old newspapers, glass, clothes and aluminium. The campaigning environmental group Friends of the Earth has been prominent in Britain since 1970, lobbying on world issues such as rain forests and global warming as well as on local British concerns including beach pollution and the privatisation of the water authorities in 1989. Greenpeace, the Campaign for Nuclear Disarmament, Earth First! and various 'New Protest' groups, sometimes associated with New Age travellers (discussed in Chapter 7), have all also been active in Britain over the last twenty years.

A further issue of the (particularly built) environment is disability. Though many people in Britain have been slow to recognise the special needs of the disabled, supermarkets now nearly always have designated parking spaces close to the entrance, theatres often have signed performances, public buildings may be denied planning permission if they do not include wheelchair access, and most employers in the 1990s claim that their equal opportunity policies mean that jobs are open to all people regardless of age, ethnicity, gender or disability. Despite this, legislation has been difficult to pass, and disabled people are not well represented in films or on television, although a regular Radio 4 programme entitled *Does He Take Sugar?* attempts to provide a platform for issues of disability and the representation of the 'differently abled'. However, with respect to people's misconceptions, a high-profile media figure like the scientist Stephen Hawking (who has motor neuron disease) or the pop star Ian Dury (who has polio) can do more than such a minority programme to raise general awareness of the difference between a physical 'disability', which usually relates to a specific aspect of life, and general, particularly mental, abilities. Overall, the campaign for responsible and fair adaptation of the natural and built environment has been seen as one of slow progress as organised groups lobby and protest on specific issues of personal or social importance against businesses whose interests are by contrast short-sightedly commercial.

As a final word, it can be said that while the Union Jack can be seen flying at international conferences and decorating lapel badges, it is as often used today as a design for underpants, a pattern for dyed hair and a favourite symbol of the far Right British National Party. In other words, it is now chiefly an emblem of Britain's past – along with those other traditional symbols of England and Britain discussed in the introductory chapter, such as John Bull, Albion and Britannia – and will be used nostalgically, ironically and even callously as a sign of solidarity against others. Britons have always defined themselves as an island people whose singularity and separateness is illustrated by the channel of water dividing them from the Continent. However, the British now have an undersea tunnel that connects them with France, they are hostile to federalism but committed to joining Europe, they are soaked in influences from the USA and are succumbing to a global culture that may leave them disunited but curiously alike. This chapter has illustrated how, in terms of place, 'Britishness' is a problematic tag for people living in the UK in the 1990s, and that it perhaps best serves simply as a national label for traditional values and issues that lie between the local or global concerns with which individuals are increasingly more likely to identify themselves.

EXERCISES

1   What different kinds of regional identity do you think there could be said to be in Britain? How many regional variations in accent can you think of?

2   Can you name any personalities or politicians who seem to you to represent of a distinctive kind of Britishness? Can you say which country or region they grew up in?

3   Do you think there is any correlation between climate and culture or character, and do you think there are any dangers in promoting such beliefs?

4   Try to locate six other British cities on the map on p. 42. What do you know about each city and how do you think cultural identities might be different in each?

5   The discussion about London (p. 61) noted that the British Museum is the second largest tourist attraction in Britain. Below is an alphabetical list of the top thirteen attractions for the year 1994, as ranked by the British Tourist Authority. Find out what you can about them and then try to rearrange them according to the number of tourists you think they attract. Incidentally, nine of these attractions are free of charge and eight are in London. Again, do you know which? What else do you notice that is significant in terms of country or region about the location of these attractions?

- Alton Towers
- Blackpool Pleasure Beach
- British Museum
- Canterbury Cathedral
- Funland, London (Laserbowl/Trocadero)

- Madame Tussauds
- The National Gallery
- Palace Pier, Brighton
- St Paul's Cathedral
- Strathclyde Country Park
- Tate Gallery
- Tower of London
- Westminster Cathedral

READING

Champion, A.G. and Townsend, A.R. *Contemporary Britain: A Geographical Perspective* Edward Arnold, 1990.
Looks at Britain in the 1980s and at the relationship of policies and practices with the land (considers the north/south divide and the rural/urban debate).

Daudy, Phillipe. *Les Anglais: Portrait of a People*. Translated by Isabelle Daudy. Barrie and Jenkins, 1991.
A French overview of the British.

Jacobs, Eric and Worcester, Robert. *We British: Britain Under the Moriscope*. Weidenfeld & Nicolson, 1990.
Analyses the results of surveys about subjects ranging from politics to drugs.

Kearney, Hugh. *The British Isles: A History of Four Nations*. Cambridge University Press, 1989.
Suggests that while English, Irish, Scottish and Welsh identites are strong, a British identity is lacking.

CULTURAL EXAMPLES ══════════════════════════

■ *Films*

Bhaji on the Beach (1994) dir. Gurinder Chadha
Film, mixing British realist and Indian musical styles, about
a group of British Asian women from Birmingham on a day
trip to Blackpool.

The Crying Game (1992) dir. Neil Jordan
An exploration of national, political and sexual identity in
Ireland and Britain.

High Hopes (1988) dir. Mike Leigh
Social comedy about class aspirations and family values in
the city.

Into the West (1992) dir. Mike Newell
Irish mythology, travellers, and inner city life.

Jubilee (1978) dir. Derek Jarman
Anatomy, and dissection, of modern urban life set around
the Queen's jubilee in 1977.

Local Hero (1983) dir. Bill Forsyth
Poignant film about a Scottish coastal community threat-
ened by a multinational oil corporation.

Riff-Raff (1990) dir. Ken Loach
Social comment, set on a building site: strong regional
characters.

■ *Books*

Martin Amis, *London Fields* (1989)
A study of contemporary urban amorality.

Margaret Drabble, *The Radiant Way* (1987)
London dinner table perspective on Britain in the 1980s.

Sue Townsend, *The Queen and I* (1992)
Fantasy about the Queen living on a Midlands housing estate.

Jeanette Winterson, *Oranges Are Not the Only Fruit* (1985)
Tensions between sexuality and religion in Lancashire.

■ *Television programmes*

Birds of a Feather
Popular comedy about the adventures of two women in London.

Brookside, EastEnders, Coronation Street.
Urban living in Liverpool, London and Manchester respectively.

Emmerdale
Previously called *Emmerdale Farm*, this is a serial about (now somewhat loosely) agricultural and village communities in England.

The Good Life
A clash between rural, ecological values and urban, materialist aspirations in middle-class suburbia.

Hamish MacBeth
Drama series about life on a small Scottish island.

Last of the Summer Wine
Comedy about three retired men in a Yorkshire village.

The Old Devils
Serial adapted from a Kingsley Amis novel about a reunion of friends in Wales (S4C provides many of the best programmes about Wales).

Pobol Y Cwm (*People of the Valley*)
Welsh language soap opera.

Take the High Road
Enduring Scottish soap opera.

Education, work and leisure

■ Mike Storry

Timeline

600	King's School Canterbury founded
1249	Oxford University founded
1902	Education Act: secondary education
1936	Television starts in England
1944	Education Act: grammar schools
1954	Independent Television Act
1967	Plowden Committee: child-centred learning
1970	Equal Pay Act
1971	Industrial Relations Act
1975	Employment Protection Act Sex Discrimination Act
1976	University of Buckingham founded
1983	Unemployed: 10% of work force
1988	Education Reform Act
1990	Student loans
1992	Polytechnics become universities
1993	Trade Union Reform Act
1994	Criminal Justice Act opposed by Ramblers' Association

Introduction

W E HAVE LINKED WORK, EDUCATION and leisure in the title of this chapter in the belief that very often people's education is a major factor in deciding the type of work they will do, while their education and work influence how they occupy their leisure time. Thus any examination of cultural identity must take into account these factors in British life.

The timeline above picks out a number of significant historical points. From it you will see that schooling for the top echelon of British people started in AD 600, through royal patronage. Concern with people's conditions of work came only gradually and change was achieved slowly through the Factory Acts of the nineteenth century. Today, the 'working week' generally covers 9 a.m. to 5 p.m., Monday to Friday, although few people still work those exact hours and many Britons are now employed on 'flexitime'; so their daily times of arriving and leaving work are not fixed. On average, Britons work the longest hours in western Europe. In the 1980s and 1990s, with more centralised state intervention in citizens' lives as detailed elsewhere in this book, people have sought to form their own identities and to derive cultural fulfilment through work and leisure activities inside and outside of the home. This chapter will look at the part played by education, work and leisure in forming British cultural identities, and will deal with those topics in sequence.

Schools

Schooling in Britain has evolved over time as a result of both state and local influences. There are separate state and private systems. The school year runs from September to July and

85

FIGURE 2.1   Children on a school playing field

children normally start school in the September following their fifth birthday. The school day is usually from 9 a.m. to 3.30 or 4.00 p.m. and children are allocated places by the Local Education Authority (LEA) in the schools nearest to their homes. Appeals against these allocations are usually on the grounds of the superior reputations of neighbouring schools. The Conservative Government has lent encouragement to the exercise of this form of parental choice by promoting competition among schools and adopting a policy of incentives for 'good' schools and a *laisser-faire* attitude to the closure of those which are becoming less popular.

The state offers 'primary' (for ages 5–11) and 'secondary' (for ages 11–18) schooling. There are a few middle schools for children aged 10–13 and some 'special' schools for children with learning difficulties. These are the main state schools, although there are others in, for example, hospitals and youth custody centres. Pupils are permitted to leave school at 16 but a majority (1992: 76 per cent) stay on or move to local authority controlled Further Education (FE) or sixth-form colleges.

The present state system evolved from a gradual move towards universal educational provision which started in the nineteenth century with poorly funded board and hedge schools (the former managed by a local school board, the latter where teaching took place in the open air) to teach pupils up to the standard leaving age of 14 years (most recently raised from 15 to 16 in 1976).

In 1944, R.A. Butler's Education Act introduced the 'eleven-plus' examination. It reflected a desire to create educational opportunity for all social classes who had to cooperate for survival during the Second World War as never before. All children took this test at the end of primary school and those who passed had their fees paid at the local grammar school. This change had significant social and cultural effects in Britain. It enabled a degree of social mobility hitherto unknown and eroded notions of those with ability coming only from higher social strata. It introduced to postwar Britain a 'meritocracy', and made a significant contribution to the affluence of the 1950s.

On the negative side, it distanced children from less well-educated parents. But perhaps the worst effect of the 1944 Education Act was that some people saw it as 'discarding' the 90 per cent of children who were assigned by the test to secondary modern schools which concentrated on technical rather than academic subjects. Children were labelled 'failures' at the age of 11 and this led to a cumulative loss of ambition, achievement and self-esteem. Many became alienated and rejected the commitment expected of them by older generations and this offered fertile ground for the growth of such youth-cultural subgroups as mods, rockers, hippies and punks. Secondary modern school pupils and teachers were demoralised by the knowledge that the most favoured students had been 'creamed off' and by the fact that despite the rhetoric of 'appropriate provision', they were part of second-class educational establishments in a system of 'separate development', a sort of cultural 'apartheid'.

Partly because of this malaise, the Labour Government endorsed a system of 'comprehensive' schools in the 1960s. These were co-educational (both sexes) and for all. Some 'comps' exchanged grammar-school type streaming (grouping pupils according to performance) for mixed-ability teaching. Here, pupils of differing capabilities shared the same classrooms in the belief that the bright would help the weak and that improved social development would compensate for any lack of intellectual achievement and that this would eventually lead to cohesiveness rather than competitiveness in society at large. Other comprehensive schools adopted what they saw as the best of existing educational practices, including intellectual rigour, while de-emphasising classics and sport.

In the private system 'preparatory' schools educate children from the age of 5, prior to their entering the 'public schools' at 13. Confusingly, famous private schools like Eton and Harrow, Winchester and Stonyhurst are known as 'public schools'. (The expression 'public' school originally referred to a grammar school endowed for the public.) That system of education is now, as *Chambers Dictionary* defines it: 'for such as can afford it'. There are also schools which have some state and some private support. By 1995 the parents of children in approximately 1000 schools had voted to opt out of the control of local authorities and be funded directly from central government, that is, to become 'Grant Maintained'.

State schools in Britain are non-denominational. Of the state-supported schools with a religious affiliation the majority are Anglican, but other denominations of schools exist, principally Roman Catholic and Jewish. Their capital expenditure is covered by the state and their running expenses are paid by the members of their congregations. A contentious issue is that the same financial support is not currently made available to Hindu or Islamic schools and this has become a major issue in Bradford and other places where there are large Muslim populations.

To monitor pupils' performance, the government has introduced a series of Standardised Assessment Tests (SATs) – taken at age 7, 11 and 14. However, the major public exams which pupils face are those taken in individual subjects at age 16 and 18 respectively: the General Certificate in Secondary Education (GCSE) and Advanced (A) levels. In Scotland students gain Lower and Higher Certificates. University entrance is typically based on good grades in approximately six GCSEs and three A levels. Other qualifications open to those school leavers who want to attend college are Business and Technology Education Council awards (BTECs), Higher National Certificates (HNCs), City & Guilds, Royal Society of Arts (RSA) and General National Vocational Qualifications (GNVQs).

Colleges and universities

On leaving school at age 18, 23.1 per cent (1991/2) of pupils become students at universities and colleges. There are eighty-seven universities in Britain: seventy-one in England, twelve in Scotland, two in Wales and two in Northern Ireland. They have 844,400 students and 176,900 lecturers. The standard length of undergraduate study in Britain is three years for a Bachelor of Arts or Science degree (BA/B.Sc.), and up to seven years for 'vocational' degrees (that is, those linked to a specific job), like medicine, dentistry, veterinary courses or architecture. Students of subjects such as civil engineering spend an intermediate year in industry on a 'sandwich' course. Many universities offer the Bachelor of Education (B.Ed.) degree which is a four-year course geared towards classroom experience. The majority of primary school teachers qualify by this route. The standard way to train to be a secondary school teacher is to do a three-year university course in a specialist subject such as biology, history or mathematics followed by a one-year Post Graduate Certificate in Education (PGCE) which includes teaching practice.

Students on Master's courses (MA/M.Sc.) study for one year and those doing Doctorates (Ph.D.s) for upwards of three years. Student grants have remained at 1982 levels and students today experience real financial hardship. Only those with parents who can afford to subsidise them are without money worries. In the

FIGURE 2.2   Punting at Oxford

mid-1990s the percentage of working-class children attending university is declining.

Oxford and Cambridge (known collectively as 'Oxbridge') are the oldest remaining universities in Britain (at one time, Scotland had four universities, all founded before AD 1600). Their student numbers are small: in 1993/4 Oxford had 8910 male and 5828 female students in residence; Cambridge: 6083 men, 4553 women. Other old universities are Durham and St Andrews, and they are distinguished from the so-called 'Redbrick' universities founded around the beginning of this century (for example, Birmingham, Liverpool, Manchester) through their emphasis on traditional subjects. Redbrick universities included in their curricula subjects such as engineering, applied sciences and business studies. They also had placements in industry. 'New' universities created in the 1960s include Lancaster, York, Keele and Sussex. In 1992 all the former polytechnics (which had evolved from technical colleges) changed their names and joined the existing forty-four universities.

Britain has two other main universities (apart from the European campuses of several American ones): the University of Buckingham (1994/95: 1006 students) and the Open University (1995/96: 95,000 students). The former was Britain's first private university; the latter offers a wide range of degree programmes delivered partly by television and radio, appealing to those who are already engaged in full-time work, and whose only all-day attendance commitment is to a week-long annual Summer School. Students have to fund themselves.

Educational changes and trends

Major recent educational changes have been: the imposition of a National Curriculum (as opposed to one agreed with local authorities and Her Majesty's Inspectors (HMIs)); the introduction of pre-GCSE examinations, and the publication of league tables of schools' performances. Opponents of a National Curriculum felt it was preventing room for individual initiative and saw it as

FIGURE 2.3 Liverpool, a 'redbrick' university, founded early this century

sinister in its regimentation of pupils. They referred to a French minister of education who boasted that he knew at any hour of the day which page of which book pupils would be turning. Supporters of a National Curriculum promoted it as a necessary educational reform which would ensure uniform standards in schools. Such reforms, including a National Curriculum, are designed to erase the divide between learning and everyday life described by George Orwell in the 1930s: 'There is not one working-class boy in a thousand who does not pine for the day when he will leave school. He wants to be doing real work not wasting his time on ridiculous rubbish like history and geography' (*The Road To Wigan Pier* 1937).

Debate on these and other educational changes has featured in *Grange Hill*, a children's soap opera set in a comprehensive school. Contrasting it, or a film like *Kes* (1969), with ones such as *Good-bye Mr Chips* (1939) or *The Belles of St Trinians* (1954) shows the extent of the changes in both education and representation that have taken place. The former relate to the everyday lives of their viewers. The latter invite audiences to peep into a privileged world to which few will ever have access.

Schools are important to people partly because it is through playground culture that children learn to share a fierce yet beneficial scepticism which holds the adult world at bay until they can come to terms with it. If female, the school nurse is 'Nitty Nora' and attendants at street crossings are 'lollipop ladies'. The playground is a concrete jungle where children learn and practise their games, where society's folk memories and myths are recycled through chants. The song 'A ring a ring a roses/ A pocketful of posies/ Ashoo! Ashoo! / We all fall down' contains memories of the Black Death which swept Europe in the Middle Ages. Another reminder comes when, on seeing an ambulance pass, children say: 'Touch your collar/Never swallow/Never catch the fever.'

Because schools are so important in the formation of national and cultural identity, great public interest centres on the way in which prominent people choose to educate their children. For example, Prince Charles was the first member of the royal family not to be educated by palace tutors. He was sent to Gordonstoun in Scotland. His own sons William and Harry have gone to Eton. There is more at stake here than entitling schools to use the famous 'By Appointment' logo. British people gain, through the media's lens, some empathy with the Royal Family who will become subjected to the same anxieties and uncertainties of sending children to school as they have. This is all the more so because, while corporal (physical) punishment has been banned from the state school sector, some private schools retain the practice. This serves as an attraction or a deterrent to parents of prospective pupils; while some worry chiefly about their children's potential academic progress, others are concerned about the prevalence of bullying, the development of life skills and the kind of social, cultural and spiritual experience offered by the school.

Some parents also consider the availability of an 'Old School Tie' network, which may help their child to get a job and to develop socially useful lifelong friendships. In Britain as elsewhere, those who have shared experiences during their formative years forge a common cultural identity which encourages them subsequently to operate along co-operative and self-help lines, sometimes known as 'jobs for the boys'. The most famous of such networks may be that grouping of old Etonians, Harrovians and others known as 'the Establishment'. Girls' schools offering access to this network would be Roedean, Benenden or Cheltenham Ladies' College. Britain works on a system of contacts among people whose business, professional, sporting and social lives are intertwined within a shared cultural milieu. This is evident in memberships of numerous clubs: business people's Rotary or Round Table; golf and sailing; political groups; children's local 'packs' of scouts, guides, cubs and brownies.

Some people fear that recent governments have encouraged a shift from education to training. The former comes from the Latin word *educo* meaning to lead out or develop qualities which are within. This is meant to produce the fully rounded individual with a healthy mind in a healthy body (*mens sana in corpore sano*). Critics suggest that because the majority of students are in the formative 18–22 phase of their lives it is obtuse to concentrate solely on instruction and ignore the students' developmental phase. Training is to do with the supply of workers, and is not concerned with the individual. Its aim is to meet society's need for workers – not to offer any kind of personal cultural fulfilment. Opponents say that education should be pragmatic and supply society's need for skills – the piper *is* entitled to call the tune.

A current trend in school and university education is that girls seem to be performing much better than boys. Various factors have contributed to their increased pre-eminence. Today more women in prominent jobs offer role models. Feminism has also changed girls' outlooks and encouraged their ambition. Debate centres on whether pupils do better in single-sex schools, where they lack the distraction of the opposite sex. These schools dominate league tables of examination success for both girls and boys.

The educational sector which has been most influential in raising Britain's profile abroad, the public (that is private) schools, has benefited from the difficulties experienced by the state sector. Some public schools have chosen to pick out the best elements of the National Curriculum. The number of pupils going to public/independent secondary schools has risen, as the public sector atrophies. The change is small – from 573,000 in 1976 to 619,000 in 1992 – but the trend is especially significant at a time of declining total school rolls. It indicates parents' wish to benefit from the fact that the private sector has always had a disproportionately high influence on British culture and society, dominating many aspects of British public life, from Whitehall to Shire Hall, from Parliament to local constituency parties, from the Institute of Directors to local Chambers of Commerce.

As regards the place held in British society and culture by universities, they have always taken criticism from both the political Left and Right. When in power, the Left has seen them as élitist nurseries for the children of the bourgeoisie. Sections of the political right have seen them as populist hotbeds of left-wing radicalism where the next generation is encouraged into the ways of socialism and opposition to authority.

Despite sometimes rancorous debate, people still feel positive about education. A wide range of them, having had the experience of being in the school play, practising team sports like hockey or soccer, or such extra-curricular activities as chess or judo, develop and retain a shared sense of pride in their schools. A competitive spirit is fostered within schools through division into 'houses' – an idea long prevalent in the independent sector and redolent of the Oxbridge college system. Rivalry between schools is felt by children who are publicly labelled by the uniforms that most British schools make them wear. When they leave school, reports of their achievements will often indicate their schools – for example, members of the Oxford and Cambridge rugby teams have their colleges *and* schools listed thus: Carr, Kenneth: Merton; St Anthony's Comprehensive, Luton. Smith, John: Churchill; Shrewsbury School. Students will often visit their old schools and join old girls' or boys' associations, which meet to arrange social functions. Primary schools also have reunions, as people feel a need to re-experience the comradeship and spirit of community of their youth. No matter how old people are, school is where they acquired their first long-term friends, developed their social personalities and gained a deep and lasting sense of a communal identity.

Employment

Education and work are linked in that an individual's success at school often determines the kind of job he or she goes on to do. The relationship is not always as crude as this, but there is often a connection between upward and downward trajectories at school and in the workplace. An important effect of the many divisions in British education – between state and private, Oxbridge and Redbrick, vocational and academic – is that the workforce faces ideas of stratification which have been superseded in many other countries. Thus the British workforce is distinguished by its divisions rather than by its cohesiveness. Remuneration replicates social division. Process or factory workers have always received (weekly) wages, while predominantly middle-class managers have received (monthly) salaries. There are still quite separate ladders of achievement in numerous workplaces and it is almost impossible for people to cross from one to another despite the fact that John Major, who did not attend university, let alone Oxbridge, rose to become Prime Minister.

Further examples of the continuing stratified nature of Britain unfortunately abound. British company reports still append names to photos of directors while referring to technical processes beneath photos of workers. The Civil Service is divided into administrative, executive and clerical grades; industry into management and shop floor; banks into directors, managers, clerks and cashiers. These divisions may not be watertight in all cases, but very few people at the top of British industry have risen from the bottom and this both reflects and determines a British cultural identity which replicates the social and economic divisions that separate groups of people from one another.

Tables 2.1 and 2.2 show, respectively, the distribution of workers between different industries and the rates of unemployment in recent years.

This is a factual record of working Britain, but attitudes to work are determined culturally and work in general has always had a low cultural profile in the UK. If we 'read' British society through literature, we can see, for example, that most novels either don't refer to work or, if they do, denigrate it. In Jane Austen's works, people who are in trade are not quite respectable; the correct thing to do is to own land and to live off one's rents. Bulstrode in George Eliot's *Middlemarch* (1871/2) is a banker and thus in a profession which is not yet entirely respectable. In Dickens's novels people try to separate their public (working) selves from their private (domestic) lives in the belief that everybody wants to escape from work. Wemmick, the law clerk in *Great Expectations* (1860/1) pulls up a drawbridge when he goes back to his home where his 'aged parent' lives. He values his private domestic space, as does the adage 'the Englishman's home is his castle', which is echoed in the children's playground chant: 'I'm the king of the castle/And you're the dirty rascal.'

Today, work is rarely portrayed seriously or in detail in British films. Karel Reisz, Tony Richardson and others of the 1950s New Wave cinema were seen as daring for approaching the subject of work at all in *Saturday Night and Sunday Morning* (1960) and *Room at the Top* (1959). In fact, although there are some 'documentary' scenes from the factory floor in the former, the film concentrates on a love story. The same is true of David Lodge's novel *Nice Work* (1988). Even 'revolutionary' drama like Alan Bleasdale's lauded television series *Boys from the Blackstuff*, which shows how work is integral to a sense of both identity and culture, feels a need to portray workers as 'cheeky chappies' who avoid 'hard graft'. On the other hand, Willy Russell's popular escapist films *Letter to Brezhnev* (1985) and *Shirley Valentine* (1989) deal directly with work in and outside the home, and yet they offer their audiences a fantasy of escape from the tedium of work into romances with 'exotic' foreigners. Russell's films drew audiences which fitted almost exactly the social classifications of

TABLE 2.1   Distribution of workers between different
industries (1994)

Agriculture, forestry and fishing	243,000
Production industries:	
Coal, oil and natural gas	76,000
Electricity, gas and water	230,000
Manufacturing industries	4,227,000
Construction	864,000
Service industries:	
Wholesale distribution and repairs	1,083,000
Retail distribution	2,275,000
Hotels and catering	1,205,000
Transport	849,000
Post and telecommunications	358,000
Banking, finance and insurance	2,666,000
Public administration	1,761,000
Education	1,848,000
Medical and health services, veterinary	
services	1,569,000
Other services	1,752,000
Total no. of men in employment:	10,634,000
Total no. of women in employment:	10,377,000

Source: Adapted from *Employment Gazette*, February 1995

the characters in them. Unlike novels and films, television,
curiously, has produced a spate of series about work. They have
accelerated beyond such hospital dramas as *Casualty* or rural
veterinary practices like *All Creatures Great and Small* to include
the military (*Soldier Soldier*), fire-fighting (*London's Burning*) and
many others.

A film which offers a useful case study because it did very
well at the box office, and therefore may be seen to reflect popular
British aspirations and values, is *Four Weddings and A Funeral*
(1994). The story pursues some friends around Britain and examines their social lives in the context of the ceremonial rituals of

TABLE 2.2   Rates of unemployment

Year	Total	Rate (%)
1980	1,363,800	5.1
1981	2,171,500	8.1
1982	2,544,100	9.5
1983	2,787,200	10.4
1984	2,915,500	10.6
1985	3,027,000	10.9
1986	3,096,900	11.1
1987	2,804,900	10.0
1988	2,274,800	8.0
1989	1,782,100	6.2
1990	1,660,800	5.8
1991	2,286,100	8.0
1992	2,765,000	9.7
1993	2,900,600	10.3
1994	2,619,400	9.4

Source: Adapted from National Readership Survey

the title. The whole is placed in the context of an Anglo-American 'special relationship', which is part shared cultural history and part wish-fulfilment designed to appeal to different agendas on both sides of the Atlantic. As in other films such as *The Remains of the Day* (1994), *A Handful of Dust* (1988) or *The Shooting Party* (1984), it adds social comment to a familiar recipe of stately homes in a timeless, upstairs/downstairs England peopled with fascinating eccentrics and nameless servants. This has been called a 'Merchant/Ivory' version of Britain (from the names of the director and producer who made *A Room With a View* (1985) and *Howards End* (1992)). *Four Weddings and a Funeral* offers a version of Britain which contains a mixture of traditional and new clichés. Bohemianism, the gay community and monarchy are all contained in the non-threatening framework of British compromise and there is practically no mention of work. The film comes from the same mould as *Chariots of Fire* (1981) and *Another Country* (1984), which ultimately praise the leisured Britain that they depict and steadfastly ignore the means of earning a living. In such pointedly socially divided worlds, work persists in its cultural representations as something the upper classes do not do and the working classes wish not to do.

To further illustrate the prevalence of this view of work, we can look at an example from recent Britpop. The 1995 Blur album is called *The Great Escape*. Its front cover has a picture of someone diving from a motorboat into a beautiful Mediterranean sea. Its back cover has the four members of the group dressed as urban professionals huddled around a computer. Here, as with most popular culture aimed at the country's mass population, the dominant British view is that work is a treadmill from which people dream of escaping (Blur's other album titles also suggest this: *Leisure, Modern Life is Rubbish, Parklife*).

The possibility of a life of leisure is also a fantasy indulged in every week as the National Lottery winning numbers are announced on television and millionaires are literally 'made' overnight. It is assumed that the winners will give up work without a regret but many have to be counselled by therapists to cope with (partly their wealth but largely) their position away from the community and working life they have known. People establish and share identity at work through participation in such incidental 'social' aspects as car pools, coffee clubs, office sweepstakes (betting on horses), company sports clubs and celebrations for engagements and birthdays. In the 1990s more people meet their future spouse through work than in any other way.

On leaving the office or the factory, there is often a shared drink with workmates and nights out to celebrate new jobs, retirements and weddings. (The latter are known as 'hen' and 'stag' nights for women and men respectively.) They take place in night clubs, pubs or working men's social clubs. Many relationships carry on outside work and workers do jobs ('foreigners') for one another, which may be called 'a busman's holiday' (doing in your leisure time what you do at work). This kind of social side to work obviously comes to an end when jobs are lost.

Despite the taboo against cultural representation of work, in practice British society is constructed so much around employment that those who are cut off from it are also isolated socially. Britain was the first country to industrialise and it looks like becoming one of the first to have to devise programmes for coping with the problems of post-industrial and even post-agricultural society (in 1950 25 per cent of the workers in Britain still worked on the land – the figure today is under 2 per cent). It will have to supply redundant workforces with a range of services, from counselling to setting up small businesses to make-work to voluntarism.

Unemployment and economic change

The work ethic is very strong in the UK and for a majority of the British population their identity is shaped by the notion that they *work*. However, one of the main features of the working classes in 1980s and 1990s Britain is that a greater proportion of them than of either the middle or upper classes is *not* working. Loss of work to a class which defines itself as *working* is traumatic and will be dealt with further in Chapter 5 on class and politics. One must not underestimate the culture shock involved in growing up within such a situation. Yozzer Hughes, a chief character in Alan Bleasdale's *Boys from the Blackstuff*, became a cult figure with his catchphrase of 'Gizza job', partly because so many people could empathise and identify with him. This has also been a major theme in soap operas such as *Brookside* and *EastEnders*.

Women in employment have fared less well than men. There is a higher percentage of women in work than there was in 1950 and there are now more women in the workforce than men. However, for a number of reasons, including prejudice and part-time working, women have often failed to gain promotion to posts of greater responsibility. The term 'glass ceiling' is applied to this consequent upper limit of women's progress in company careers. Their rate of unemployment at 4.7 per cent is less than half that

FIGURE 2.4   Women office workers

of men but their average pay is only 75 per cent of men's in similar occupations. However, unemployed women *and* men from ethnic minorites are even more disadvantaged than mainstream workers with rates of 17 per cent and 24 per cent of the workforce. The rate of unemployment for Muslims is estimated to be 27 per cent, whereas for Christians it is under 10 per cent.

Not surprisingly the above climate has led to a decline in a sense of job security. According to a government report [23 August 1995], unlike previous generations middle-aged people now do not feel secure about their financial prospects. When the chairman of a major bank predicts job losses in his industry of 20,000, others see *their* jobs as precarious, and people are cautious about spending. For example, the percentage of disposable income that people now save at 12.2 per cent is 50 per cent more than in the 1960s. John Major's prediction of 'wealth cascading down through the generations' has a hollow ring for this generation.

Karl Marx's predictions about the 'casualisation of labour' appear to be coming to pass and certainly many more people are being employed on temporary or part-time contracts. Instead of seeing this as the apocalyptic end to capitalism however, some business analysts prefer to interpret it as following the pattern of the United States and supplying a more flexible productive base which ultimately regulates more efficiently the balance between supply and demand in the labour market.

For the last hundred years the south of England has been the most prosperous part of Britain and for a time in the 1980s, people there enthusiastically endorsed the concept of a corporate Britain. They were enabled to participate in company share purchase schemes, and they supported the under-priced privatisation sales of utilities such as electricity, water and telephone companies. The majority of small shareholders (they were known as 'Sids', because of a British Gas privatisation advertising campaign with a character of that name) took their profits and sold out, in the spirit of the entrepreneurialism which was being recommended to them by government. Some did sense themselves for a time as empowered and as part of corporate Britain. Other people felt that, because the industries were owned by the country, *their* national assets were being sold off to those sufficiently well off to have money to invest in them.

In a social democracy there is a widespread belief that the state has a duty to its citizens so that, if society cannot offer them jobs, the government should provide them with the means of coping with the demands made on them as useful citizens and consumers. The state has a responsibility towards them and, partly through such welfare support, they retain as individuals a sense of social responsibility despite society's failure towards them. People on the political Right argue that Britain has become a poor country because it has created a climate of dependency: its citizens lack initiative, rely on the 'nanny' state to look after their every need and thus avoid their personal responsibilities. Contrary to this view, however, are those indications that recent government policy has clearly led to failure in many people's lives. For example, after government drives to increase home ownership, there are up to 1.4 million people in Britain today with 'negative equity', that is, the loan they have taken out with a bank is greater than the value of the house they borrowed it for. Other people in the 1980s, who were encouraged by the government to buy their state-owned homes (council houses) on very good terms, have not been able to keep up the payments and so homes are being repossessed at the rate of 1000 per week.

A further under-discussed factor in Britain's economic malaise may be the decline in religious observance which, through Protestantism, has a particularly close relation to work. A belief in the moral importance of work was especially notable in the late eighteenth century, with the growth of commerce in London, and in the early nineteenth century, with the start of the industrial revolution. The popularity of a novel like Daniel Defoe's *Robinson Crusoe* (1741) shows how ingrained in the culture was the idea of the 'self-employed' individual who, out of a sense of religious duty, struggled alone against odds to succeed. This ideology appealed to a population which until recently had been largely rural and self-employed but who, because of the 'division of labour', was now forced to do single unsatisfying jobs in the city.

In *Religion and the Rise of Capitalism* (1926), R.H. Tawney drew attention to the link between people's religious beliefs and their relative wealth. He attributed Britain's economic well-being to the Protestant work ethic – the idea that we are put on earth, not just to live and to eat, but to work hard (partly as descendants and inheritors of the sin of Adam and Eve (work as 'punishment')). People who believe in the sanctity of work become rich. Conversely, the more unworldly the religion the less likely the religious congregation is to become rich. The situation is undoubtedly circular – economic decline may test religious commitment, which in turn limits adherence to the work ethic. The latter is based on a religious belief, but in practice, people of all persuasions have come through habit to believe in work as a good thing and as a defining characteristic of being British, rather than 'foreign' (a word which is much more xenophobic than the *étranger/estrangeiro* found in most romance languages or the German *auslander*). Again this has increased psychological and social trauma for those unable to find jobs.

If for one reason or another, both culturally ingrained commitment to work is eroded and opportunities are taken away and replaced with the mentality induced by enforced dependency upon the state (ironically under a Tory government), people have to find outlets elsewhere. Their energies have been channelled into leisure and this displacement has taken place in Britain progressively throughout the years of unemployment. The graph of the decline in the number of permanent jobs is crossed by the ascendant one of ownership of video recorders, the practise of sports and other indoor and outdoor leisure pursuits.

Leisure around the home

In dealing with leisure we are concerned not just with how people occupy themselves but with the cultural significance of their hobbies and practices. This applies to group and individual activities. We may divide the leisure pursuits which British people engage in into domestic and public. These are crude designations, but they do offer a way in to understanding how leisure affects cultural consciousness and identity.

As mentioned in the Introduction, the dominant medium for cultural exchange in Britain is television. It is difficult to pinpoint the moment at which television became a significant part of the national cultural consciousness, but many oral histories of older people refer to the novelty of watching the June 1953 Coronation of Queen Elizabeth II on television. This they did in company with friends, relations and neighbours. The transition from listening to the Football Association Cup Final on 'the wireless' (radio) to watching it on television marked a further important change. Particularly since the 1960s, daily consumption of television has risen as broadcasting expanded from evenings only, to daytime, to the mornings – so-called 'breakfast television'. Television watching is now effectively available 24 hours a day, especially with video and over forty cable and satellite stations.

The average time spent watching television is 230 minutes a day. The young and the old will watch a lot more than that, the middle-aged a lot less. Television is a powerful social adhesive in Britain. Following stories on television provides people with topics of conversation, allows them to get to know one another's tastes and preferences, but mainly enables them to explore the kind of current social and cultural preoccupations that television deals with. Workmates and friends are bonded together by their responses to the News or football matches that they have seen on television.

It is clear that the change in the importance to their lives that people attach to television had come about by 1974. At that time Edward Heath, Britain's then Prime Minister, made two mistakes in devising strategic responses to the emergency of the oil crisis. In order to save electricity, he brought in a three-day working week, and he made the television companies finish broadcasting each evening at 10.30 p.m. In other words, he prevented people from working and he interfered with their television viewing. They were not prepared to put up with either of those changes. There was widespread opposition to the government and undoubtedly these were factors in Heath's loss of the General Election in 1974.

Television is not a complete national obsession however; for example, pubs introduced large-screen televisions for specific sports events and promotions in order to increase custom, but their success has been limited, because pubs are more places for social interaction than for 'watching the box', which is a private, domestic pastime. Many people prefer to attend football matches and get much more of a sense of a shared identity from their support for the same team. There is a 'family' atmosphere at some of the big clubs, despite the fact that there are 40,000 people present. Such large attendances indicate a craving for a shared sense of community which television alone cannot provide.

However, in a country with all sorts of signs of social breakdown (from child murder and random knife attacks in the cities to rural suicides and abduction) people cling to electronic expressions of community and watch their own society through television

TABLE 2.3 Most popular soap operas/series (1994)

	Total potential audience (%)
Coronation Street	45.4
The Bill	42.9
EastEnders	37.0
Keeping Up Appearances	36.3
London's Burning	35.3
Neighbours	28.6
Wish you were Here	27.5
Lovejoy	26.4
Drop the Dead Donkey	17.2
Cheers	16.9
Cosby Show	12.7

dramas such as *Casualty* or *The Bill*, which offer excitement set in an everyday context, or soap operas like *Emmerdale* or *Heartbeat*, which convey an idealised rural past. Young people especially relate to soap operas. Reference was made above to *Grange Hill*, but the most popular soaps followed by people in the age group 14–25 are the Australian series *Neighbours* and *Home and Away*. A slightly older age group watches *EastEnders*, *Brookside* and *Coronation Street*. Given the success of US culture in numerous areas of British life, there is a surprising lack of interest in American soaps. Exceptions are ones set in ostensibly coherent communities, for example, *Cheers* or *Northern Exposure*, and are usually comedies. Characters in these programmes supply viewers with topics of conversation which provide the potential glue for their own social community. Table 2.3 shows the relative popularity of television programmes.

Besides television, the major leisure activity of many British people is their 'hobby'. The hobbies or minority interests pursued by Britons are numerous, wide-ranging and passionately (obsessively even) indulged in, because they are part of the forging of

TABLE 2.4 Readership of selected newspapers/magazines (1994 to 1995)

	'000s	Potential readership (%)
Sun	10,168	22.3
Daily Mirror	6,695	14.7
Daily Telegraph	2,579	5.7
The Times	1,455	3.2
Guardian	1,270	2.8
Radio Times	5,050	11.1
Take a Break	4,985	11.0
Just Seventeen	941	2.1
Cosmopolitan	2,409	5.3
Private Eye	750	1.6
Viz	3,354	7.4
The Economist	547	1.0
BBC Gardeners' World	1,672	4.0
What Hi-Fi?	686	2.0
Motorcycle News	591	1.0
Practical Photography	467	1.0
Horse and Hound	400	1.0
The Face	433	1.0

Source: National Readership Survey

individual identity. Such 'minority' activities include philately, train-spotting, ferret-keeping, fishing, pigeon-fancying, bird-watching, scouting, swimming, cycling, fell-running – on a rising scale of physical activity. Most of these hobbies will have magazines to accompany them, or at the very least a newsletter. The number of browsers in high street stationers demonstrates the range and diversity of British people's leisure interests and perspectives, as does Table 2.4.

Book-buying ironically is stimulated by television. Both *Brideshead Revisited* (first published 1945) and *Pride and*

TABLE 2.5 Most popular types of books bought

Rank	Type	Rank	Type
Women		**Men**	
1	Cookery books	1	Crime/thriller/detective
2	Romance/love stories	2	English dictionaries
3	Crime/thriller/detective	3	Car repair manuals
4	English dictionaries	4	Cookery books
5	Puzzle/quiz books	5	Computer manuals
6	Gardening/indoor plant books	6	Sports/games books
7	Food/drink books	7	Gardening/indoor plant books
8	Historical novels/ romance	8	Sports/games instruction books
9	Classics/literature	9	Road atlases of Great Britain
10	Baby and childcare books	10	War/adventure stories

Source: Books and the Consumer 1994, Book Marketing Limited

Prejudice (1813) sold many more copies after their television series than they had before. Table 2.5, which covers books people buy for themselves, is divided along gender lines and concludes this section on 'indoor' entertainments.

Public entertainment

Pubs

The principal place of entertainment outside the home that people automatically think of in relation to Britain is the public house or pub. In the past, pubs have performed different social functions. Traditionally they were male preserves. Various sociological

FIGURE 2.5 Pub scene showing a broad age range socialising together

studies have suggested that until the 1950s the British pub was a more welcoming place for a man than was his home. It was familiar and cosy (small bar rooms were called 'snugs'), with a fire and games such as darts and dominoes. This changed in the 1950s, a period of increasing affluence, when houses were brought up to date and made more attractive with higher standards of draught-proofing, labour-saving appliances, new furnishings and even central heating in some cases. Studies of the 1950s refer to the 'home-centred society'. It was then less acceptable for a woman to go into a pub on her own than it was for a man. Some city centre pubs specified 'men only' and many covertly discouraged single women. Now they are much more welcoming to people of both sexes but few women will say they feel comfortable going into a pub on their own.

Like cinemas, pubs have been through periods of boom and bust in English social life. Cinemas are currently resurgent, with

98 million attendances in 1992 despite the competition of television. Pubs on the other hand, with the percentages of men and women who never drink alcohol at 16 per cent and 20 per cent respectively and rising, are struggling. However, with the churches in Britain in decline, with congregations ageing and Sunday attendances falling, there is a new role for the pub. It often fills the social vacuum created by this change, and performs the function of community meeting place and so is still, in the 1990s, very much central to British life. That this is the case is shown by the many pubs in soap operas, including 'The Vic' in *EastEnders* and 'The Rover's Return' in *Coronation Street*.

Pantomimes

At Christmas time, pantomimes form an important aspect of British cultural experience. Unknown on the Continent, they are staged in theatres, village halls and community centres of all sorts, both amateur and professional. Well-known television personalities or even politicians often appear in them. Parents attend with children, and in a controlled dramatic environment pantomimes offer a 'safe' form of initiation into the adult world. They have always contained a number of standard ingredients: cross-dressing (the 'Principal Boy' is always a woman; the 'Dame' is a man); *double entendre* (parents can understand lewd meanings which pass over the heads of their children); contemporary reference (current politicians, or aspects of daily life such as the National Lottery are ridiculed); ritualised audience participation, where children shout; 'He's behind you', or 'Oh yes it is'/'Oh no it isn't'. They often involve reworking of myths as in *Babes in the Wood*, or *Cinderella*, where the poorly treated individual wins justice and their rightful place in the world.

Sport

Another major outdoor leisure outlet in Britain is sport. The main sports practised in Britain during the winter are rugby and soccer. Rugby is controlled by the Rugby Union and the division between

111

FIGURE 2.6   Poster advertising the Football Association Cup as a holy grail

lower social status soccer players (who need to be paid) and higher social status rugby players ('gifted amateurs') has been eroded by the Union's decision in 1995 to relax its rules to allow professionalism into the game. People in Britain spend a great deal of their leisure time either participating in or watching sport. Attendances per soccer Premier League match averaged 23,040 nearly every Saturday during the 1993/4 winter season. Football in Britain is commonly referred to as 'soccer' to distinguish it from either rugby football or American football and is controlled by the Football Association. Soccer is known as 'a gentlemen's game for roughs' and rugby as 'a roughs' game for gentlemen'. One of the many paradoxes of British society is that although most of the Public (that is private) schools in Britain play the middle-class game of rugby as their main sport, both Eton and Harrow, Britain's most exclusive schools, have always played soccer.

There are two major groups of professional clubs which play in either the Premier or the Football League. There are also two main competitions: the League Cup which is based on points won and the FA Cup which is a knockout competition. Supporters of rival teams are segregated at football matches and they often ritually taunt one another. For example, supporters in the Kop (a terrace at Liverpool named after a lookout hill from the Boer War, Spion Kop) used to sing: 'See them lying on the runway . . .' to Manchester United supporters – to remind them of their team's plane crash in Munich in the late 1950s. Most of the chanting is not so vicious; a milder taunt nowadays is to sing 'Always look on the bright side of life . . .' to your rivals, when your team has just scored a goal. Much debate centres on whether football supplics a safety valve for, rather than an encouragement to, violence and it is argued that aggression is harmlessly released in these ritualised verbal exchanges between supporters. Supporters are thought to feel a necessary sense of shared community through loyalty to their team and local pride when it wins. A measure of the seriousness with which supporters take their soccer is contained in a Liverpool manager's remark: 'Football isn't just a matter of life and death. It's far more important than that.'

The summer game of cricket is played widely on village greens and is a genuinely popular grass-roots game about observance of rules, fairness and a pitting of wits and talent between equally matched teams. However, there are class associations to all British sports and in the case of cricket there is a history of contention for 'ownership' of the game. For example, many British stately homes have an adjacent cricket pitch and pavilion where over the years encounters have taken place between 'gentlemen and players'. This again underlines the British distinction between the upper classes (gentlemen), who are leisured and admirable, and the lower classes (players) who work and are disparaged. Significantly, professional soccer is associated with Britain's cities while cricket, which may well be played in urban centres such as Old Trafford (Manchester), Headingley (Leeds) or Lords (London), is associated with rural Britain. So while football clubs are named 'Leeds United' or 'Manchester City', professional cricketers play for counties, such as Kent, Somersetshire and Gloucestershire.

Variations occur in the terminology used to describe people watching leisure entertainments. Those who watch soccer, rugby, cinema, television, theatre or opera are known respectively as 'crowds', 'spectators', 'audiences', 'viewers', 'theatre-goers' or 'opera-buffs'. These terms form part of a spectrum of cultural snobbery. Soccer fans are traditionally working class and are called 'crowds', suggesting that they are amorphous. Middle-class people who watch rugby are 'spectators' – they are dispassionate onlookers. 'Audiences' are more sophisticated again because they listen. 'Viewers' is a euphemism which denies the passivity of the television 'couch potato'. 'Theatre-goer' implies some form of dynamism and the word 'buff' comes from the uniform (made of buffalo hide) worn by smart regiments.

There are many high-profile outdoor sporting events in Britain, particularly in the summer, which attract national and international interest. However, there are many more less publicised ones which supply the high point in individual enthusiasts' years. Local events are invariably more interesting and can sometimes surprisingly be better patronised than national events. For example, 30,000 runners take part in Gateshead's Great North Run, compared with the 26,000 who take part in the London Marathon. The former is hardly alluded to in the national news media with their metropolitan emphasis, but the latter is hyped and televised. Impressionistically, the degree of health consciousness, fitness and dietary awareness is higher among the British young than the Americans, but young Swiss, Germans or Canadians are much more likely to swim or ride bikes than the British. There are few British equivalents to the continental 'parcours' (outdoor fitness areas in national parks), and facilities such as the National Rowing Centre at Nottingham or the Manchester Velodrome (for cycling) are over-stretched and of no help in keeping the majority of people fit. Most women exercise indoors, and so increasingly do men. Health and fitness clubs or gyms have become very popular throughout the country in the

114

FIGURE 2.7   The Glastonbury Festival

1990s, and large numbers of people regularly attend aerobics or 'step' classes. Despite this focus on fitness, cigarette smoking among the young is again on the increase – particularly among young women.

Festivals

Arts festivals take place annually in most large cities, and smaller places like Glyndebourne and Buxton have their own opera festivals. Pop and rock festivals in particular have become a feature of youth culture. The best known are at Glastonbury and Reading. Entrance fees are relatively expensive at £65 for two or three days but they are extremely well attended with upwards of 20,000 people.

Museums

In this survey of communal leisure activities, we can also say that a traditional version of British culture is nurtured in a range of public institutions, mainly museums and art galleries. In the past it has tended to be high culture which is conserved here and they were places of obligatory pilgrimage for schoolchildren, who in the course of their subsequent lives never returned. This has changed in recent years. These institutions have become more imaginative, and their collections have been partially devolved to the regions. There is a Tate Gallery in Liverpool and a branch of London's National Portrait Gallery at Bodelwyddan Castle in north Wales. Instead of a single unchanging stock, museums now tend to stage more 'thematic' exhibitions, such as Liverpool Maritime Museum's slavery exhibition, or its Labour Museum which deals with the material conditions of people's existences rather than high culture.

Holidays

Leisure was originally the preserve of the upper classes. Only they had the time and the money to tramp their own grouse moors in Scotland, or sail their yachts with professional crews at Cowes. For example, the industrialist Sir Thomas Lipton was able to finance his own Americas Cup yachting challenges and pay his crews in the 1930s. So when leisure became available to ordinary people through decreased working hours and paid annual leave, by and large in the 1950s, it gave social status to those benefiting from it. This soon changed, as catering for larger numbers of leisured people on a year round basis became an industry. Treatment of holiday-makers became more systematic, more professional, less deferential and less status dependent.

Since the 1960s the two-week annual holiday is more likely to be spent abroad. 'Package tours' have brought these holidays within the price range of ordinary people. The beneficiaries have been the hoteliers of Spain, Greece and Florida; those losing out have been, British seaside landladies at traditional resorts. David Lodge suggests in *Paradise News* (1992) that tourism is the new world religion. British people have become obsessed with holidaying abroad, principally in Spain and France, but increasingly in Florida. The Hoover Company, when it promoted a holiday scheme in 1993, so underestimated the public's response that it lost £200 million.

New patterns in leisure

Gambling

Betting on horse-racing, the sport of the rich, has always been practised by the working rather than the middle classes, whose puritanism in regard to gambling has been tempered only by government sponsored Premium Bonds and the National Lottery. The latter has become a major national talking point in Britain, which for reasons largely to do with inherited puritanism was the last country in Europe to introduce the game, in November 1994. As a social and cultural phenomenon it is especially interesting. It generates comment in the media, between politicians and among people in general. It has brought a whole new clientele into gambling. Tickets are sold through newsagents and post offices – where everybody goes – whereas other forms of gambling such as horse-racing are contained within betting shops where passers-by may not even see in through the windows and from which the family is virtually excluded. Once a year many people will place a bet on the Grand National or the Derby, but with the Lottery and its sequel, 'Instant' scratchcards, millions have a 'flutter' (a bet) every week.

Since its introduction Britain's National Lottery has become an important social and cultural phenomenon. Its revenues, at £65 million per week, are well above initial estimates of £14–35 million, and it is claimed that nine out of ten adults have bought tickets at some point. It is clearly a financial success. This is especially striking since the bookmakers Ladbrokes have likened the chance of winning the jackpot to that of Elvis landing a UFO (Unidentified Flying Object) on the Loch Ness Monster. The odds are about fourteen million to one.

George Orwell, writing in 1948, imagined the Lottery with quite uncanny accuracy:

The Lottery, with its weekly pay-out of enormous prizes was the one public event to which the proles [workers] paid serious attention. It was probable that there were some millions of proles for whom the Lottery was the principal if not the only reason for remaining alive. It was their delight, their folly, their anodyne, their intellectual stimulant. Where the Lottery was concerned even people who could barely read and write seemed capable of intricate calculations and staggering feats of memory.

(Orwell: *1984* (Penguin, 1949), p.71)

It is tempting to say that the Lottery is really about the possibility of social change. It has highlighted potential for social upheaval and division. Predictably, some people have not been able to cope with huge winnings. Many legal cases have centred on breaches of trust among workmates, within families and between friends.

The weekly television programme on Saturday nights when the draw takes place draws twelve million viewers with its mixture of orchestrated hype and celebration of greed. The proceeds are devoted to 'good causes', many of which are associated with heritage or 'high' culture like Sadlers Wells Ballet, or the Royal Opera Company. It has introduced the word 'rollover' (un-won prizes carried forward) into the dictionary. It has increased the number of what were previously (football) 'pools winners' (in its first year it produced more than a hundred millionaires) and so raised their profiles as social and cultural phenomena.

A number of lobbies have predictably come out against the Lottery. Church leaders, directors of charities helping the poor, other charities whose revenues have fallen and the companies who previously received the money gambled on football via their weekly 'pools coupons'. These groups raise the following main objections: people are spending money they cannot afford; revenues are being diverted from the poor to the rich; the state is encouraging gambling, and less money is going to charity overall.

Public acceptance of the Lottery and people's enthusiastic identification of themselves as prepared to take a risk, may none the less represent a sea change in Britain's attitudes to gambling, entrepreneurialism and the new rich. In much British middle-class culture and entertainment – from the novel to plays to television sitcoms, the most reviled characters have been the *nouveaux riches*, whether as individuals or as a class. Mrs Malaprop, Josiah Bounderby and Hyacinth Bucket are examples of people whose wealth and pretensions exceed their level of cultural attainment and sensitivity but mainly their good manners. A series like *Fawlty Towers* acknowledges the idea that however rich you are, there are still proprieties to be observed and limits beyond which you may not go in requiring standards of service which people do not choose to give you within the context of their own home or 'guest house'.

Much of the criticism of the Lottery is based on the fear that one class will be subsidising another's pleasures. A major complaint about the disbursement of funds is that places of entertainment for the rich have benefited.

What irks many people is that winning the Lottery goes against their idea of 'natural justice', as defined by the middle classes, in terms of the work ethic discussed earlier: 'unearned' money is frowned upon. Furthermore, when someone with a criminal record won several million pounds, the *Daily Telegraph* expressed its readers' sense of outrage that such 'undeserved' luck should happen. Yet the paper itself is caught in the bind of accepting and promoting such aspects of capitalism as free enterprise and entrepreneurialism yet not liking one of the inevitable consequences.

Trends in entertainment

There have been major shifts during the twentieth century in the cultural influences which British people cite as reflecting their tastes. In the past, common reference points would be individual musical hall performers like Marie Lloyd, or singers like Vera Lynn or Gracie Fields – people giving live performances in theatres around the country. With technology and the growth of radio and television, *groups* of entertainers came to predominate. The Beatles or Rolling Stones are obvious examples. The same is true of radio and television comedy shows where a team (the Goons, Monty Python, the Goodies) was involved in making the show. Now, on the other hand, possibly because of a new cult of individualism, the emphasis has moved away from the group to the individual in entertainment. Young people in Britain today name as their formative cultural influences such lone stars as Vic Reeves, Jo Brand, Ruby Wax or Steve Coogan.

There is now also a noticeable preference by young people for inanimate over animate sources of entertainment. This is evident not just in the decline of such live arts as theatre, or home pastimes like card playing or in the preference for night clubs with DJs over live gigs. Technophiliac 'Generation X' (from Douglas Coupland's 1991 novel of that name) prefer things to people: cash machines to bank cashiers; computers to socialising; cyber cafés to coffee houses; virtual reality to reality; the internet and technological gizmos such as pagers and answering machines to live individuals. Nor do people simply prefer television and cinema to live entertainment. Within electronic media they prefer cartoons to 'real' representations of people. By the early 1980s Britain was already fertile ground for the revival of puppetry – the American Jim Henson's *The Muppet Show* was based in London. *Spitting Image* had enormous popularity on British television and is credited politically with destroying the leadership of the Liberal Party. In sum, people now seem to prefer electronic representations of life to ones which purport to offer more 'real' slices of life through film or video.

Technology has proved that it can deliver the 'real world', yet people want even more overtly 'manufactured' images than are contained in traditional representation. They prefer animated characters in television adverts. Illustrations for a Boddingtons' Beer television advertising campaign are supplied by Dan Clowes, who is better known for his 'grunge' illustrations. Puppets and cartoons have replaced people on hugely successful television shows such as *Wallace and Gromit*, *Beavis and Butthead* and *Crapston Villas*. Television has had huge successes with animation. Several shows have followed the age curve for children brought up on *The Muppets* and *The Simpsons* and they imitate both clever advertising and the cartoon figures of Japanese Manga comics.

Cartoons have always been directed at children, but recently television cartoon series have been developed, characterised by seriousness of purpose and directed at adults. The advent of Disney's computer generated *Toy Story* is no doubt the start of a whole trend. This is the age (certainly for Generation X) of electronic entertainment. Many young people brought up on games arcades *prefer* artificially animated films to ones inhabited by human beings.

Another notable change in the pattern of people's leisure is a move away from socialising at home to frequenting public places of entertainment: 'fun pubs' and multiplexes (containing cinemas, bowling alleys, fruit machines and night-clubs). There are regional variations but generally the fact that British socialising took place in the pub or club made it difficult for new people to integrate into British society in the 1950s. Asians in particular preferred to socialise at home, and this exacerbated cultural differences and kept groups separated. In time however, as in so many aspects of culture referred to elsewhere (body piercing, casual clothing, rap music, use of marijuana), while young mainstream people adopted immigrants' practices, young people from minority backgrounds joined the move to socialise outside the home.

So young people of all ethnic origins now mix in places of public entertainment. One can see the influence of McDonald's in this, where premises, balloons, party poppers and so on have been supplied free of charge for children's parties. Operators of multiplex cinemas, bowling alleys and night-clubs benefit from this groundwork and cater to a young population brought up on 'canned' culture and dedicated to Britain's consumer society.

In a consumer society, people, undoubtedly feel an enhanced need to express a sense of unique identity. This is illustrated by the fact that some will pay large sums of money (up to £100,000) for personalised number plates. Since 1986, the Department of Transport has allowed people to pay extra when licensing their cars in order to buy these special plates. Registrations such as ME 1 or A5 enable people to draw attention to themselves – to assert their identity – and are much sought after.

The older generation meanwhile, which saves 13 per cent of its disposable income (3 times the level of the 1950s) continues to opt for home entertainment. Eighty-nine per cent of British households have video machines and are catered for by an estimated 2000 video shops – supplying a market which didn't exist twenty years ago.

Irish pubs

Finally in this section on leisure, a revealing debate has been taking place about the introduction of Irish pubs into the British high street. This trend, a 'simple' commercial phenomenon, is seen to have all sorts of other implications. Irish pubs are financially successful, but people ask: 'What are they saying about Britain? Do they suggest it is a soulless place which needs an infusion of Celtic culture?' CAMRA (the Campaign for Real Ale) resists the trend as part of a commercialising of the English institution of the pub – a dilution of authentic English values. Others are unhappy about the ideological implications of raising of the profile of a 'minority' culture in the war for hearts and minds in relation to an Ulster political settlement. Others are concerned that national identity is being exploited for purely commercial ends. Some see the trend as one more illustration of a postmodern phenomenon that uses elements of the past and elsewhere as a vocabulary with which to write the new Britain. In that respect Irishness has only a surface significance – it could as easily be an American influence like McDonalds, or a Japanese one like Karaoke – and they suggest that the trend should be welcomed as more evidence of tolerant multicultural Britain.

However, perhaps the most significant thing is that the forum in which this nationalistic venture is being played out – the high street – is a more democratic one than parliament, whose legislation cramps and controls people. (The post-war Labour administration, which produced 1000 pages of legislation per year, was seen as 'interventionist'. The present government produces 3000 pages per year.) People want to liberate themselves through culture and believe that cultural change cannot be legislated for. *Laissez-faire* capitalism will produce stampedes of commercial developers to out-of-town shopping centres or a situation where all high streets have more or less the same shops: Halfords, Boots, Marks & Spencer and so on. In other words, a homogenising commercial process will take place which will ultimately dampen rather than enrich culture and cultural identity.

Conclusion

To sum up this chapter: the cultural ambience is not neutral, it is a plain on which warring factions contend. Education, work and leisure are defining aspects of British cultural identity. Schools place a distinctive stamp on their pupils – a past pupil will be defined both in society at large *and* by the individual him or herself as a *grammar school* boy or girl, or more specifically as a product of Shrewsbury School or King Street Primary. This pattern is repeated in the work arena when society labels people 'owned' by particular industries or by the state as a *Ford* worker, a *Civil* Servant. People acknowledge these descriptions of themselves, because they also define themselves by their schools and their work functions. The rhetorical question 'How do you do?', on being introduced to people, is very shortly followed by 'What do you do?' and soon thereafter by 'Where did you go to school?' So education and work are significant defining aspects of identity. As we have seen, people will always try to take control of their lives and define their own identities through the exercise of individual choice in their leisure activities. Finally, we have highlighted a number of debates which arise in relation to these issues.

EXERCISES

1   Reading checklist. Answers to, or information on, all
     of these questions can be found in the chapter.

     ■   Why are public schools so called?
     ■   What is the origin of the word 'education'?
     ■   What is the difference between wages and
          salaries?
     ■   Are average female earnings the same as those of
          males?
     ■   What are 'hen' and 'stag' nights?
     ■   What is the Protestant ethic?
     ■   What is a 'glass ceiling'?
     ■   What is a wireless?
     ■   Where is the Kop?
     ■   How are soccer and cricket teams differently
          named?
     ■   When is the Sabbath?
     ■   What is a Merchant/Ivory representation of
          Britain?
     ■   Who plays the Principal Boy in a pantomime?
     ■   What is CAMRA?
     ■   Which was the last country in Europe to have a
          National Lottery?

2   What kinds of schools are more likely to be portrayed
     in films? Why is this? You might consider viewing on
     video some of the films referred to in this chapter: *Kes,
     The Belles of St Trinians, Another Country.* How do
     these representations differ from the school in, say,
     Dead Poets' Society?

3   Why are portrayals of work so rare in British
     novels/plays? Is American writing more likely to deal
     with work? Are British cultural forms more or less
     escapist than American ones?

4   Is it healthy or unhealthy to watch soap operas?

5   Questions for discussion.

- What is the effect on individual identity of pupils attending state or private schools?
- Does education always involve the imposition on one group in society of the values of another?
- How is unemployment related to identity?
- Does self-employment confer more dignity on workers?
- This chapter has referred to the presence in Britain of McDonald's and Japanese Manga comics. Are overseas influences in a culture to be welcomed or resisted?
- Should the state fund culture? If so, should it aim to encourage high or popular culture? If not, why not?
- How important are tradition and traditional ways in a culture?

━━━━━━━━━━━━━━━━━━━━━━━━━━━ READING

Deem, Rosemary. *Work, Unemployment and Leisure.* Routledge, 1988
A study and analysis of the relation between time in and out of work.

Giles, J. and Middleton, T. *Writing Englishness 1900–1950.* Routledge, 1996
A useful sourcebook of traditional material relating to the construction of the concept of Englishness.

Marwick, A. *A Society At Odds With Itself.* Forthcoming
Updated historical account which plays on John Major's goal of 'a society at one with itself'.

Storey, John. *An Introductory Guide to Cultural Theory and Popular Culture*. Harvester, 1993
An accessible book on culture and cultural studies set in a British context.

CULTURAL EXAMPLES

■   *Films*

Another Country (1984) dir. Marek Kanievska
Speculative drama about the claustrophobic public school life of two future British spies, Guy Burgess and Donald MacLean.

Clockwork Mice (1995) dir. Jean Vadim
Gentle drama about a young teacher starting at a Special Needs School, his relationships with pupils and staff, and his attempt to involve the children in a cross-country running club.

Educating Rita (1983) dir. Lewis Gilbert
A working-class woman, unfulfilled by life at home with her husband, tries an Open University English course and develops a strong relationship with her tutor.

How to Get Ahead in Advertising (1989) dir. Bruce Robinson
Satire on the advertising and marketing professions.

■   *Books*

Bill Bryson, *Notes from a Small Island* (1995)
Idiosyncratic but informed view of Britain offered by a resident American journalist with experience of British work and leisure.

David Lodge, *Changing Places* (1975)
Deals with insights into human nature gained by academics from Britain and America who exchange jobs, houses, educational experiences and much more.

Muriel Spark, *The Prime of Miss Jean Brodie* (1961)
Powerful story of the effects of education on impressionable young people.

■ *Television programmes*

As Seen on TV
Comedy programme of very talented comedienne, Victoria Wood. Includes sketches, stand-up, piano songs. Satirises specific idiosyncracies of British life.

The Bill, London's Burning, Casualty
Popular drama serials about work set in, respectively, a police station, a fire brigade, and a hospital. All provide tension and excitement through their focus on one of the three emergency services.

Boys from the Blackstuff
Sympathetic portrayal of unemployed people who work on the side, and their encounters with officialdom.

Drop the Dead Donkey
Award-winning weekly comedy series set in a newspaper office. Written by Andy Hamilton.

Porterhouse Blue
Series set in Cambridge·academe with David Jason and Ian Richardson – from the novel by Tom Sharpe.

Gender, sex, and the family

■ Roberta Garrett

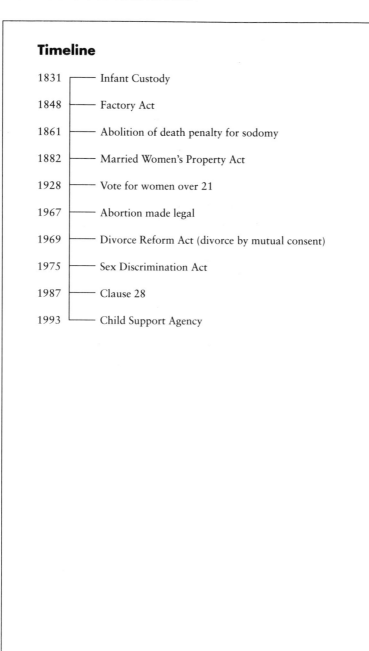

Timeline

1831	Infant Custody
1848	Factory Act
1861	Abolition of death penalty for sodomy
1882	Married Women's Property Act
1928	Vote for women over 21
1967	Abortion made legal
1969	Divorce Reform Act (divorce by mutual consent)
1975	Sex Discrimination Act
1987	Clause 28
1993	Child Support Agency

Introduction

SINCE THE INDUSTRIAL REVOLUTION, rapidly changing employment patterns coupled with demographic and social movements have challenged the beliefs, laws and customs governing notions of family and gender. As the timeline indicates, there has been a long series of legal reforms affecting sexual behaviour, kinship structures and the social status of women.

On the one hand, these reforms were the result of progressive, humanitarian social movements such as feminism, which, in less than two hundred years, has secured rights of guardianship, property ownership, political representation and reproductive control for British women. On the other hand, protective legislation – such as the 1848 Factory Act limiting women and children to a ten-hour working day – countered the exploitation of women workers in the newly developing manufacturing industries primarily in order to ensure their allegiance to motherhood and wifely duties. In this sense, nineteenth-century parliamentary reforms went hand-in-hand with a gradual acceptance of the state's right to directly intervene in and regulate the domestic sphere. During the 1960s and 1970s 'permissive' legislation such as the legalisation of abortion, the introduction of the no-fault divorce and the decriminalisation of homosexuality have reversed this trend, reflecting the higher priority awarded to personal choice and freedom as opposed to public morality and duty. In recent years the pendulum appears to be swinging back, with legislation such as the Child Support Act, which enforces parental responsibilities by law, and calls to reintroduce more restrictive divorce laws.

Over the next few decades, there will undoubtedly be further contentious reforms in legislation concerning sexual discrimination, abortion, divorce and sexual practice. All of these affect, and are in turn affected by, social attitudes and cultural activities.

Their strongest impact, however, will be perceived in terms of the British family unit and so, when looking at trends in attitudes towards gender and sex, it is here that we must begin.

The family unit

At present, there are factors pulling in opposite directions in terms of the size of the British population. While the average lifespan has increased in the UK, British fertility rates have been steadily declining since the population boom of the immediate postwar years. A higher number of couples do not have children (20 per cent) and those who do generally have smaller families. This is largely attributed to both improvements in female education and career prospects and greater social acceptance of contraception. Childbearing is frequently postponed until the late twenties or early thirties and the majority of women work outside of the home both before and after having children, regardless of marital status. Consequently, the often-quoted average British family with 2.4 children has now dwindled to 1.8: a trend which reflects the overall decline in the proportion of 'conventional' family units. Only 24 per cent of contemporary British households fall into the 'two adults plus dependent children' nuclear model, and this figure includes not only married couples but the increasing number of long-term cohabitees.

Perhaps one of the most significant shifts over the last twenty years has been in attitudes towards marriage, which, though still popular (around 75 per cent of people marry at least once) is less so than at any previous time in British history. The decline in registered marriages has also been mirrored by a sharp increase in marital breakdown. One in every three British marriages currently ends in divorce, making UK rates the highest in Europe (Table 3.1). As a result of these changes, the number of single-parent families (90 per cent of which are headed by women) has risen dramatically, comprising one in five of all family units and generating the latest in a long line of perceived threats to the fabric of British family life.

TABLE 3.1 Divorces in the UK: 1971 and 1992 (by duration of marriage)

	1971	1992
All divorces	79,200	175,100
0–4 years	10,296	40,273
5–9 years	24,552	47,277
10–14 years	15,048	31,518
15–19 years	10,296	22,763
20+ years	19,800	33,269

Source: OPCS, NTC

If the statistics indicate a rapid decline in allegiance to the traditional family unit, these figures need to be balanced against other interrelated changes in life experience and cultural norms. For example, while the liberalisation of the divorce laws and the (albeit limited) possibility of female economic independence has undoubtedly done much to make divorce a realistic option for greater numbers of people, the extended life expectancy of both partners is also an important contributory factor. A couple who marry in their twenties are now committing themselves to stay together for the next fifty or so years, whereas a century ago, when people rarely lived beyond their mid-forties, a lifelong marriage would have covered only thirty years. When these differences are taken into account, it appears that the length of the average marriage has stayed fairly constant over the last century, settling at around fifteen to twenty years before either death or divorce.

Ethnicity is also an important factor in accounting for different British family structures. For example, many Vietnamese and Bengali families still retain an extended family structure, while a higher than average proportion of Afro-Caribbean families are mother-led. In addition to this, the relatively low proportion of 'normal' British families does not reflect the symbolic or ideological importance of the conventional family unit, which remains strong despite its minority status. The two-parent, patriarchal family continues to be regarded by many as the most important of all social institutions, bearing the brunt of responsibility for producing well-adjusted, law-abiding citizens. And although the Conservatives have assumed the role of 'the party of family values', the family tends to occupy an elevated position within the rhetoric of all major political parties. Public discussion of the family is generally concerned with the best means of defending it and ensuring its continuation, as opposed to whether other forms of socialisation – such as communal child-rearing – might prove to be a healthier or more practical model for most people. In short, the overall desirability or legitimacy of the institution itself is rarely questioned, at least within mainstream political debate.

But as with any social institution, notions of what constitutes a healthy, normal family unit vary according to contemporary cultural practices and social concerns. In the 1970s, the 'teenage bride' became the subject of much moral concern, whereas such debates in the 1990s have instead focused on the growing numbers of single mothers. It would seem that, whether young women are in favour of or against marriage, their marital status constitutes an ongoing cause of anxiety (the insistence on and resistance to the use of Ms instead of Mrs and Miss illustrates this). In this sense, shifting conceptions of gender identity and, in particular, women's greater participation in public as opposed to domestic life, has been a key factor in generating fears about the collapse of the family throughout the last two centuries. In a similar manner, notions of the family are closely linked with debates over national identity and cultural cohesion; at all points of the political spectrum, commitment to 'the family' is frequently evoked as a source of national unity.

In attempting to understand the symbolic importance of the contemporary nuclear model, it is useful to examine its historical development. This is usually traced to the late Victorian period, when, as religious influence declined, the family took up the mantle of moral guardianship. It was expected to provide both moral guidance and social stability, or as early twentieth-century social anthropologists put it, to function as a 'Nursery of Citizenship'.

FIGURE 3.1 A family wedding. Guests surround the couple in their 'going-away' car as they leave for their honeymoon

As mentioned in the introductory chapter to this volume, despite being more of a cosmopolitan dynasty than a cosy nuclear group, the British Royal Family swiftly came to symbolise the ideal British family unit. Even today, the Queen is sometimes referred to as 'the mother of the Commonwealth', just as England, the imperial centre, was once viewed as 'the mother country'. The ideological importance of the Royal Family goes some way towards explaining why the recent spate of acrimonious partings and kiss-and-tell scandals (Charles and Diana's troubled relationship in particular) blighting the present House of Windsor are a cause of such consternation within the UK, but provoke only mild amusement in other countries.

Given this weight of expectations, it is not surprising that the family, as an institution, seems always to be in crisis. Nevertheless, while fears of its erosion are often exaggerated and vary according to cultural context, there is no doubt that the last twenty years have witnessed a particularly turbulent period of

135

change in family structure and gender roles. To consider these transformations in more detail, this chapter will next examine the changing status of British women and then move on to look more broadly at attitudes towards marriage, parenting and sexuality.

Gender and British institutions

Despite the strength and longevity of the British women's movement, many traditional British institutions remain remarkably male-dominated, although this is slowly beginning to change. We will begin to examine both institutionalised sexism and the attempts to challenge it, by looking at predominately male institutions such as the political and legal systems and the Church of England. The culture of Westminster is often likened to that of a boys' public school. Not only are there very few female Members of Parliament (9 per cent) but the House of Commons thrives on an atmosphere of masculine combat. Heckling, jeering and the routine exchange of insults are so much part of the daily proceedings that the Prime Minister John Major and the Leader of the Opposition Tony Blair recently discussed the possibility of a ban on name-calling and a new emphasis on 'mature' debate (at present, only a few insulting words, such as 'liar', are not allowed, and so not heard, in the House).

However, for aspiring female members, the macho culture of Westminster is a minor problem compared to that of getting elected, or even selected to stand, in the first place. Not surprisingly, local constituency executives nominate the candidate with the best chance of getting elected, which, given the age-old prejudices of both sexes, is less likely to be a woman. Of course, there are always notable exceptions. Margaret Thatcher's eleven-year reign proved that a female leader could be quite as confrontational and bloody-minded as any man. During her years in office, Thatcher was frequently described as both 'the best man for the job' and 'the iron lady', perhaps indicating the degree of unease and confusion produced by the presence of a female leader in a traditional male enclave. As it made her the first female British prime minister, Thatcher's election was of symbolic importance, although it may be noted that the overall number of female MPs fell during her term in office and that she herself was outspoken in her opposition to women's rights. Thatcher's appointment was shortly followed by another, no less historic female appointment, when Betty Boothroyd was made the first woman to occupy the powerful position of Speaker of the House of Commons – the arbiter of Commons debate.

Of the major political parties, Labour has the strongest commitment to and historical identification with feminist politics. Recent party initiatives have aimed to counter discrimination by promoting a high number of women to powerful-positions within the party (such as the Shadow Cabinet) and devising all women electoral shortlists for some constituencies. These policies have aroused much controversy, for while many think it necessary to take positive action to achieve equal political representation, others have argued that the policies undermine the achievements of the women they favour. Furthermore, labour's pro-feminist sympathies have never guaranteed the largest share of the female vote. In fact, the Conservative Party's endorsement of strong law-and-order policies, combined with a commitment to traditional family values, appeals to a higher proportion of (particularly older) female voters.

The British legal system is one of the country's oldest, most traditionalist institutions. As such, it is often accused of gender bias in terms of proceedings, sentences and professional opportunities. Although women are now entering the legal profession in ever increasing numbers (half of all British law students are female), they are less likely to reach the top of their profession, more often becoming solicitors than higher ranked and (generally) better paid barristers. There are few British female QCs (senior barristers, known as Queen's Counsel) and even fewer female judges. It is therefore less surprising that the judiciary has come in for particularly harsh condemnation regarding its attitudes towards sexual assaults and other forms of violence against women. British judges have been accused of letting rapists off lightly and apportioning an inexcusable degree of blame to female victims. Indeed, one of the main reasons so few sexual assaults are reported in the UK is that women feel anxious that they, and not their attacker, will be made morally, if not legally, culpable for the crime. This fear is exacerbated by well-publicised comments made by prominent members of the judiciary concerning the style of clothing and sexual history of victims.

Another contentious issue has been that of domestic violence. Again, the judiciary have been condemned for showing leniency towards men who perpetrate it, but have little sympathy with women who retaliate. In response, women's groups have mounted lengthy campaigns for the release of women convicted of killing violent, abusive husbands, arguing that even in cases in which the death was premeditated, years of persistent abuse amounted to provocation, and thus could not be regarded as cold-blooded murder. Interestingly, while these campaigns have proved largely ineffective, the 1995 dramatisation of a similar case in the socially conscious soap opera *Brookside* resulted in a groundswell of public opinion in favour of such women and helped to secure the release of Sara Thornton, who had served five years of her life sentence for just such a crime.

On 11 November 1992 the General Synod of The Church of England voted in favour of the ordination of women priests. This decision was the result of over a century of struggle on the part of women's rights campaigners, and ended a lengthy and divisive battle within the Church. The initial demand for female ordination began in the late nineteenth century (Florence Nightingale was an early supporter) as part of the first wave of the British feminist movement. As a result of this pressure, the Church of England created the somewhat ambiguous order of 'deaconess' which entitled women to preside over certain rituals, but was not regarded as part of the holy triumvirate of bishops, priests and deacons. The Church of England did not permit women deacons until as late as 1987, by which time Anglican church-women in Canada and the US had been taking the priesthood for around ten years. In this respect, the Church of England was somewhat out of kilter with other branches of the Anglican Church and, indeed, the British public at large, 80 per cent of whom had been in favour of the ordination of women for some time. The fiercest clerical opposition to female ordination came, not surprisingly, from the church's influential Anglo-Catholic wing, many of whom either renounced the priesthood altogether or converted to Catholicism when the decision was announced. Since the vote was taken around 1,300 women have been ordained in Britain.

Women and employment

Probably the most important factor in the transformation of British gender identities has been the long-term and seemingly irreversible trend towards female participation in the paid labour force.

Women have continued to enter the labour force in ever-increasing numbers throughout the twentieth century, but many fears are voiced about changing gender roles and a perceived deterioration of family life. Women's paid employment may be an accepted fact of modern life, but it is still regarded by many as an undesirable one. In the first half of the twentieth-century government policy reflected the widely held view that the female population constituted a reserve labour force, only to be drawn on in times of dire necessity. During the First World War, the vast numbers of women who were encouraged to enter the labour force had to fight bitterly to achieve the same wage as their male counterparts, a privilege which was granted to women workers during the Second World War, in which, for the first time, state-run nurseries were also provided. But, like the previous generation of women war workers, they were expected to relinquish both their jobs and their state childcare facilities during peacetime.

The immediate postwar period saw a forceful reassertion of traditional roles; women were enticed back into the home as sociologists and psychologists warned of the dangers of maternal

TABLE 3.2 UK employment status by sex (%)

	All	*Men*	*Women*
All in employment	100	100	100
Traditional workforce (figures are rounded): Full-time permanent employees	61.8	73.2	47.9
Flexible workforce (figures are rounded) Full-time temporary employees	2.6	2.8	2.3
Part-time permanent employees	18.6	3.7	36.7
Part-time temporary employees	2.5	1.2	3.9
Full-time self-employed	10.2	15.6	3.7
Government training schemes	1.4	1.7	1.1
Unpaid family workers	0.6	0.3	1.0
Miscellaneous	0.6	0.3	1.0

Source: Spring 1993 Labour Force Survey estimates

deprivation caused by the working mother's absence. Fears concerning the welfare of so-called 'latchkey kids' (those who had no mother to greet them from school) reinforced the notion that children could not be properly cared for without a home-based mother, heightening public hostility towards such women (to reinforce this, in 1995 there were several high-profile attacks in the tabloids on mothers who left their children at 'home alone'). But in spite of these attitudes, women's participation in paid employment rose dramatically in the late 1950s and has continued to increase in every decade since. Shifts in patterns of employment, particularly the expansion of secretarial, administrative and clerical occupations in the 1960s and 1970s, and the rapid growth of the service sector in the 1980s, opened up new areas of female employment. Table 3.2 indicates the breakdown of the workforce by gender and type of employment.

Coupled with the demise of heavy industry, and a subsequent drop in the male-dominated areas of unskilled manual work for the first time ever, the balance has tipped towards an almost evenly divided male and female British labour force. Moreover, there is a marked difference in the composition of the female labour force: in the first half of the century the majority of working women were either young and single or middle-aged with grown children, whereas the greatest increase in the 1970s and 1980s has been amongst those with partners and dependants. But these statistics can be misleading: British women are still far from achieving equality in the workplace. Despite the legacy of hard-won women's rights legislation, such as the Equal Pay (1970) and Sex Discrimination Acts (1975), women in the mid-1990s are still earning just under 80 per cent of men's pay. In practice, equal

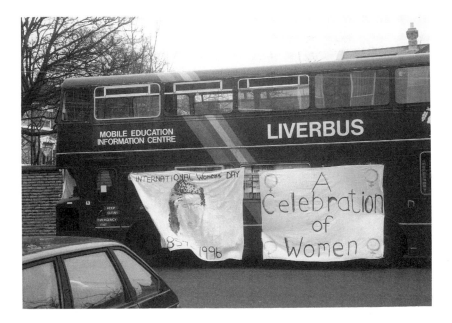

FIGURE 3.2 International Women's Day was celebrated on 6 March 1996

141

pay legislation is difficult to enforce and discrimination hard to prove. Women are still much more likely to be discriminated against on grounds of age or physical attractiveness, although clearly, employers are no longer able to openly specify gender in a job description. The affix 'man' – as in postman, salesman, fireman – has either been replaced by 'person' (salesperson) or dropped completely (firefighter).

It is also the case that a small number of women are now working in previously male-dominated areas, but sex segregation persists. Female employees tend to be heavily concentrated in non-unionised, unskilled areas of work, with an overwhelming majority (81 per cent) working in service industries, as cleaners, waitresses, bar and hotel staff. The catering industry for example, relies largely on part-time and casual labour, precisely the kind of low-paid, low-status, 'pink collar' occupations, which women with small children and limited childcare assistance are often forced into accepting. But even predominantly female skilled occupations – such as secretarial or administrative work – tend to command less pay and status by virtue of their 'feminine' associations. Probably the most serious example is that of British nurses, who earn considerably less than those in most other parts of Western Europe, chiefly because, in this country, nursing is still viewed more as an extension of woman's natural 'caring' role than as a skilled profession. In addition, there is little evidence to suggest that women's increased participation in the labour force has been accompanied by a corresponding shift in domestic responsibilities. Working women continue to do the lion's share of housework, child-rearing, and caring for elderly relatives. Surprisingly, this rule applies even in situations where women are the primary earners. Studies of areas of high male unemployment, such as Wearside in the post-industrial North East, show a rise in stay-at-home husbands and working wives. But they also indicate that while husbands are prepared to perform 'light' domestic duties (such as shopping and cooking) they still draw the line at cleaning and other 'menial' domestic tasks. In short, traditional gender identities persist and role reversal was regarded as temporary and pragmatic.

As we might expect, female employment opportunities are also heavily influenced by other factors such as region, class and race. For example, although a higher than average number of Afro-Caribbean women go on to further education, levels of unemployment within this ethnic group are significantly greater than amongst their white female counterparts. Predictably, the greatest career gains have been made by white, middle-class, university educated women, who are now beginning to make significant inroads into previously male-dominated professions such as law and medicine. But even they fare badly in private industry, and despite the much-touted success of a handful of British female entrepreneurs – Body Shop boss Anita Roddick in particular – less than 10 per cent of British businesses are currently owned by women.

All in all, employment opportunities for British women certainly exceed those of previous generations, but they are still far from equal with those of British men. Nevertheless, if the reality of women's employment opportunity is not as rosy as it is often assumed to be, this does not diminish its impact in terms of cultural representation and notions of female identity. British advertising and television are now beginning to represent women in a much wider spectrum of roles than just girlfriend, wife or mother. In recent years there has been an abundance of television programmes featuring women in traditionally male or exciting, 'high-powered' professional jobs; for example, *The Manageress* (about a woman football manager) and *Prime Suspect* (about a police chief inspector). These can be seen as presenting new role models or as adding a new twist to well-worn fictional formulas such as the police procedural or hospital drama series.

Perhaps as a result of these images, young women now have far greater expectations than ever before. A recent study of British teenage girls revealed that many now confidently expect to have both a career and a family, although given present working conditions, they are unlikely to achieve both these aims.

Marriage and divorce

Prior to the implementation of the 1969 Divorce Reform Act, a legal separation required a guilty party. Adultery was by far the most frequently cited reason and the 'wronged' wife or husband had to provide evidence that an affair had taken place. Not surprisingly, this emphasis on moral culpability heightened any existing bitterness between parties, as lurid details were dragged out in court. In fact, when divorce became available through mutual agreement (albeit after a five-, and later, two-year separation) the majority of British private detective agencies went bankrupt as a result. From that point onwards divorce rates have soared, causing many to argue for stricter divorce laws.

This view was widely endorsed by the present Conservative Government, who launched a 'moral crusade' in the early 1990s – popularly known as the 'back to basics' campaign. This initiative implored the public to stand firm in their commitment to marriage and family life, but was discredited by the disclosure of a string of sex scandals involving prominent MPs. From then on the phrase 'back to basics' became almost synonymous with sexual hypocrisy and corruption.

Those who uphold the sanctity of marriage view Britain's one-in-three divorce rate as an indictment of its commitment-shy national culture: divorced people are sometimes castigated as selfish and fickle, putting their needs above those of their children. On the other hand, while few regard it positively, many argue that it indicates a more realistic, tolerant attitude towards the breakdown of relationships. From whichever viewpoint, it is clear that while a high percentage of the population continue to marry, people's expectations of what this entails are vastly different from those of their parents.

Until the late nineteenth century, British women, unlike those in Islamic or Hindu societies, were required to relinquish all property rights upon marriage. Divorce was virtually unheard of amongst anyone except the upper classes. Nevertheless, it was still more easily accessible to men, who had only to establish that adultery had taken place. A wife needed proof of adultery plus desertion, bigamy, incest or cruelty to divorce her husband. It was not until 1923 that women and men could bring a divorce suit on the same grounds, and women were denied a share of their ex-husband's income until as late as the mid-1960s. Given that many had no independent means of support, divorce was clearly not an attractive or realistic prospect for large numbers of women. Even today, a woman's credit rating usually drops following a divorce while the reverse is true for her ex-husband. But in spite of this disparity by far the majority of divorces are instigated by women, who are also much less likely to marry again. In part, the higher divorce rate is therefore an inevitable consequence of women's increased financial autonomy, but it also corresponds to more general shifts in the structure of the family and the relative importance attached to the heterosexual couple.

At least until the mid-twentieth-century, the dominant form of family structure was extended rather than nuclear, with parents and even grandparents, uncles and aunts living in close proximity to their grown-up children. It was also considered normal for women and men to inhabit quite different worlds in terms of both work and social activities. Due to the increased geographical and social mobility of the population, this often romanticised family unit has gradually disappeared and is now found mainly in soap operas based in traditional working-class communities: Albert Square in the 'cockney' soap *EastEnders* is a good example.

One consequence of the decline of the extended family has been the emergence of stronger adult friendship networks; a development explored in the popular recent British film *Peter's Friends*. Another has been the emergence of a more 'companionable' idea of marriage. Within the contemporary companionate model, mutual respect, emotional fulfilment and shared 'quality-time' have, at least in theory, replaced the old model which assumed separate spheres and female dependence.

But if higher expectations and better alternatives have done much to increase the divorce rate, the financial incentives to marry are also not what they used to be. Over the last fifteen years, tax relief for married couples has been gradually reduced. Meanwhile, unemployed married people are disqualified from certain state

benefits if their partners are in work. This also applies to cohabitees, but clearly, it is rather more difficult to establish their
domestic arrangements. As one in three children is now born out
of wedlock, proposals to further extend the legal rights of long-
term cohabitees are currently under review, as are plans for
one-year no-fault divorce, although this has met with stiff opposition.

Parenting

Compared with other European states, Britain could hardly be
regarded as a child-orientated society. There has undoubtedly been
a rejection of the often harsh child-rearing methods favoured in
the UK a century ago, but children are still not welcomed or
adequately catered for in public places such as pubs and restaurants. More serious perhaps is the fact that British nursery
provision is the poorest in Europe, with only half of pre-school-
age children able to obtain a place. Yet, at the same time, the
family is revered and the popular media is dominated by debates
about the falling standard of British parenting. We can begin to
consider this paradox by focusing on two particularly contentious
issues: first, the increase in single parent households, and second,
children's exposure to violence both within the family, and as
depicted within forms of popular entertainment.

In 1993, arguments came to a head over Britain's high
proportion of single-parent families when a government minister
claimed that an over-generous state benefit system was encouraging young, single mothers to 'marry the state' and embark on
a 'benefit career'. This controversial statement came shortly after
suggestions that teenage girls were becoming pregnant chiefly in
order to secure scarce local authority housing. At the heart of
this issue was not only the assumption that many young women
preferred not to work, but the fear that rather than becoming
single mothers through male abandonment – and thus worthy
recipients of state support – young women were actually choosing
to live without men, in communities of single mothers. In order

to lower the tax burden and reinstate traditional family values, the government considered developing a system (already operating in some parts of the US) whereby single mothers are penalised for the birth of a second or third child. In response to these suggestions, groups such as the Association of Single Parents swiftly pointed out that although many single parents relied on state subsidies, this resulted from difficulties in finding a decent enough job to cover childcare expenses, rather than a disinclination to work. In addition to this, it was revealed that two-thirds of lone parents had become so through divorce or separation rather than choice, and that far from enjoying a high standard of living at the taxpayers' expense, as many as 75 per cent were surviving below the official poverty line. Due to these and other criticisms, plans to cut benefit for single parents were shelved. But in the same year, an even more explosive parenting debate arose over the establishment of the Child Support Agency.

This government-funded body was set up to fix maintenance payments and pursue absent fathers after the discovery that fewer than one in three were supporting their children. The agency soon came under fire for fixing payment rates at an unrealistically high level, often destroying amicable agreements in the process. Critics also argued that the agency was more concerned with raising the payments of those who were already contributing rather than finding those who were not. The furore intensified after the occurrence of two well-publicised suicide cases, in which financial stress caused by the agency's demands was thought to be a contributory factor. Eventually, a House of Commons Select Committee was formed to review the workings of the agency. Stricter guidelines were introduced to ensure that fathers were left with sufficient funds to live on and, as was often the case, support second families.

While the single-parent and the Child Support Agency controversies highlighted the financial responsibilities attached to being a parent, there has also been a growing awareness of the widespread extent of child abuse and the long-term psychological effects on its victims. This has led to much debate concerning the difference between legitimate expressions of parental authority and malicious ill-treatment. For example, many thought that a recent poster campaign, run by the Society for the Prevention of Cruelty to Children, went too far in emphasising the damaging effects of verbal as well as physical abuse. Questions have also been raised as to how far the state is entitled to intervene in family life, leaving the social services to tread a dangerous path between accusations of unnecessary and disruptive interference and negligence.

The most serious debates about British parenting arose in 1993, after 2-year-old James Bulger was abducted from a shopping centre in Bootle, Merseyside and murdered by two 11-year-old boys. Not surprisingly, the horrifying case caused a national outcry and much attention was given to seeking an explanation for the boys' behaviour. While a good deal of blame was apportioned to the two boys' parents, questions were also raised as to what extent the murder reflected a rising tide of British violence and how far this could be traced to the corrosive influence of violent, American 'video nasty' imports. It was suggested that the children's behaviour had been influenced by a horror film – *Child's Play* – which the pair were alleged to have watched shortly before the murder. In this respect, the Bulger case rekindled a much older debate about popular entertainment and British crime rates, centring on the wide availability of violent American videos and their moral 'contamination' of the nation's youth. As there has never been any substantial evidence to suggest that behaviour is dictated or even strongly influenced by viewing habits (despite numerous studies) other commentators looked closer to home for causes. A study authorised in the wake of the Bulger case by The Commission on Children and Violence found that the key determinants linking young, violent offenders were parental abuse and poverty rather than excessive exposure to television or cinema violence.

One of the more positive results of debates on child abuse has been the organisation of a twenty-four hour free-of-charge phone counselling service for distressed children and teenagers – the National Childline – which was set up in 1993.

Sexuality and identity

The British are famed for both their prurience and sexual reserve, a stereotype which, though exploited within many British cultural forms (for example, Merchant/Ivory 'heritage' cinema) probably derives less from contemporary cultural attitudes than from England's former role in the global imposition of repressive middle-class norms and values. It is certainly true that British censorship laws are still stricter than in many other European states, and that it is one of the few countries in which a government minister will be forced to resign over a minor sex scandal. But in other respects attitudes are fairly liberal. The shift towards so-called 'permissiveness' is associated with 'swinging London', the explosion of British youth culture and the legalisation of homosexuality, abortion, birth control and divorce reform in the 1960s. The Obscene Publications trial of 1960, in which it was finally decided that D.H. Lawrence's sexually explicit but critically acclaimed novel, *Lady Chatterley's Lover*, would be made available to the British public, is generally regarded as something of a watershed, dividing prudish 'Victorian' Britain from permissive, contemporary Britain.

However, while the majority of permissive legislative reforms date from the 1960s (when registered marriages actually increased), the social effect of this legislation was not really felt until the 1970s and even 1980s, by which time permissiveness had begun to acquire a pejorative meaning, denoting the collapse of moral authority and the traditional family unit. Aside from concerns about single mothers, absentee fathers and rising divorce rates, the backlash against permissiveness was given a new impetus by the AIDS crisis, with much attention focused on the British gay community.

Britain's first official AIDS-related death, that of Terrence Higgins, occurred in 1982 and led to the establishment of what remains Britain's biggest AIDS/HIV education and advice service, the Terrence Higgins Trust. The British Government, however, was much slower to respond to the crisis. This reluctance was not only due to its disinclination to mount costly HIV prevention campaigns, but also related to the problems of censorship which preventive education created. Addressing the problem of HIV transmission necessitated the acknowledgement of a range of sexual practices and an extent of extra and premarital sexual activities which a 'family orientated' administration did not want to be seen to endorse. Only when the heterosexual risk factor became very apparent did the Department of Health launch a full scale, £5 million television, cinema, poster and house-to-house leafleting campaign in 1987. Although the Health Department's ubiquitous slogan was 'AIDS: don't die of ignorance', preventive education tended to be both oblique and alarmist, stressing promiscuity as a central factor, despite overwhelming medical evidence that viral transmission was related to particular sexual practices rather than sheer numbers of partners.

The early years of the crisis produced a wave of anti-gay hysteria, exacerbated by the popular press, which was quick to (wrongly) identify AIDS as an exclusively homosexual 'plague'. Many British newspapers actually went so far as to support such draconian measures as the recriminalisation of sodomy or the forced quarantine of those suffering from the disease. For example, speculating on the predicted growth in HIV infection, Auberon Waugh's 1985 *Daily Telegraph* column asked why: 'No one has mentioned what might seem the most obvious way of cutting down this figure (of one million by 1990) – by repealing the Sexual Offences Act of 1967 and making sodomy a criminal offence once again.'

British rates of infection have not reached these initial predictions, and ten years on such attitudes are less prevalent. However, recent surveys continue to indicate that while 'safe' sexual practices have been widely adopted within the gay community since the mid 1980s, the majority of heterosexuals still do not regard themselves as seriously at risk. Furthermore, the climate of homophobia created by the initial burst of AIDS scare-stories did much to undermine growing acceptance of the gay community. In Britain, it has never been illegal actually to be a homosexual, only to participate in homosexual acts, while lesbianism has not been

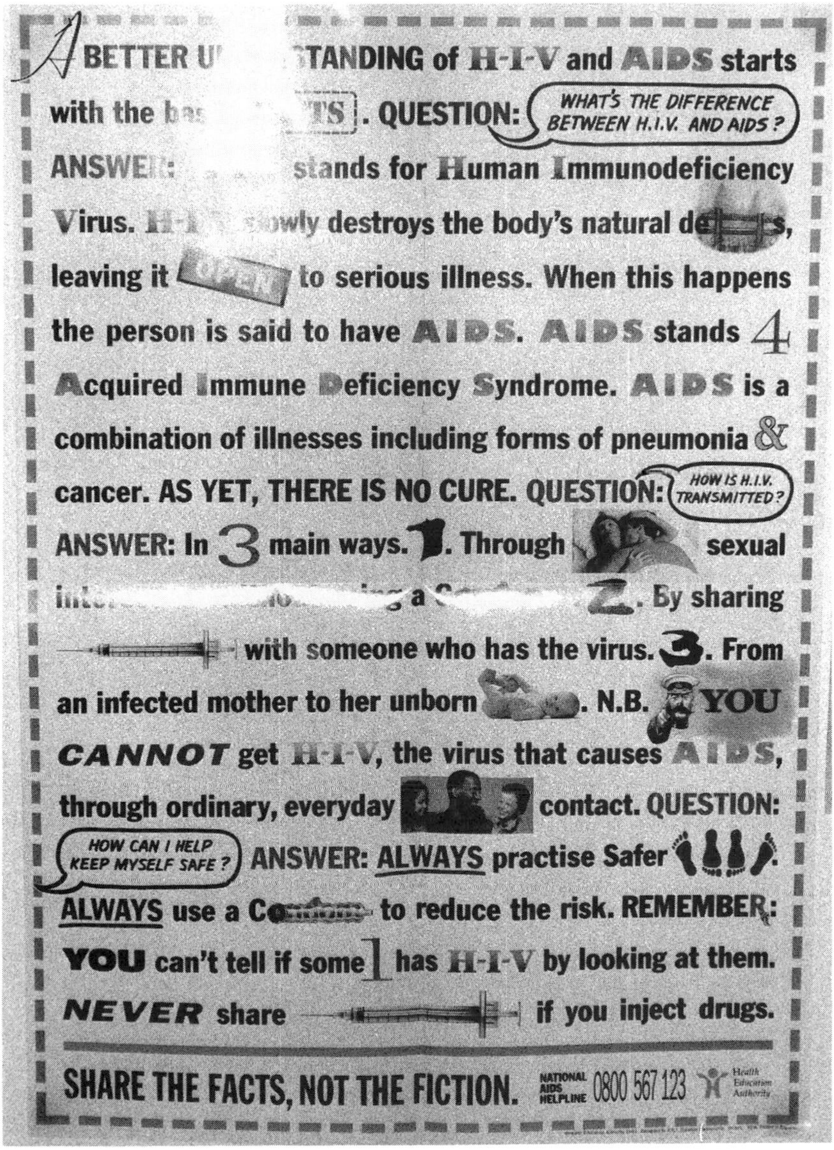

FIGURE 3.3 AIDS campaign poster

recognised by the law, supposedly because Queen Victoria refused to acknowledge its existence.

Following the 1967 Sexual Offences Act, which decriminalised homosexual activities in England (extended to Scotland in 1980 and Northern Ireland in 1979) a lively gay and lesbian subculture flourished in urban areas of England in the late 1970s and 1980s. Soho, for example, famous for its gay-owned shops, pubs, clubs and cafés, has become one of London's biggest nightlife attractions. Moreover, the widespread media adoption of the word 'gay', a term denoting positive self-identification, as opposed to 'homosexual' or more pejorative terms, suggested a growing acknowledgement of gay identity as an alternative lifestyle choice, rather than just a sexual preference.

The first indication that British gay lifestyles were seriously under threat was an addition to the Local Government Bill of 1987 inserting the notorious Clause (aka Section) 28. This amendment stipulated that local governments could not 'Promote homosexuality or publish material for the promotion of homosexuality' or 'promote the teaching in any maintained school of the acceptability of homosexuality as a pretended family relationship by the publication of such material or otherwise'.

The act was eventually passed, but rather than silencing the gay community, it had the effect of mobilising and reaffirming British gay identity. The annual Gay Pride march – always the biggest, though generally one of the least publicised, demonstrations in the capital – recorded a much higher than usual attendance in the year following the introduction of the clause. Ranging from 'professional' pressure groups like Stonewall to more militant organisations such as Act Up (AIDS Coalition to Unleash Power) and Outrage (who sometimes adopt the term 'queer' to distinguish themselves from more moderate, assimilationist gay groups), there has been a resurgence of British gay activism in the late 1980s and early 1990s. Two specific issues – that of the gay age of consent, and that of the forced exposure (outing) of homosexuals and lesbians – have commanded particularly high levels of public interest and will be examined in turn.

Initiatives to bring the gay age of consent (which was 21) in line with that applied to heterosexuals (16) was part of a broader gay equality package drafted by the Stonewall group, and inspired by the European Union's social charter commitment to ending all forms of discrimination. An uneasy compromise was reached in February 1993 when the homosexual age of consent was lowered to 18 but proposals are already under way to lower it further. At the other end of the spectrum, groups such as the Faggots Rooting Out Closet Sexuality Group (FROCS) have adopted the more controversial tactic of outing allegedly gay public figures – specifically those perceived to have lent their support to discriminatory practices. Outing is often associated with the exposure of pop stars and media celebrities, but in Britain (if not in the US), gay outing groups tend to target more establishment figures, such as eminent clergymen or Members of Parliament. This has to be distinguished from the routine exposure of gay media celebrities more commonly practised by the tabloid press, who are also, ironically, almost unanimous in their opposition to 'political' outing. A recent example was the tabloids' revelation that Britain's most popular television comedian, Michael Barrymore, was gay. Despite being front-page news for a full two weeks, the story does not seem to have seriously damaged his career. On the contrary, a particularly vicious, homophobic press campaign can often generate a good deal of public sympathy for its victim. In fact, Britain has a long tradition of camp entertainers, many of whom have both exploited and challenged gay stereotypes as a source of comedy. A recent example is that of openly gay comedian Julian Clary, whose bawdy game show *Sticky Moments* has taken smutty jokes and gay sexual innuendo to the point of self-parody.

British attitudes towards homosexuality and lesbianism have to be considered in relation to the overall political climate. The AIDS crisis increased prejudice, but current attitudes appear to be more tolerant than ever before. Amongst younger age groups in particular, the distinctions between gay and straight culture are more blurred than ever. Gay male dress codes have been widely adopted by heterosexual men and gay clubs are now more mixed in terms of both gender and sexual orientation.

If gender roles are learned first and foremost within the family, they are reinforced or challenged in our choice of social activities and leisure pursuits. Indeed, if the family is less central in most people's lives, these roles may provide a greater source of identification. One of the clearest indications of the collapse of polarised gender identities is the slow decline of exclusively male or female British institutions such as the Women's Institute or working men's clubs. Although it is often dismissed as a backward-looking, traditionalist organisation, the Women's Institute (WI) was formed in 1915 with the intention of informing and broadening the horizons of housewives, many of whom, at that time, received little or no conventional education. In fact, many of the Institute's early philanthropic patrons, such as the first chairperson, Lady Denman, were inspired by the first-wave feminist movement. But as women's educational and career opportunities have increased, the Institute has come to be associated with one particular aspect of its work: the appreciation and preservation of traditional 'feminine' crafts such as cookery and needlepoint. Clearly, as the majority of women now work, not only do they have less time to devote to pursuing home-based crafts, but these have become less important as an indication of gender identity. Consequently, membership has fallen from 500,000 in its heyday in the late 1950s and early 1960s to the contemporary figure of 272,000. The WI is still involved in raising awareness of contemporary women's health issues, such as breast cancer or environmental risks to children, but as membership is largely drawn from the over-fifties age group and the Institute has little appeal for younger women, it looks set to fade away in time.

Like the Women's Institute, the formation of working men's clubs harks back to a period in which male identity (particularly that of working-class men) was primarily constituted through the kinds of manual trades and blue collar occupations which have receded in the postwar period. With an annual membership of 350,000 around the country, working men's clubs are still popular. But most have evolved into mixed social clubs and are now only tenuously linked to the workplace. Only 2 per cent

FIGURE 3.4   A women-only health club

exclude women from the premises, although they are barred from participating in organisational responsibilities in 35 per cent, and, like the WI, the clubs now appeal more to older people. Amongst the under-25 age group, leisure activities are becoming virtually indistinguishable. Pubs, still the most popular of all British social environments, are no longer male-dominated territories, although many women still do not feel comfortable visiting one alone.

The health and fitness culture which has flourished in Britain over the last ten years has also opened up a new range of cross-gender leisure activities. Women are still less likely to compete in team sports and tend to favour fitness classes, but activities such as running, swimming and weight training are becoming increasingly popular with both sexes. The gym, once a strictly male domain, is now frequented by almost equal numbers of men and women. Furthermore, while it is often maintained that women's participation in fitness activities is motivated by vanity and men's by health concerns, there is much evidence to suggest that British men are becoming increasingly preoccupied with appearance and body shape. This can be understood as part of a more general shift in perceptions of British male identity. British men have often been characterised, perhaps unfairly, as badly dressed and proudly indifferent to common standards of style, taste and personal grooming. In the 1980s, the expansion and diversification of the menswear retailing industry, coupled with a growth in men's grooming products, revolutionised attitudes towards British masculinity. A new range of fashion and beauty products were targeted at men and more sexualised male images began to circulate in advertising and in 'new men's' style magazines, such as *Arena* and *GQ*.

At other times such images may have carried distinctly gay connotations, but their contemporary appeal is ambivalently cross-gender. Male bodies were more crudely objectified in the new women's porn magazines, and male strippers became a regular feature of the hen-party or girls' night out. It is not surprising that British men are now beginning to develop the kinds of body-image disorders, such as anorexia and bulimia, which were once confined to women. As a result of these developments, British men have finally been cajoled into spending a greater proportion of their leisure time engaged in that most 'feminine' of activities – shopping, which now takes up a fair proportion of leisure time for both sexes, augmenting more traditional male activities, such as Saturday afternoon football.

Conclusion

Today, the British population comprises 51 per cent female and 49 per cent male subjects. However, the higher numbers of women are heavily concentrated in the over-60 age group and do not reflect the gendered composition of the population as a whole. Recent studies also suggest that male life expectancy is catching up (it is currently about five years lower) and that over the next century this imbalance is likely to be reversed in favour of men.

FIGURE 3.5 Children's Society poster reflecting fears over children and drugs

Such predictions may be altered if all parents in the future are allowed, as some argue they should be, the right to choose the sex of their children. Either way, the gender composition of the population will undoubtedly affect attitudes towards age, marriage, children, and women in paid employment.

However, the overall picture which currently emerges is one in which gender roles are becoming somewhat more flexible and the two-parent, patriarchal family is gradually becoming less dominant. This has produced a variety of responses. Right-wing politicians and many prominent Church leaders tend to blame permissive legislation and the new social movements of the 1960s and 1970s (such as feminism and gay liberation) for the decline in traditional family life and conventional gender roles. From this perspective, the nuclear family unit is evoked as a symbol of social cohesion, and its breakup is regarded as the root cause of many contemporary social ills, from vandalism to drug addiction.

ISLE COLLEGE
RESOURCES CENTRE

Yet fears about the future of the family cross traditional party lines, and while the more conservative sectors of society tend to blame liberal reforms, others have argued that if permissiveness weakened the family, it was Thatcher's right-wing revolution which really killed it off. The rampant individualism and consumer greed associated with the 1980s economic boom are, in this version, responsible for undermining the moral values necessary to sustain family life.

Finally, we must consider whether the decline of the traditional family has actually led to a more atomised, alienated society. There is also evidence to suggest that new, more flexible family structures and systems of community support are beginning to take its place. Single mothers, for example, often rely heavily on one another for both childcare assistance and emotional support. Similarly, while children of divorced parents are generally regarded as disadvantaged, it has also been suggested that many actually benefit from drawing on a wider support network of two families. It is also important to recognise the new range of identities which the decay of the traditional British family has opened up. For women in particular, the decline of the traditional family unit clearly coincides with greater social freedom and status, and increased financial autonomy.

EXERCISES

1   What is the difference between a nuclear and extended family? Do you know or can you think of other kinship structures? How do family structures vary according to (a) class, (b) ethnic background? Which, if any, is most commonly represented in popular television film?

2   What is the meaning of the following popular phrases: back to basics; Victorian values; family wage; white wedding; lie back and think of England? How did they originate, and in what sense are they specific to British culture?

3   The recent British blockbuster film, *Four Weddings and a Funeral*, featured three traditional English and one Scottish wedding. What do you think are the staple ingredients of a British wedding? What is the significance of each?

4   In recent years there has been much debate about non-sexist language. Can you think of gender-neutral alternatives for the following occupational titles: Seaman; Ombudsman; Dustman; Craftsman; Fisherman; Postman; Signalman? Do you think it is important to adopt non-sexist language?

5   Do you think 'outing' is a fair practice? Under what circumstances? Consider arguments for and against.

READING

Banks, O. *Faces of Feminism*. Basil Blackwell, 1981.
An introductory guide to the development of nineteenth- and twentieth-century feminist politics in Britain.

Holdsworth, A. *Out of the Dolls House: The Story Of Women in the Twentieth Century*. BBC Books, 1988.
An analysis of popular culture, modernity and women, looking at changing British attitudes towards motherhood, marriage sexuality, politics and work.

Jeffrey-Poulter, S. *Peers, Queers and Commons: The Struggle for Gay Law Reform from 1950 to the Present*. Routledge, 1991.
An examination of the British legal and political system in relation to its treatment of homosexuals and lesbians.

Wilson, F. *Organisational Behaviour and Gender*. McGraw-Hill, 1995.

An industry based sociological and statistical analysis of employment discrimination against women in Britain.

CULTURAL EXAMPLES

- *Films*

Carrington (1995) dir. Christopher Hampton
Film exploring the relationships between members of the Bohemian 1930s artistic circle, the Bloomsbury group, focusing on little-known female artist Dora Carrington.

Dirty Weekend (1992) dir. Michael Winner
A harassed woman turned serial killer runs amok in British seaside town.

Four Weddings and a Funeral (1994) dir. Mike Newell
Courtship and marriage rituals amongst the English middle classes.

GoldenEye (1995) dir. Antonia Bird
Updated James Bond movie which knowingly flaunts its sexism.

Orlando (1993) dir. Sally Potter
Feminist costume drama spanning five hundred years in the life of a gender-bending English aristocrat.

Paris by Night (1988) dir. David Hare
Thriller charting the rise of a ruthless female politician.

Raining Stones (1993) dir. Ken Loach
Gritty view of male unemployment and its effects on two working-class families.

To Die For (1994) dir. Peter Mackensie
London-based exploration of AIDS and its aftermath amongst the gay community.

Young Soul Rebels (1992) dir. Isaac Julien
Alternative view of punk and the Silver Jubilee year, focusing on black disco and gay subcultures.

■   *Books*

Alan Hollingshurst, *The Folding Star* (1994)
Witty depiction of growing up gay in the home counties.

Kazuo Ishiguro, *The Remains of the Day* (1989)
Dissection of repressive English manners centred on a 1930s butler.

Adam Mars-Jones and Edmund White, *The Darker Proof: Stories from the Crisis* (1987)
A collection of short stories exploring the AIDS crisis in the UK.

Timothy Mo, *Sour Sweet* (1982)
Chinese family life in inner city London.

Fay Weldon, *The Life and Loves of a She-Devil* (1983)
A female revenge fantasy.

■   *Television programmes*

Absolutely Fabulous
Hit comedy depicting the outrageous antics of two 1960s generation women as they reach middle-age.

Byker Grove
Serious children's drama giving an adolescent perspective on family breakups, teenage sex, drug problems, etc. – set in the north-east.

Gaytime Television
Upbeat gay and lesbian magazine programme.

Jake's Progress
Tragi-comic drama focused on the dynamics of a dysfunctional British family.

The Manageress
Trials and tribulations of a female football manager.

Men Behaving Badly
Post-feminist situation comedy exploring traditional and contemporary ideas of masculinity.

The Politician's Wife
Four-part drama depicting an adulterous government minister and the actions taken by his vengeful wife.

Prime Suspect
Acclaimed police procedural series centred around a female detective and exploring sexism in the British Police Force.

Two Point Four Children
Popular situation comedy featuring an 'average' British family.

Chapter 4

Youth culture and age

■ Jo Croft

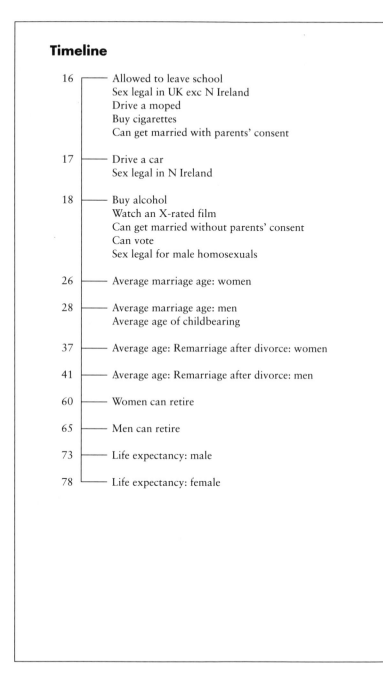

Timeline

16 — Allowed to leave school
Sex legal in UK exc N Ireland
Drive a moped
Buy cigarettes
Can get married with parents' consent

17 — Drive a car
Sex legal in N Ireland

18 — Buy alcohol
Watch an X-rated film
Can get married without parents' consent
Can vote
Sex legal for male homosexuals

26 — Average marriage age: women

28 — Average marriage age: men
Average age of childbearing

37 — Average age: Remarriage after divorce: women

41 — Average age: Remarriage after divorce: men

60 — Women can retire

65 — Men can retire

73 — Life expectancy: male

78 — Life expectancy: female

Introduction

W HEN WE ATTEMPT TO DESCRIBE someone else, or when we are required to describe ourselves (for example, on an official form) age almost always seems to be a crucial component to such descriptions. Age shapes and sets limits upon the way we live our lives in a way that we very much take for granted. As the timeline shows, age dictates such things as when we can leave school, when we can legally have sex (cither homosexual or heterosexual), when we can drive, when we can marry, when we can join the army, when we can drink alcohol, when we can retire, and of course when we can vote. In an obvious sense, age is a 'fact' we cannot alter because it literally describes how long we have been alive: however much advertising campaigns for beauty products, vitamins or health foods might try to convince us otherwise, it is something which fixes our position in society as much as, and often more than, other factors such as race, gender or class.

Nevertheless, once we begin to consider the different ways in which age underpins the identity of any given individual, it emerges as a category that is far from being simply a biological given. The social effects of age have implications far beyond the explicit classification of a person's physical, chronological status. Age, consequently, is an aspect of identity which powerfully reflects the particular character of life in any national culture and we can learn a lot about a nation's values and cultural practices by paying attention to the significance it attaches to certain life stages. It's worth noting, for example, that – unlike the United States and many European countries – Britain in the mid-1990s has no specific legislation governing 'age discrimination'.

As the timeline demonstrates, the official landmarks of age in Britain seem to become fewer and further apart once you reach the age of 18, though there is a slight reversal of this trend during old age (driving licences, for instance, have to be reapplied for when you reach the age of 70). In any case, the period between the ages of 11 and 21 is a time when life is most punctuated by changes in status – when the rules about what you can do and where you can go are shifting most dramatically. Therefore, in terms of understanding British cultural identities, the age groups that fall broadly within the category of 'youth' offer some of the most interesting insights – not least because British institutions seem to subject young people to such close scrutiny. It is almost as if young people in this country are – consciously or unconsciously – regarded as guarantors of the nation's soul, for whenever anxieties surface about moral or social decline, the first target for concern is British youth.

Britain is a nation which seems to attach particular importance to 'tradition'. 'Britishness' in both the upper class and the working class tends to be characterised by an adherence to 'old values', and it could be argued that the British see themselves (and are viewed by the rest of the world) as having an 'old' (established, aged or even ancient) culture. In consequence, it might also be claimed that, precisely because of this British conservatism, young people are regarded as both threatening and vulnerable. One of the issues which will be explored in this chapter is the extent to which British notions of social stability are explicitly associated with the stability of relationships between generations. A claim, after all, might be made that the massive changes in people's lifestyles in postwar Britain have been felt most acutely in terms of 'age relations'. 'The generation gap', juvenile delinquency, loss of community, the fragmentation of the nuclear family and disappearance of the extended family: all these much-debated social phenomena seem in one way or another to be associated with a perceived deterioration in relationships between different age groups.

Along with the rest of Europe, Britain will soon have to cope with some drastic changes in the age distribution of its population. Over the next thirty years, the average age will increase considerably. By the year 2025 the number of pensioners is predicted by a European Commission report to rise by 43 per cent. Meanwhile the working population is set to decline by nearly 3 per cent. The number of young people under 20 will also fall, by 8 per cent. Additionally, along with many other European countries (France, Holland, Denmark), Britain's fertility rate has fallen over the past twenty years, so that now it is not sufficient to maintain the current level of population (in the EU as a whole, immigration of seven million people a year will be necessary to retain current levels).

The changes expressed in these figures will have profound implications. At the simplest level, when a declining workforce has to support more people it can easily lead to inter-generational tensions. Further, as the proportion of people in retirement grows, the strain on state social and health services increases. The effect of these additional expenses will be to lower people's spending power which will in turn threaten industries which produce or sell goods. The decline in the numbers of young people may also significantly disrupt the housing market which depends on new entrants at the bottom to enable others to move up. Such changes and their likely implications will probably add to the importance attached to youth and its conduct.

It could perhaps be argued that in earlier epochs of British history less emphasis was placed upon youth as a time of crisis because there was less legislation governed by age, and hence fewer official turning points or transitions in a person's life. In other words, age is a component of identity which is very much tied to cultural factors such as the education system, health or marriage practices. This is probably most acutely exemplified by British attitudes towards children in the nineteenth century: the Victorian era was a time of great sentimentality and also great cruelty towards children, when the infant mortality rate was much higher than now, and when mass poverty meant that children had to 'earn their keep' in working-class families.

In this chapter, while other aspects of age in Britain will be touched upon, the focus will be on late childhood, adolescence and youth culture, because it is in these fast-changing periods of life that British people absorb and challenge accepted cultural identities. It is also here that the direction of present and future British identities can be apprehended, as a range of new ideas and beliefs are added to those associated with the traditional social values attaching to work, class and the family: the staple ingredients sustaining cultural identity for older British citizens.

Youth, teenagers and adolescents

At first glance, the terms 'adolescent', 'teenager' and 'youth' seem to mean exactly the same thing: they all refer to young people who are not children, and yet who are also not quite adults. However, there is also a sense in which these words suggest different forms of identity, different groupings of the British population. For example, 'youth' is generally used to refer to young people operating in the public sphere, as part of a social group, and most typically it is associated with boys rather than girls. We talk about 'youth clubs', 'youth training schemes', 'youth unemployment' and of course, 'youth culture'. 'Adolescence', on the other hand, is a term which is more likely to be used in connection with an individual's identity – to refer to a private, psychic realm of experience, as in such common expressions as 'adolescent angst', 'adolescent diary', or 'adolescent crisis'. The term 'teenager' first emerged in the 1950s when young people were newly identified as a distinct group of consumers, and since then it has typically been associated with certain kinds of products or markets: for example, 'teenage fashion', 'teenage magazines' and 'teen pop idols'. With respect to gender, we should note that the expressions 'teenage pregnancy' and 'gang of youths' suggest that 'teenage' is feminine and 'youth' is masculine.

The three fundamental natural events – birth, procreation and death – offer the most succinct summary of the human life cycle. However universal these events may be though, there are inevitably massive differences in the ways that they are experienced by people from one culture or community to the next. In the contemporary context of Western capitalist societies, 'consump-

ISLE COLLEGE
RESOURCES CENTRE

tion' best illustrates some of these differences. Whenever statistics are sought on the details of people's lives (to answer the question 'How do people live?'), the most plentiful and perhaps scrupulous sources of information are provided by market research. In other words, the ways in which money is spent and the kinds of things that people choose to buy tell us quite a lot about the identities of British people and cultural formation is partly reflected in patterns of consumption: we may not be a 'nation of shopkeepers', but – as a capitalist nation – 'we are what we buy'.

In order to gauge how age shapes patterns of behaviour, it is important to read between the lines of facts and reports which detail how people spend their money and time at different stages of their lives. The term 'lifestyle' itself seems to have become inextricably linked to the notion of patterns of consumption. The phrases 'lifestyle politics' or 'lifestyle magazines' therefore tend to be used (often derogatively) to refer to middle-class preoccupations with 'consumer choice'. Following in America's wake, Britain seems, in the 1980s and 1990s, to be characterised more explicitly as a 'consumer culture'. In this context, the typical British teenager is viewed as the consumer 'par excellence', and is seen by some, often older commentators as a 'fashion victim' dominated by larger forces. But others see the teenager as a supple negotiator of the minefields both of contemporary style trends and of technology. Knowing the price of a 'Big Mac' from McDonald's is sometimes the limit of an older person's familiarity with youth culture, which is in fact more about empowerment than victimisation.

Famously, the teenager was supposed to have been an invention or symptom of shifting consumer markets in the 1950s, both in Europe and in America Because of postwar economic prosperity, young people now had money, rock'n'roll, dress styles, and a separate culture from their parents. Many studies of British youth which have been carried out since the 1950s have focused, in one way or another, upon the way young people express themselves through the clothes they wear, the music they listen to, the films they watch and the places they go to. When Richard Hoggart wrote (rather apocalyptically) about the state of the nation's youth in his well-known book *The Uses of Literacy* (1957), he summoned up an image of the modern British teenager being almost literally consumed by a 'mass culture' which in turn was linked to the saturating effects of 'Americanisation'.

More recently, social commentators have argued that it is precisely through their role as consumers of popular culture that young British people express themselves most powerfully and creatively, not least because they feel excluded by the more traditional realms of the arts. There is a widening gap between the officially sanctioned practices of 'high art' and the forms of self-expression and creativity that young people choose to explore in their everyday lives.

An acute example of this is young people's use of graffiti in the UK, an art form initially borrowed from the inner city subcultures of black Americans. From the mid-1980s onwards, complex, brightly coloured designs produced with spray paints became a

FIGURE 4.1   American-style graffiti under a motorway bridge

common sight on 'spare' bits of wall in many towns and cities, especially along railway tracks and under motorway bridges. Typically, these motifs would be based around a single word, name or phrase with obscure connotations, and an important element of the appeal of graffiti within British youth culture is that you have to know *how* to read its messages, and above all to recognise the 'signature' of the artist. For many young people, the explicit association between British graffiti and urban America seems to imbue this art-form with the power to 'glamorise' mundane environments of UK housing estates or shopping malls – to make these spaces both more exotic and more hard-edged. Perhaps this accounts, then, for the particular prominence of the graffiti scene in new towns such as Crawley (just south of London), where (generally) white working-class youths became minor celebrities and where police would regularly search teenagers for incriminating spray cans.

In the following sections, this chapter will focus on the way that British young people spend their money and their time, both when 'going out' and when 'staying in'.

Going out: 'dressing up and dressing down'

It may seem all too easy to characterise British youth cultures in terms of fashion styles. Nevertheless, dress codes are obviously crucial keys to understanding how the lines are drawn between different identities in Britain. After all, the way that we dress can serve either to confirm or to subvert various facets of our identities, such as our gender, race, class and age. Clothes also reflect our perceptions of the historical epoch in which we live – how we relate to the cultural mood of the day. The postmodern preoccupations of the last decades of this century, for example, are linked to nostalgia, pastiche and what might be better described as cultural hybridity (mixing different styles of fashion, music, or anything else). Contemporary fashions conspicuously play upon these cultural themes and, in the 1990s, styles from every previous decade have resurfaced to evoke the spirit (or *zeitgeist*) of late twentieth-century Britain. 'Now' is in many ways a recycling of previous *zeitgeists*.

One way of thinking about different subcultural groupings within young British fashion is in terms of class identities. Subcultures such as punks, hippies, crusties, bikers and goths have tended – in one way or another – to challenge the traditional values of smart and respectable dress. On the other hand, mods, soul boys (and girls), teds, skinheads and home-boys have usually emphasised a 'sharper' style of dress, though of course in diverse ways. This opposition between 'smart' and 'scruffy' clothes bears some relation to class allegiances insofar as dress codes which place greater value on clothes 'looking new' are more often adopted by working-class young people, while scruffier 'bohemian' styles are more likely to have middle-class wearers. But often, subcultural styles of dress confront and confound mainstream expectations about people's position in the social structure.

The above is too simplistic a formula to apply to all UK youth subcultures, especially as these styles in themselves are not necessarily mutually exclusive, and most young people, in any case, are likely to draw on a range of possible influences. The enormous increase in the student population, for instance, is bound to affect the class delineations of subcultural style, as many more working-class young people enter a terrain which had previously been a middle-class preserve.

As Dick Hebdige points out in his book *Subculture: the Meaning of Style*, black subcultures have been a central factor in the formation of many white working-class subcultural styles such as that of mods (short for moderns). Both Afro-Caribbean and Afro-American influences have been critical in shaping British youth culture since the 1950s, not least because more and more young people in this country are growing up in multi-ethnic (multicultural) environments. In the late 1970s and 1980s, the Afro-Caribbean Rastafarian style influenced both black and white youth subcultural fashion, with red, green and gold Ethiopian colours commonly featuring on T-shirts, hats, badges and jackets. In the 1990s, more than ever before, black subcultural styles tend to lead the way in British street fashion, especially those derived

FIGURE 4.2 Purple Ronnie sells three million cards a year and is the most popular poet in Britain
(Reproduced by permission of Giles Andreae)

from the Afro-American Rap scene: the 'home-boy' look of baggy jeans, big hooded jackets and baseball caps is almost ubiquitous among teenage boys, especially the under 16s. Nineties 'clubwear' styles (for example, tight lycra, shiny fabrics and bright colours) also seem to be strongly influenced by black street fashions. Perhaps most significantly, Asian youth culture in 1990s Britain seems to draw very much on Afro-American and Afro-Caribbean subcultural styles (as in the music of Apache Indian). Identifications and cultural allegiances in late twentieth-century Britain are much more complex, in other words, than is suggested by traditional models of assimilation.

When considering what people wear, we need also to think about where they go, as the two are usually connected. In 1994, 34 per cent of adults in Britain visited a pub at least once a week. However, for young people between the ages of 18 and 24, the figure was much higher at 64 per cent. It is therefore perhaps not surprising that UK pubs seem to be becoming more overtly geared towards a youth clientele. Nevertheless, pubs still have a unique status in British culture as places where people of different ages and, to a lesser extent, different classes, are likely to socialise. British soap operas such as *Coronation Street* and *EastEnders* have long played on the pub's function as a place where many different types of people could plausibly meet. This, in turn, has led to complaints from television monitoring groups that soap operas might encourage viewers to drink more alcohol, because characters are so often portrayed having a drink in the pub.

In the 1990s, it has been argued, clubs rather than pubs are the focus of many young people's social lives. The growth of the 'rave' scene in Britain (which began with 'Acid House' parties in the late 1980s) has meant that dancing has again become a central activity, as it was in the dance halls of the 1950s and early 1960s and the discos of the 1970s. In contrast to these earlier dance scenes however, alcohol has tended to be a peripheral element of UK dance culture in the 1990s. Instead, rave places much more emphasis on taking drugs such as 'Ecstasy' (the effects of which tend to be cancelled out by alcohol). People dancing constantly for several hours are more likely to drink fluids to avoid dehydration and to restore energy levels, which no doubt accounts for the cultish popularity of the soft drink Lucozade in the rave scene.

At the outset, a key element in the appeal of raves was their illegality: events where thousands of people would come together were often publicised by enigmatic flyers, and by messages transmitted on pirate radio stations such as Kiss. The counter-cultural status of raves could be compared to 'blues parties' or 'shebeens', which became particularly popular in Afro-Caribbean communities in the 1980s. Like raves, these parties blurred the boundaries between private gatherings and public events insofar as they tended to be held in 'unofficial' or even squatted venues, with entrance by informally sold tickets or invitations. Like raves, blues parties were associated both with a specific type of music (reggae and ragga) played through enormous sound systems, and with drugs (cannabis) more than with alcohol – though cans of beer or other alcohol would usually be sold or included in the entrance price.

Significantly, though, raves were one of the key targets of the Criminal Justice Act (1994), and this no doubt partly accounts for the decrease in their popularity now, their place arguably being taken by big ('legitimate') clubs such as Cream and The Ministry of Sound. More than anything, however, these shifts in the popularity of different venues reflect the fast-moving, changeable nature of British youth culture: new scenes or styles quickly transmute from 'subculture' to 'mainstream' trend, and with equal rapidity they also fade from favour or disappear altogether. This ebb and flow in subcultural activity informs most young people's cultural identities in one way or another, but this is by no means to suggest that everyone's lives follow the same patterns. For instance, even though clubs and parties might well represent a central (and glamorous) social activity in 1990s Britain, many young people on a 'night out' will still often start the proceedings by visiting a pub. The more traditional activity of 'pub crawls' – where many different pubs are visited in one evening – also persists in Britain, particularly among students and groups of 'laddish young men' (such as the members of a rugby team or a 'stag' party).

In the 1980s and 1990s, traditional features of pubs such as bar billiards have often been superseded by CD or video juke-boxes, and wide-screen televisions tuned to MTV or Sky Sport. And yet, whether or not loud music is played in pubs, most still retain the same function in this country. The pub remains *the* primary leisure institution for white British culture but is generally much less popular among Afro-Caribbeans and Asians. It could be argued that pubs are bound up with British ideas of 'rites of passage', insofar as a young person's 'first legal drink in a pub' is often treated as a landmark. Growing concern about under-age drinking has meant that more attention is paid to young pub customers providing proof that they are over 18, and the major companies which run pubs have introduced their own ID cards. It is perhaps not surprising therefore that, since the late 1970s, increased emphasis has been put on eighteenth birthday celebrations rather than on twenty-first birthdays.

In large cities, especially northern ones such as Liverpool, Manchester or Newcastle, there is a whole ritual which revolves around 'going out on the town' on a Friday or Saturday night. Long queues form as hundreds of people gather around the pubs, clubs and wine bars – young women often dressed glamorously in thin-strapped or backless evening dresses, gauzy tunics or very short skirts, and young men in more casual (but nevertheless immaculate) shirts and trousers. In the context of 'a night out on the town', the mythical British predilection for queuing acquires another significance. The more popular clubs, for instance, sometimes hire 'queue spotters' who look out for particularly stylishly dressed 'punters' – the best dressed may well be allowed to go to the front of the queue, while those guilty of certain 'fashion crimes' (for example, wearing white socks or the 'wrong' kind of shoes) may not be allowed in at all. Like the cinema queues in the heyday of cinema-going, these queues of clubbers function as a kind of social scene, a place to meet your friends, to flirt or compete with your peers. Young people also might end their evening in another queue, waiting to buy chips or a kebab, or standing in line for a taxi.

This kind of Friday or Saturday night spectacle is not often regarded as being part of any specific subculture (apart from what might be broadly described as 'clubbing'), and yet it is still governed by a distinct set of codes – for example, in many cities, Friday night is girls' and boys' night out but Saturday night is for couples. One of the most striking aspects of these weekly events is the disregard most of the young people appear to have for the weather – the rule seems to be that jackets or coats are not worn even on freezing winter nights (this is also a question of money, as it is a luxury to buy an impressive coat or jacket which will only be 'checked', hung out of sight, at the club). Perhaps most noticeable, though, is the fact that men and women tend to go out not with boyfriends or girlfriends, but with their 'mates' of the same sex. For women especially, this seems to be an important element in the way they choose to dress – the flamboyance and overtly sexual nature of the outfits that many young women wear are apparently in some way legitimated by the fact that they are dressing up 'for fun', rather than explicitly to attract men. Indeed, it is often said that women on these occasions are 'dressing up' for other women – that an integral part of the ritual is be identified as part of a female subculture, and to gain the approval of other members of that social group. None of these so-called 'rules' or codes of dress are clear-cut however.

Staying in: young people and the media

On average, people in Britain spend 230.6 minutes watching the television or video every day, which is more than in any other European country. These days, rather than talking about the weather, it is probably more accurate to say that television programmes provide a favourite topic of conversation for British people (according to market research, 46 per cent of the UK population discuss television programmes with their friends or family). In many ways, television now seems to be at the hub of 'the British way of life', offering a structure and rhythm around which people may shape their leisure time. Nowadays, the success or otherwise of major national holidays such as Christmas and Easter is less likely to be talked about in terms of the quality of church services, than about the quality of programmes on television. In the 1990s, in fact, there is a mood of nostalgia about the 'good old days' of family viewing on television, especially in connection with Christmas. From the 1950s through to the 1970s, there was actually a regular BBC programme broadcast from a theatre in Leeds called *The Good Old Days* which simulated a night out at the music hall in Edwardian England (complete with audiences in fancy dress Edwardian clothes, singing along with the performers). In the 1990s, however, equivalent viewing slots are more likely to show archive footage of old television shows, and now there is even a satellite television station called UK Gold which is entirely devoted to reruns of British programmes from the 1970s and 1980s. So, whereas thirty years ago older people might sentimentally reminisce about 'happier' times when the family would make their own entertainment, singing songs around the piano or playing charades, these days people are more likely to recall nostalgically 'the golden age of television' during the late 1960s and early 1970s – a time when adults and children would supposedly sit together to watch favourite programmes (such as *The Morecambe and Wise Show*, *Dr Who* or *The Generation Game*), comfortable in the knowledge that it would all be 'good clean fun'.

A traditional British Christmas has been characterised (or caricatured) through images of the family (ranging across three generations) sitting in front of the television after Christmas dinner, watching the Queen's Speech at 3 p.m. and then a classic film such as *The Sound of Music* or *The Wizard of Oz*. It is important not to underestimate the status of these televisual myths in relation to the attitudes which British people themselves express about national identity, and as a corollary of this, it is often the case that anxieties about social decline are most readily articulated in terms of 'falling standards' on television. The concept of family viewing is a central stake in debates about the role of the BBC, a public-owned institution known to the country as Auntie (suggesting its cosy, nanny-like persona – one programme which shows out-takes from BBC television series is called *Auntie's*

Bloomers). It is often deplored in the press that current American or American-inspired television shows, such as *Baywatch*, *Blind Date* and *Gladiators*, are usually the most popular programmes, shown in the prime time family viewing slots on early Saturday evenings. In effect, programmes that are associated both with youth and American culture often seem to be regarded as anathema as far as British family values are concerned. In an attempt to recapture the all-round entertainment of twenty or thirty years ago, the BBC now has nostalgic television shows such as *The New Generation Game*, and a family quiz show called *Telly Addicts* which tests the contestants' knowledge of television's 'good old days'.

Young people nowadays watch more television than did preceding generations. However, as far as television programmers and advertisers are concerned, 'youth audiences' are potentially the most elusive segment of the population in this country, for although television may play an influential role in the identities of young British people, they generally spend less time watching television than people over 25 or under 12. British youth, implicitly, are less likely than any other section of the population to be seen as inhabitants of the domestic environment. In response to this, there has been a growing movement towards 'youth television' in Britain, which aims to 'catch' young people either before or after they go out to socialise. Youth television was famously pioneered in the 1980s by the cockney television producer Janet Street Porter and is sometimes satirically referred to as 'Yooff TV'. The kinds of programme that fall into this category tend to have a fast-moving magazine format with young, fashionably dressed presenters often speaking in 'non-standard' English. A peak-time viewing programme such as *Blind Date* also targets a youth audience, not least because it is shown on Saturdays, fairly early in the evening so that people can watch before they go out on the town (to increase the programme's cross-generational appeal it also occasionally sends middle-aged or older people on blind dates).

Other television programmes which seek to reflect youth lifestyles are shown late at night on Fridays and Saturdays:

The Word, *Fantasy Football League*, *Euro-Trash*, *Bad Ass TV*, *Beavis and Butthead*, obviously working on the assumption that they will be watched by young people returning from a night out. The fast and furious style of these kinds of programmes, with their heavy emphasis upon 'chat', music and mildly outrageous sexual behaviour seems to suggest that young people in Britain do not want to watch more 'serious' television, and have very short attention spans. Another way of interpreting 'youth television', however, is to argue that it is watched in a different way: less as a central activity than as a backdrop – more akin, say, to having the radio turned on than watching a film at the cinema.

However, whereas youth television seems to anticipate (or fantasise about) an audience which is caught up with the demands of a hectic social life, other activities such as computer games, reading or listening to music suggest a more solitary vision of the teenager at home. Uncommunicative teenagers playing with their gameboys or listening to their personal stereos acutely exemplify this. The 1990s has seen the emergence of a whole new range of concerns about the state of the nation's youth which focus upon the dangers of children and adolescents inhabiting private fantasy worlds, accessed through computers. Jokes and anecdotes are commonplace about the technology 'generation gap', whereby children are deemed to be more adept than their parents at operating machines like videos and computers (many television adverts play on this discrepancy). However, the internet has rendered such jokes a little more sinister, in that they suggest a loss of parental control. Above all, fears seem to centre upon the fact that the internet enables children to communicate not only with other children but also with adults, without supervision. The much publicised emergence of pornographic and paedophilic 'pages' on the World Wide Web has created a mood of pessimism about what might otherwise have been greeted more optimistically as a communication system which encourages the breakdown of many traditional boundaries, including those between different ages and generations. In terms of computer games, since the early 1990s 'shoot-em-ups' such as *Doom* and the *Star Wars*-inspired *Rebel Assault* have acquired a cultish popularity, particularly with teenage boys. Unlike surfing the internet, playing these games involves no human communication, and so is an activity which seems to provoke different anxieties because it is deemed to be antisocial and introspective, plunging the player into a violent fantasy world.

Aesthetically and thematically, computer games have a close relationship to comics and magazines. Since the mid-1980s, comics – especially 'graphic novels' – have spawned a whole subcultural scene, and most British towns now have a specialist comics shop (Forbidden Planet, for instance, are a nationwide chain of shops). Virgin Megastores, which principally serve as music outlets, also sell comics and magazines aimed at this cultish readership, thus suggesting further subcultural cross-overs between computer games, music and comics. However, when people in Britain talk about 'teenage magazines', they are most likely to be referring to publications aimed at girls – for example, magazines such as *Just Seventeen*, *19*, *Sugar* and *Looks*. This is significant in that adolescent femininity in the UK tends to be associated – more than any other aspect of youth culture – with stereotypical consumerism. While things have definitely moved on since the days when British teenage girls were represented almost solely in terms of 'teeny-bopper' culture – screaming at pop stars or gazing at posters on their bedroom walls – it is still the case that young women are more explicitly identified as a 'market', rather than as a series of subcultures. Surveys about how much money is spent on clothing and footwear in the UK actually tell a very different story. For instance, around 6 per cent more clothes and shoes are bought by young men over 15 than by young women in the same age group. The point to make here, perhaps, is that the cultural activities of British young women are interpreted less positively, in that women are more likely to be stereotyped as passive consumers (of clothes and pop stars) than as creative participants in a subcultural scene.

Many parents tend to expect their children to buy and enjoy the same magazines as they did – shifts, as with music and youth fashion styles, are almost always perceived negatively by older generations. In the 1970s, *Jackie* was by far the highest selling magazine for teenage girls, selling an average of 605,947 copies per week in 1976. In the 1990s, this pole position has been taken up by *Just Seventeen* which had a readership of 941,000 in 1994. Comparing the content of *Jackie* in the 1970s with *Just Seventeen* in the 1990s, you can infer some sense of the kinds of changes which have taken place in the lives of British teenage girls over the last twenty years. The most notable, and perhaps optimistic difference is that teenage girls today seem to be far less exclusively associated with a private, domestic space (the adolescent girl in her bedroom, dreaming about love). *Jackie* by and large used to be concerned with romance, whereas contemporary teenage girls' magazines focus much more on actual relationships (most are dominated by their problem pages where readers' questions are answered). Far more attention is now paid to music and fashion, which can be interpreted in a number of ways. These preoccupations would seem to confirm the idea that the adolescent British girl's identity is almost wholly shaped by her status as a consumer. However, it could also be argued that these features imply that young women now participate more actively in the public domain – they are no longer 'stuck in their bedrooms'. Above all, perhaps, the images of British young women offered by contemporary teenage magazines suggest cultural identities which are far from straightforward, insofar as they often negotiate conflicting concerns between sexual relationships and autonomy.

In 1996, two new television programmes, *Pyjama Party* and *The Girlie Show*, appeared under the auspices of late-night youth television. These shows are supposedly an attempt to counter the 'laddishness' of many 1990s television shows aimed at young adult audiences. However, with their emphasis on sexual outrage, such programmes offer a vision of young women in 1990s Britain which is a far cry from the 'cropped hair and dungarees' of 1980s feminism. Features such 'wanker of the week', where the behaviour towards women of one well-known male personality is exposed, or a section of the show where women in the audience offer up their boyfriends' soiled underpants for public scrutiny, suggest a vogue for countering and parodying traditional 'girlie' gossip and confession.

Advice

Nick Fisher

a boy's view

GIRLS WILL THINK I'M A FREAK

I'm a 13-year-old boy and was recently diagnosed as having cancer of the testicles. Although the doctor thinks the cancer has been caught in time, he's also warned me that I might have to have one of my testicles removed. I'll still be able to function sexually, but I'm terrified that no girl will want to go near me after the operation. I feel like a freak.

A W, Norwich

● Having a testicle removed is really scary to you now, and the prospect of being left with only one must seem horrifying. But the truth is, you can function perfectly well with only one testicle. It's also possible, if you want, to insert a false one which makes everything look absolutely normal. You need to talk to your GP and the surgeon about this.

Don't let the fact that it's a genital operation stop you talking about it. If you don't want to talk to your parents, call ChildLine on 0800 1111 (everything you say will be kept confidential). As for girls rejecting you, it's far less likely than you think. If a girl loves you for who you are, one testicle is not going to change that, believe me.

BEING SINGLE DEPRESSES ME

I'm 17 and have never had a boyfriend. You may think it's not a problem, but I can't stop feeling depressed. It's not that I'm really shy or anything, but every time I let a lad know I like him, he says he's seeing someone else. I don't think I'm ugly, but no-one ever notices me. It's getting to the point where I feel life's not worth living. What am I doing wrong?

Victoria

HE DUMPED ME OVER FALSE RUMOURS

I've never had a problem with my boyfriend, only with his friends. Basically, they've never been that nice to me, but I didn't want this to come between me and my boyfriend so I just ignored them. But recently they started spreading rumours that I fancy a lad two years above me at school. It's such a lie, but my boyfriend believed them! I've tried to convince him it's not true, but it hasn't worked. Now he's dumped me, and I'm devastated. I still love him, so how can I get him back?

Ethan Hawke fan (14)

● If you've tried to convince your boyfriend that these rumours aren't true, yet he still believes his mates is what you said, then you need to ask yourself if the relationship is really worth it. Can you really love someone who has such little faith in you? Besides, for all you know he could be using the rumour as an excuse to wriggle out of the relationship and make you look like the wrong-doer. It seems like a stupid way to end things, but you might have to accept that that's what he's doing. He's the one with the problem, not you. If he's not prepared to listen to you, then you're truly better off without him.

● You aren't doing anything wrong. Basically, finding a boyfriend is a hit-and-miss affair. As the saying goes, you have to kiss a lot of frogs before you find a prince! But if a boyfriend is what you want, the best way to get one is to be open-minded and friendly, to mix in groups and get to know boys as mates first. And, of course, to ask out ones you fancy. If you keep doing this, eventually you'll find someone.

But don't believe a boyfriend will answer all your prayers. If you're unhappy inside, it's far better to deal with it before starting a relationship. It's hard to get someone to love you before you learn to love yourself. If you want to talk to someone anonymously about this, call the Samaritans on 0345 909090. Boyfriends come and go, but you'll always have to live with yourself.

I DIDN'T GET TURNED ON

This term, my year went on a school trip to France. I sat next to my girlfriend and I don't remember much about the journey as I slept for most of it. When I woke up, she acted sulky, as if I'd done something wrong. Finally she explained that she'd put her hand on my trousers, but I hadn't woken up. The trouble is, I didn't feel anything and now I'm really worried that my nerve endings aren't working. Please help!

Scott (16), Somerset

● Just because you didn't wake up when your girlfriend touched you doesn't mean there's anything

wrong with you. She expected her touching to be the most exciting thing in the world for you – and maybe it would have been if you were awake! I think she sulked because you slept through what sh felt was a big moment. She's hurt because she thinks you aren't properly turned on by her.

Make sure she knows how sexy you find her, but explain that it only arouses you when you're awake. And don't think there's anything wrong with your nerve endings – your body's working fine.

I HATE HIM TALKING TO GIRLS

I've been with my boyfriend for over two years. During this time, I've developed a major jealousy problem and it's ruining our relationship. I know trust is really important, but I find it so hard when he's talking to other girls. I can't help myself – I always end up telling him how I feel, and this is really starting to annoy him. He always used to say how much he loved me, but lately he's stopped telling me. I'm sure it means he's going off me.

Worried (15)

● Being honest about your feelings is a good thing – up to a point. But if you tell him you're jealous every time he talks to a girl, then he will get annoyed. You see, he has every right to talk to girls. And when he does tell you he loves you, you hav to accept that part of that love comes from the fact you trust him. By saying you're jealous, you're telling him that you don't trust him. No wonder he feels hurt.

You need to stop worrying and trying to control him. Try to talk about your feelings to a close frien or relative. There's only so much honesty your boyfriend can take. If you don't work on controlling your jealousy, it could become a problem in other areas of your life.

remember: to be suffed if a must **but** sex under 16 is illegal

---

FIGURE 4.3 Advice page from the magazine *Just Seventeen*
(*Reproduced by permission of* Just Seventeen)

Overall, the crucial point to make about youth culture is its speed of change and its difference from more mainstream representations of British identity, whether those of children at school or adults at work. Youth identities are more commonly associated with pleasure and leisure, but they are crossed by other crucial factors in cultural positioning discussed in this book: gender, ethnicity, region and class.

Sex and drugs and Rock 'n' Roll

It is both clichéd and true to say that the lives of young people in the UK in the postwar era have been characterised on the basis of the rather unholy trinity of 'Sex and Drugs and Rock 'n' Roll'. This concluding section will therefore focus on these three aspects because they are associated more excessively and more apprehensively with British youth culture than any others.

Although the poet Philip Larkin suggested that 'Sex began in 1963 . . .', anxieties about the sexual mores of the younger generation certainly preceded the so-called sexual revolution of the 1960s. Nevertheless, sex is undoubtedly a realm of contemporary British life where the mythical 'generation gap' is felt particularly keenly, and this is no doubt exacerbated by a perceived difference between what is sexually common now and what was acceptable thirty or forty years ago. Nostalgia at the end of the twentieth century is expressed with peculiar intensity in relation to notions of childhood innocence, whereby today's children and teenagers are regarded as both more vulnerable and as more sexually 'knowing'.

Whereas a hundred years ago, fears were rife about the social dangers of adolescent masturbation, since the 1970s the key areas of concern surrounding young British people have been: the role of sex education, the availability of contraception, HIV, teenage pregnancy, sexual abuse and homosexuality. In Britain's increasingly secular climate on the other hand, the issue of sex before marriage or cohabitation is no longer hotly contested.

More than anything, sexual knowledge seems to be the central stake in debates about young people's sexuality. Since the 1980s, for instance, UK campaigns and initiatives such as 'Childline' and 'Kidscape' have increased public awareness of childhood sexual abuse. The fact that these issues are now more openly discussed has sometimes been taken as an indication that the British nation is being overwhelmed by an epidemic of paedophilia. However, this is not the case, and it is probably much more accurate to say that British people are now less inclined to draw a veil of silence over these kinds of problems. Social services policy, as well as the less official influences of magazine problem pages and television shows such as *That's Life* (in which Esther Rantzen launched 'Childline') have been key factors in bringing about this shift. Changing attitudes towards child sexual abuse in the United States have also been extremely influential in the UK, especially with the increasing popularity here of American talk-shows such as *Oprah*.

Until the 1980s, the general perception in Britain had been that sex would inevitably be subject to fewer and fewer restrictions for each subsequent generation. However, concern over HIV and AIDS has obviously put paid to this vision of an unstoppable machine of sexual liberation. It could even be argued that today many young people have more restricted sex lives than their parents had as teenagers. It may be the case that young British people have less sex with fewer partners than did teenagers in the 1970s and early 1980s, the heyday of the contraceptive pill. Certainly there are more fears about sex, and unwanted pregnancy no longer necessarily represents the worst possible scenario for sexually active teenagers. Campaigns to educate people about 'safer sex' have meant an increased openness about referring to sexual practices which fall outside the scope of 'straight sex' (for example, dressing up or using 'sex toys'), and the idea of conventional sex as being the only kind has ceased to dominate. Glossy media representations of sex are far more likely nowadays to play on fetishistic imagery, and it is telling, for example, that ice-cream has acquired a voguish association with sex, mainly because of the erotic Haagen Daas advertisements. As if, perhaps, to detract attention away from the fact that sex is now more circumscribed by risks, contemporary British youth culture seems to place a premium on the idea of experimental or imaginative sexual practices, and is perhaps less ready to equate 'experience' (that is, of penetrative sex) with sexual pleasure and knowledge. Teenage magazines like *Just Seventeen* are littered with slogans such as 'to be sussed is a must', and most young people in this country over the age of 11 (and often younger) now know what a condom is. Since the late 1980s, numerous youth projects have been set up in Britain to educate young people about safe sex, workers often distributing free condoms as well as leaflets. 'Condom buses' have even been enlisted in the service of health education, a phenomenon which plays on the mythically clean-cut images of British teenagers 'having fun on buses' featured in the early 1960s film *Summer Holiday*, and the children's television series *The Double Deckers*.

Sex, for young British people at the end of the twentieth century, is double-edged. Talking about sex, listening to other people talking about sex, reading about sex and even watching sex on television or video has become progressively easier. In a sense though, actually having sex in 1990s Britain is becoming more complicated, not least for teenagers. In 1996, controversy erupted about the content of magazines aimed at teenage girls in the UK after a Tory backbench MP, Peter Luff, made an unsuccessful attempt to introduce a 'Periodical Protection Bill'. Luff's main objection to magazines such as *Just Seventeen*, *TV Hits* and *Bliss* was that they encourage young girls to be obsessed with sex because they deal too explicitly with sexual issues. What is most telling about the debates which surrounded Luff's crusade is the polarisation of the arguments. For some people in 1990s Britain, childhood is in danger of becoming entirely eroded, while for others, young people can never know too much.

Drugs are another area of life where the generation gap appears to be wide. In postwar Britain, youth subcultures have always been associated with the use of particular (usually illegal) drugs: mods with amphetamines ('speed'), hippies with cannabis ('dope', 'pot', 'blow', etc.) and LSD ('acid'), ravers and clubbers with 'Ecstasy'. In the 1990s however, drug use has become fairly mainstream among the UK youth population, and it is estimated that more than 50 per cent of young people will have tried at least one illegal drug by the time they are 18. The drugs scene of 1990s Britain has been characterised, rather ambiguously, as being about 'recreational drug use' rather than as a small alienated enclave of drug addicts, as in the past. British youth seem yet again to fulfil their role as 'sophisticated' consumers who make discriminating choices from, in this case, a whole menu of intoxicating substances. In his book *Street Drugs*, for instance, Andrew Tyler argues that 'value for money' influences the decisions young people make about using drugs: 'They will judge a pint [of beer] against, say, the psychoactive clout of a £2 LSD blotter.' This may account for the fact that while overall alcohol consumption rose by more than 30 per cent between 1961 and 1991, pub and club sales of beer have dropped by more than a quarter since 1979. Drinks with a relatively high alcohol content, including alcoholic lemonades such as 'Hooch', and fruit cocktails such as '20/20', seem to be aimed, by and large, at a youth market which appears to prioritise both 'cheapness' and 'coolness' and a guaranteed 'high'.

Set against this image of British youth as adept 'recreational' users of drugs are the media portrayals of young people either as hapless victims or as crazed addicts. Such representations do not offer an accurate overall perspective. In the 1980s there was a huge increase in heroin (or 'skag') use among working-class British youth, especially in urban areas, and this 'skag' culture was often the target of sensationalist news stories. Heroin was, somewhat exaggeratedly, rumoured to be as easy to get hold of as tobacco in some cities, and was undoubtedly a major cause of rising property crime. Although there has been no drastic change in the numbers of people using heroin in the UK in the 1990s, however, media attention has almost completely shifted towards other drugs. In the early 1990s, concern was focused upon the possibility of a cocaine ('crack') epidemic, and numerous stories were run in the press and on television about crack-related crime in the United States. However, while crack has become more common in this country, particularly in inner city areas, the spot-light has shifted once again: Ecstasy (which first appeared on the British drugs scene in 1988) prompted a number of media-led moral panics in the mid-1990s, based around the widely publi-cised deaths of teenagers using the drug (the most notable case being Leah Betts's death in 1995 on her eighteenth birthday). Though fewer than sixty people died in Britain from Ecstasy use between 1988 and 1996 (that is, fewer than 1 per cent of alcohol related deaths of young people), national publicity has focused on this drug in particular. One of the most commonly expressed concerns is that British parents no longer 'know what their chil-dren are doing', and the relative novelty of Ecstasy seems to exacerbate older people's sense of estrangement. However commonplace drugs may be in the social lives of many young people in this country, they are seen as both alien and threat-ening to much of the British population over 40, even those who were teenagers in the 1960s.

Most British youth subcultures have been aligned, at some stage, with a particular type of music. Consequently, as delin-eations, cross-overs and fusions between different styles of pop music have become ever more complicated, so too have the criteria distinguishing one subcultural scene from another. In 1990s Britain, rock'n'roll music is certainly no longer (if it ever was) a single unifying symbol of youth rebellion. At one level, it is almost as if British pop music has become so diverse that the differences between music scenes now seem to be blurred and indistinct. The 'tribalism' of the 1960s and 1970s, whereby musical taste was often inextricably bound to much broader allegiances, seems to be fading in the 1990s. Music nevertheless still plays a critical part in the construction of identities for British youth, but in more fluid ways. In 1978, British 15 year olds may well have used musical taste as a means of declaring themselves to be punks or mods. In the 1990s, 15 year olds are probably more likely to say that they like 'a bit of Jungle, House, Techno or Garage' than to use music to ascribe a specific subcultural identity to themselves. The phenomenon of Britpop is a good example of this historical shift in the constituency of youth subcultures, insofar as bands

FIGURE 4.4   Student party

such as Oasis and Blur are not closely linked to a fixed subcultural identity, despite their associations with 'mod' style. This contrasts with bands of the late 1970s such as The Jam which inspired a more distinctly 'mod' following.

An article by Gavin Hills, in the *Observer* in February 1996 argues that the ascendancy of the dance music scene in Britain 'could signal the end of youth culture'. However exaggerated such a claim may be, there does seem to be a definite shift in Britain away from the oppositional youth subcultures of the previous three decades. Hills describes 'the dance generation' as multi-ethnic, unisex and intergenerational. This broadly optimistic vision of the 'dance generation' can be linked to what the American writer, Douglas Coupland, describes as 'Generation X': a postmodern, post-industrial grouping of people who embrace the idea of diversity and who do not strictly fall into a specific age group. 'Generation Xers' are associated with a more flexible attitude towards clothes, music and peer groups as markers of identity.

At the end of the century, and of the millennium, age seems be a less rigid, though perhaps no less significant aspect of British cultural identity. This can be seen as a positive effect of the fact that Britain has become a far more diverse culture since the Second World War. However, it can also be seen as an effect of more negative cultural changes, brought about by mass unemployment in the UK: transitions between life stages are now much less stable for many people because the 'adult' status formerly incurred through work is no longer guaranteed. The labour market as a whole is much less stable, and British cultural identities are generally far less securely rooted in the jobs that people do. At some level, youth culture in Britain may well still be based around 'Sex and Drugs and Rock'n'Roll', but it's also worth bearing in mind that 'Rock'n'Roll' is rhyming slang for 'The Dole'.

Conclusion

To conclude, we will look briefly at two aspects of culture which are in many ways opposed to each other: fashion and New Age culture (you will find out more about the New Age in relation to religion in Chapter 7). Both are associated with youth, but both also in fact stretch across the generations and provide intriguing case studies for analysing the production and consumption of contemporary British identities.

A recent morning television programme focused upon the 'street style' of young people in Britain. The discussion emphasised the flexibility, eclecticism and originality of British fashion and, above all, the refusal of most stylish British teenagers to be 'slaves' to the dictates of the catwalk or the high street fashion chains. While the newsagents in this country are filled with row after row of women's magazines giving the latest tips about 'what's "in" this season', and while *The Clothes Show* (a BBC television programme all about fashion) has become almost an institution in Sunday afternoon viewing, the British seem to maintain a rather ambivalent attitude to the very concept of 'fashion'. There is a sense, of course, in which this ambivalence can be linked to British conservatism or reserve – to the nation's reputed resistance to anything new. However, there is another, equally important, strand to the way in which many British people seem to approach fashion, which is the almost mythical 'eccentricity' of the British (or perhaps more precisely the English). In fact, the most famous of British designers – Vivienne Westwood, 'Red or Dead', Katherine Hamnett and Paul Smith – are often characterised specifically in terms of their eccentricity and their lack of conformity to the broader trends of the global fashion industry. There is even a clothes company called 'English Eccentrics'. As was noted in the introductory chapter to this volume, 'reserve' and 'eccentricity' are attributes which are famously associated with 'the British character', and as qualities – albeit stereotypical ones – they possess a particular resonance in relation to British fashion, not least because they seem almost to cancel each other out. 'Classic' British clothing, of course is characterised by muted colours (especially brown, navy blue and green), sensible/comfortable tailoring, fabrics such as wool or corduroy, and the obligatory, 'understated' string of pearls for women. Above all, perhaps, this style of dress is associated with an upper-class lifestyle of 'hunting, shooting and fishing' (as well as sailing), readily mythologised through media representations of the Royal Family striding over moors, walking dogs and so on. It is probably not surprising, then, that these kinds of clothes tend to conjure up conservative, non-urban identities (and often Conservative with a capital 'C'), though they are far from being the exclusive preserve of the aristocratic, landowning echelons of British society. Rather, the 'wax jacket and brogues' way of dressing seems to be identified with what we might call an 'aspirational lifestyle' (cf. 'young fogies', *Country Life*, Marks & Spencer, etc., and shops for women like Laura Ashley). Perhaps most significantly, this 'classic' style of British dress has been readily exported and is almost certainly more popular with young people abroad than it is with their British contemporaries.

The way people dress in Britain is often explicitly informed by distinctions of social class, and yet certain articles of clothing have much more ambiguous class connotations. The cloth cap for instance (which is typically made of woollen cloth in a small check pattern) is associated both with traditional working-class men (especially in northern working men's clubs) and with upper-class gentlemen (especially when out shooting, etc.). In a far more specific and self-conscious way, clothes such as Burberry raincoats and even 'deerstalker' hats have crossed certain cultural divides insofar as they were adopted in the late 1980s and early 1990s as part of black street fashion – a gesture which seemed at the time both to mock the complacency of white home counties style and to challenge the monopoly of designer sportswear in black Afro-Caribbean fashion itself. In a way, this tendency within British fashion to play with or parody familiar images of British tradition represents a central element in the dress codes of several youth subcultures in this country: for example, teddy boys, Wigan soul, skinheads and punk.

In the last few decades the Doc Marten boot or 'DM' has probably exemplified the shifting, playful moods of British fashion more than any other single item of clothing. Skinheads in the late 1960s adopted DMs as part of a dress code which seemed to be an exaggerated version of the clothes worn by manual labourers (drainpipe Levis, Ben Sherman check shirts and braces). A particular brand of workboots therefore acquired a significance far beyond the bounds of their initial function, and by the late 1970s the divisions and subdivisions between different subcultures such as punks and rudeboys were marked out not only by haircuts and music but by the way people wore their DMs (the number of holes, the colour, customised versions and so on). As part of a more general impetus among feminists in the early 1980s to reject the trappings of a 'stereotypical' femininity, DMs became more and more popular with young women, especially students, who tended to adopt a kind of 'proletarian' chic of baggily practical clothes – overalls and donkey jackets – as a gesture of rebellion against both sexism and the materialistic excesses of Thatcherism. Now, in the 1990s, the Doc Marten boot seems to have entered yet another phase, having been adopted, briefly, by the catwalks of international fashion houses at the beginning of the decade. The omnipresence of the DM in high street chains of shoe shops has robbed it of much of its potency as a symbol of non-conformity, and nowadays it's as likely to be worn to school by a middle-class 11-year-old (or by a schoolteacher for that matter) as it is to be worn by an 'indie' musician or an anarchic art student. Even the Pope has a pair. You can now buy velvet or silver or brocade Doc Martens but somehow they seem to have lost the power to shock, acquiring instead the more dubious accolade of a British 'design classic', which of course is readily exportable and hence less likely to be popular in Britain.

Finally, we need to note how youth culture can become softened and anaesthetised, but also transformed and diffused. It has now become a kind of truism that more or less every town or even village in Britain is bound to have its resident punk, a figure as much a part of the repertoire of stock British types as the bowler-hatted city gent. Like most myths though, this scenario of 'a punk in every high street' represents only a very partial truth, one which fails to register the complex differences between particular communities and the constant mutations in the ways different subcultures identify themselves. Elements of punk can be found in various British subcultures, the most notable probably being New Age travellers. Crucially though, the style of clothes worn by many New Age travellers (sometimes known as 'crusties' because of their unwashed or encrusted look) also draws heavily on a hippy aesthetic – ethnic clothes, beads and bangles. New Age hairstyles similarly seem to draw on a range of cultural references such as dreadlocks (rastafarianism), bright hair dye (punk), shaved (skinhead), Mohican (Native American/Hari Krishna/punk) and shaggy, matted long hair (hippy). Any subcultural identity can of course be dissected into its component parts of 'key' motifs and symbols, but the example of New Age/crusty subculture in Britain today also acutely demonstrates how problematic such checklists of cultural identities can be, not least because contemporary British cultural identities seem to be so

enmeshed and hybrid – often self-consciously playing with or parodying the styles they adopt.

New Age/crusty subculture is perhaps the most recent indication of an extra-social trend that does not react or rebel
from within mainstream culture but seeks a mode of life outside
of society, and has consequently been portrayed negatively and
ignorantly in most media. People tend to get lumped together
according to very superficial criteria, and what is interesting about
the phenomenon of New Agers/crusties in the 1980s and 1990s
is that certain marginalised elements of the population which
may have previously formed far more distinct groupings such
as hippies, travellers, political activists, the urban homeless and
young unemployed people from both urban and rural communities, have come to be bracketed together, albeit in an
impressionistic way. In fact, the very vagueness of the boundaries
which surround this subculture suggests that the label of 'Crusty'
or 'New Age traveller' is more likely to be invoked as a deroga-
tory/disapproving term to describe scruffy youths or homeless
people.

Despite the fact that such disparate kinds of people might
potentially be described as 'Crusty' or 'New Age', there seem to
be marked regional differences between the north and south in
that towns in the north are far less likely to have any conspic-
uous 'Crusty' culture. The south-west, on the other hand –
particularly old rural cities like Bath and Winchester – has large,
highly visible 'Crusty' communities.

Though many people who identify with New Age lifestyles
may originally come from urban areas, there are several reasons
why the subculture is generally associated with more rural areas.
In the 1980s, a group of travellers known as 'The [Peace] Convoy'
received a lot of coverage in the British media, partly due to
clashes with police over access to the ancient standing stones at
Stonehenge. A festival had been held annually over the summer
solstice period at Stonehenge and had come to acquire the status
of an 'alternative' to the well-known Glastonbury Festival, which
had first taken place in 1970. Whereas Glastonbury had developed into a much bigger, more organised event, with an entry fee

and big name bands, Stonehenge remained steadfastly 'unofficial' – a free festival with a greater emphasis upon drugs and anarchism. Both Stonehenge and Glastonbury festivals seem to offer strangely powerful conjunctions between modern folklore and the ancient myths of pagan Britain. Events such as the Battle of the Beanfield at Stonehenge in 1983 and the more recent road protests at Twyford Down and elsewhere highlight a conflict of interest between those who claim institutionally to speak in the name of a national heritage and those who might make another, very different kind of claim to be protectors of an ancient land. Some of the campaigners who fought unsuccessfully against the construction of a bypass at Twyford near Winchester in the early 1990s called themselves 'the Donga' tribe and protested not only against the destruction of the landscape but also against what they believed to be the desecration of a sacred site – the tombs of King Arthur's legendary knights. Although archaeologists working in the area disputed the existence of these tombs, the road protesters' political campaign nevertheless remained tied to a mystical vision of the ancient kingdom/law of the land being destroyed by invasive industrial machines (graffiti on the road builders' equipment read 'Earth Rape'). As part of a more recent road protest, campaigners near Newbury literally took to the trees to prevent the felling of centuries-old woodland. These tree camps obviously served a very practical purpose, but in doing so they also evoked romantic images of Robin Hood and his merry men in Sherwood forest.

In such a way, the most recent cultural practices, and their representations in the press, will often draw on some of the oldest, and in many ways most powerful, British identities available. However, in this chapter overall, we have seen how Britain's youth culture since the 1950s has generated a varied range of subcultures. The images and assumptions of fifteen or even ten years ago can no longer be applied to the way teenagers and youths see themselves today, just as today's styles and identities will be changed or discarded in a few years' time.

EXERCISES

1 How important do you think age is within British culture? Would you say that the differences between age groups are becoming more or less distinct?

2 What kinds of music do you associate with the following British youth subcultures? Name specific bands/artists where possible:

Hippies
Goths
Skinheads
Crusties
Bikers
Rastas
Rudeboys

3 Why do you think Britain has produced such distinct subcultural styles and groupings? What, if anything, does this tell us about British culture as a whole?

4 What do the following phrases mean? Comment on the possible insights they offer into British attitudes towards age.

- 'Mutton dressed as lamb'
- 'Put out to pasture'
- 'Trying to teach your grandmother to suck eggs'
- 'Toyboy'
- 'One foot in the grave'
- 'Whippersnapper'
- 'Wet behind the ears'
- 'Darby and Joan'
- 'Long in the tooth'
- 'Cradle snatcher'
- 'Pushing up the daisies'

5   Discuss the implications of the term 'ageism'. Is it possible and/or desirable to avoid ageism in contemporary British society?

6   To what extent do you think that young people have more in common with the youth of other nations and cultures, than with older people from their own country?

━━━━━━━━━━━━━━━━━━━━━━━━━━━━━━━━━━ **READING**

Griffin, Christine. *Representations of Youth: The Study of Youth and Adolescence in Britain and America.* Polity, 1993
Academic analysis of youth and its influences across the Atlantic.

Hebdige, Dick. *Subculture: The Meaning of Style.* Routledge, 1979
Influential review of youth and alternative culture.

McRobbie, Angela. *Feminism and Youth Culture: From 'Jackie' to 'Just 17'.* Routledge, 1991
Looks at the effects of the feminist movement on magazine contents and on teenagers.

Redhead, Steve. *The End of the Century Party: Youth and Pop Towards 2000.* Manchester University Press, 1991
Short and often sweeping, but still a punchy cultural politics review of rap, rave, and youth culture.

Thornton, Sarah. *Club Cultures: Youth, Media, Music.* Polity, 1995
An exploration of subcultures across the main areas of youth activity and performance.

CULTURAL EXAMPLES ━━━━━━━━━━━━

■ *Films*

A Clockwork Orange (1971) dir. Stanley Kubrick
Futuristic cult film about gang violence, still unavailable in
Britain since its withdrawal by the director following
supposed 'copycat' brutality.

The Great Rock'n'Roll Swindle (1980) dir. Julien Temple
Portrait of the punk rock group the Sex Pistols.

Jubilee (1977) dir. Derek Jarman
Anarchic, decadent depiction of punk subcultures in
Thatcher's Britain.

My Beautiful Laundrette (1985) dir. Stephen Frears
Film, with touches of magic realism, looking at sexuality
and racism in the 1980s 'enterprise culture'. Focuses on the
relationship between two youths – one Asian, one white
working class.

Quadrophenia (1979) dir. Frank Roddam
Film about mod culture, featuring Sting and based on the
album by The Who.

Rita, Sue and Bob Too (1986) dir. Alan Clarke
Realist portrayal of sexual relationships between two
northern working-class teenage girls and an older man.

Scum (1980) dir. Alan Clarke
Brutal portrayal of life for young men in the Borstal system.

Summer Holiday (1963) dir. Peter Yates
The archetypal sixties British teenager, Cliff Richard, goes
to France on a London bus with his friends, singing all the
way (worth comparing with the subculture of Nicholas
Roeg's *Performance* (1970), starring Mick Jagger).

FIGURE 4.5   The generation gap: a contemporary cult film poster of *Trainspotting* is displayed on a bus shelter

■   *Books*

Richard Allen, *Skinhead* (1970)
Teen novel about violent youth subculture.

Maude Casey, *Over the Water* (1990)
Teenage novel about the problems of growing up as a second generation Irish immigrant girl in the UK.

Leonore Goodings (ed.), *Bitter Sweet Dreams* (1987)
Anthology of writings by a cross-section of British teenage girls.

Nick Hornby, *Fever Pitch* (1992)
Amusing account of growing up as an obsessive football supporter.

Hanif Kureishi, *The Buddha of Suburbia* (1990)
Growing up in and around London, in the 1970s and 1980s, between different cultures.

Colin MacInnes, *Absolute Beginners* (1959)
Cult novel about swinging teenage life in London. Also made into a film in the 1980s.

Sue Townsend, *The Secret Diary of Adrian Mole 13¾* (1982)
Bestselling humour about growing up in Thatcher's Britain through a schoolboy's fictional diary.

Irvine Welsh, *Trainspotting* (1993)
Grim, darkly humorous novel about heroin subculture in Edinburgh. Made into a film in 1996.

■ *Television programmes*

Bad Ass TV
Late night black youth programme, with music and outrageous stories.

Live and Kicking
Saturday morning programme with music and competitions.

Top of the Pops
Long running chart music show.

The Young Ones
Anarchic, surreal 1980s comedy about student life in a shared house.

Chapter 5

ISLE COLLEGE
RESOURCES CENTRE

Class and politics

■ Frank McDonough

Timeline

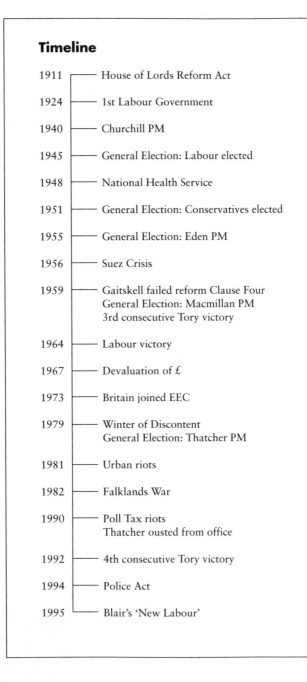

1911	House of Lords Reform Act
1924	1st Labour Government
1940	Churchill PM
1945	General Election: Labour elected
1948	National Health Service
1951	General Election: Conservatives elected
1955	General Election: Eden PM
1956	Suez Crisis
1959	Gaitskell failed reform Clause Four General Election: Macmillan PM 3rd consecutive Tory victory
1964	Labour victory
1967	Devaluation of £
1973	Britain joined EEC
1979	Winter of Discontent General Election: Thatcher PM
1981	Urban riots
1982	Falklands War
1990	Poll Tax riots Thatcher ousted from office
1992	4th consecutive Tory victory
1994	Police Act
1995	Blair's 'New Labour'

Introduction

I T WAS ONCE COMMONPLACE to portray Britain as a class-ridden society. Class was a staple part of the British way of life. Each class had unique characteristics. The upper class had stately homes, aristocratic backgrounds and posh accents; the middle class, semi-detached houses, suits and bowler hats; the working class, common accents, fish and chips and council flats. This produced a society divided between 'Us' (the workers) and 'Them' (the rich and the bosses). Pubs always had a public bar and a lounge. Even railway carriages were divided into first, second and third class compartments.

In recent years, many writers have begun to speak of the 'decline of class' in British society. The term 'classless society' has become commonplace. The rise of both Margaret Thatcher, the daughter of a Grantham shopkeeper, and John Major, the son of a garden-gnome salesman, to the post of Prime Minister, has been seen as evidence that anyone can rise to the top in British society, whatever their social origins.

The credit for this transformation is mostly given to Mrs Thatcher, Prime Minister from 1979 to 1990. Accordingly, many political commentators have suggested that the 'Thatcher Revolution' removed class from the political landscape, by shifting power through government reforms away from the Establishment, the bureaucrats and the trade unions to individual consumers and the free market. Many of Mrs Thatcher's reforms were delivered in the rhetoric of 'empowerment of the people'. Parents were encouraged to become school governors and to take control of their schools, while teachers faced the imposition of a National Curriculum to ensure that children in both state and private schools received a core course of study. The Community Charge (Poll Tax) was designed to recoup money for local amenities more

FIGURE 5.1 Upper, middle and working class represented by
(a) the elegant mansion, (b) the mock-Tudor semi-detached house

evenly across the total adult population. It was also promoted to
make local authorities more accountable to local people, but
revenue-raising limits were effectively imposed by the Treasury.
Privatisation ended up turning public utilities like gas, electricity,
telephone and water into private monopolies. Nevertheless, a large
number of commentators have argued that the Establishment (the
monarchy, Church of England, Oxbridge and the BBC) no longer

FIGURE 5.1   *(continued)* (c) the inner-city brick terraced house

exists. The middle-class bureaucrat is made to work much harder, often implementing reforms which are designed to 'get government off the backs of the people'. The working class has retreated from collective action towards domestic pleasures. The one source of collective working-class unity today is the purchase of a weekly National Lottery ticket. Even the railways now only have two classes: first and standard.

'Hurricane' Thatcher has seemingly blown class off the face of British society. Many writers now view Britain as a socially fragmented society, with life revolving around the individual, his or her family, and the idea of a better life through home ownership and consumer goods. But pronouncing the death of class is premature. A recent wide-ranging survey of public opinion found 90 per cent of people still placing themselves in a particular class; 73 per cent agreed that class was still an integral part of British society, and 52 per cent thought there were still sharp class divisions. Thus, class may have become culturally and politically invisible but it remains an integral part of British society.

FIGURE 5.2 Newspaper readership is sharply defined between those (right) which appeal to the 'serious' reader and the tabloids (left) which have a more popular appeal

One unchanging aspect of a British person's class position is accent. The words which an individual utters immediately reveal class position. A study of British accents during the 1970s found that a posh voice, sounding like a BBC news-reader, usually spoken by a person from the south-east of England, was viewed as the most attractive voice. Most respondents said this accent sounded 'educated', 'soft' and 'mellifluous'. The accents placed at the bottom in this survey, on the other hand, were regional city accents: Liverpool (scouse), Birmingham (brummie), Newcastle (geordie) and London (cockney). These accents were seen as 'harsh', 'common' and 'ugly'. No great prejudice was expressed against well-spoken Scottish and Irish accents. However, a similar survey of British accents in the US turned these results upside down and placed scouse and cockney as the most attractive and BBC English as the least. This suggests British attitudes towards accent are, to a large extent, based on ingrained class prejudice. Can it be mere coincidence that British people reserve their most negative comments for accents associated with areas containing large groups of working-class people?

In recent years, young, upper-middle-class people in London have begun to adopt fake cockney accents (estuary English), in order to disguise their class origins. Perhaps this is because they aspire to the more American image of the self-made person from humble beginnings. This is another sign of class becoming invisible. A good example of the desire to hide a privileged background is displayed by Nigel Kennedy, the brilliant violinist (who studied for several years in New York). He adopts the accent of a 'cockney lad', even though a national newspaper reported that he was the product of a very 'posh' middle-class family. However, the 1995 pop song 'Common People' by Pulp puts forward the view that though a middle-class person may 'want to live like common people', and 'sleep with common people', they can never appreciate the reality of a working-class life.

In the power stakes, however, if you want to get ahead in Britain, you would be well advised to lose a regional accent. A recent example of the importance of accent to upward mobility is Mandi Norwood, appointed editor of *Cosmopolitan* magazine at the age of 31. When she began her career in journalism she had a Geordie accent. Her London friends advised her to drop it if she wanted to get on. Two years on she admits to 'speaking like Lady Di'. From that point on, her career went swiftly upward. Even more significantly, a recent survey of recruitment managers of major corporations found that, although the majority of them knew it was wrong to discriminate against people because of a regional accent, they did. Despite all the talk of a classless society, it is still possible to divide British society into three broad classes – upper, middle and working – even though the nature and composition of each class have undergone change.

The upper class

The traditional upper class was always closely associated with the aristocracy. They lived in stately homes and had their character shaped on the playing fields of Eton. They were an hereditary élite whose wealth and position were based on property and title. These were both used to gain substantial political privileges. For example, the House of Lords, an unelected second chamber, held a veto over House of Commons legislation until 1911. However, during much of this century the power and position of the aristocracy has been steadily weakened. As long ago as the 1930s Noel Coward commented that the 'Stately Homes of England' were 'rather in the lurch'. By the 1960s the aristocracy were lampooned by Harold Wilson, the then Labour Leader, as the 'Grouse Moor tendency'. Over time, therefore, the aristocracy have been gradually replaced by a new upper class of businessmen who emerged with 'gentlemanly characteristics' and settled in London and the south-east. These 'gentlemanly capitalists' have come to dominate the financial and political heart of British society. By the 1980s Denis Healey, a leading Labour politician, was able to suggest that Mrs Thatcher had transferred power from the 'aristocracy to estate agents'.

However, most writers would put wealthy families involved in the control of major banks, insurance companies, pension funds and stocks in the City of London at the core of the modern upper class. These families still pass on wealth from generation to generation and enjoy a dominant position in society. But the nature of the modern upper class is very complex. Most vast family businesses are becoming increasingly global and are run by a highly paid managerial élite, often dubbed 'City Fat Cats'. The modern upper class is not as visible as the former owners of the stately homes of England who sought to impose standards and demanded deference. The new upper class is much more culturally invisible. Highly paid managers, PR people and the Conservative Party now represent their interests. It has been shown that a numerically small number of powerful families wield enormous power over the business life of the City of London. The Conservative Party has increasingly become the party of this City business élite, and downplays its past association with the monarchy, the Church of England and aristocracy. Many of Mrs Thatcher's reforms in the 1980s, including sharp reductions in the highest rates of personal and company tax, the removal of exchange controls, City de-regulation, the expansion of the private sector through privatisation and the weakening of trade unions have clearly benefited the business élite. The result is an upper class which has never been more wealthy. A recent study, for example, showed the top 1 per cent of wealth owners possessing 33 per cent of the nation's total wealth. Similarly, a glance at the richest 500 people in Britain shows that over 60 per cent of them inherited their wealth.

Thus, the modern upper class is still based on individuals with a common background and close social contacts. Power is still kept in the family. For example, 45 per cent of bank directors with a listing in *Who's Who* could boast a father with a previous entry. Moreover, 75 per cent of bank directors attended fee-paying public schools and 50 per cent had been to Oxford or Cambridge. Furthermore, a study of the top 250 companies in Britain recently revealed multiple directorships in the hands of a few wealthy families.

Hence, the upper class is largely made up of wealthy families. It is not exceptionally large. In 1986, for example, 43,500 people (less than 0.1 per cent of the population) held 7 per cent of the nation's wealth – or £740,000 each – while the wealthiest 10 per cent in Britain owned 50 per cent of all marketable property. Yet the numerical smallness of the upper class only serves to add to its exclusivity. It is a self-selecting élite, closed to outsiders – and money cannot buy someone into it. Networking is much more important. Contacts occur so frequently within the upper class because of their common background. The first point of entry is family background. The second is a public school education, privately funded by parents. The ethos of British fee-paying public schools such as Eton, Harrow and Rugby is geared towards lifelong friendship. At boarding schools, pupils live with each other during school terms. This allows the development of extremely close social friendships between pupils and their families. This is followed by an Oxford or Cambridge education which expands the networking process still further. It is quite remarkable to note that though public school pupils account for only 5 per cent of the total school population, they take over 50 per cent of Oxbridge places. A public school/Oxbridge education moulds an integrated élite.

The question of whether the upper class acts in unison is extremely difficult to answer. There are clearly powerful families who wield power in the City of London, and have influence over the Conservative Party. The increasingly competitive nature of business suggests conflicts of interest are likely to develop between elements within this ruling group. However, the close networking ethos of the upper-class business élite is able to make life difficult for the 'new rich' such as Richard Branson (owner of the Virgin group of record label, airline, radio station, cola), Alan Sugar (business tycoon behind Amstrad and chairman of Tottenham Hotspur) and Anita Roddick (creator of the Body Shop). These brilliant entrepreneurs, who have truly gone from 'rags to riches', are still considered 'outsiders' by the upper class. This partly explains why Richard Branson decided to withdraw his Virgin group from the stock market, because he feared its independence was being compromised by powerful City groups.

For all the talk of an 'enterprise culture', much of British business is dominated by companies set up well over a hundred years ago. Upper-class families, who own these companies, have enormous power over investment, markets, companies and shareholders. The fate of any self-made business person ultimately lies in their hands. Hence the upper class, like the public schools, may be small in size but they occupy positions of leadership in the major businesses in Britain. The upper class uses its wealth to confer social advantages and to retain a privileged position for its future generations. The closeness of the upper class ensures over-representation by this group in all the key positions in society. For example, 65 per cent of Conservative MPs in 1987 had been to a fee-paying public school. Thus, the upper class can be seen to be a relatively closed, coherent and self-recruiting élite. It may have become an invisible élite in cultural terms but its underlying power and influence have never been stronger.

The middle class

In recent times, it has become fashionable to be a middle-class hero. This was not so in the 1960s. In those days, the lifestyle of the middle-class was derided in pop songs such as 'Semi-Detached Suburban Mr Jones' by Manfred Mann and 'Matthew and Son' by Cat Stevens. These songs suggest that a suburban middle-class lifestyle is boring and repetitive. In the 1970s prejudice against a conformist life continued. The popular comedy show *The Fall and Rise of Reginald Perrin* portrayed the dull life of a middle-class executive who takes the same route from his semi-detached house to work each day. At work, Reggie grows tired of life with equally dull people, at home he despairs of his boring relatives whose idea of fun is to drink prune wine and visit a safari park at the weekend. To break free of this middle-class Alcatraz, Reggie Perrin fakes his own suicide and disappears.

In the 1980s, however, Reggie Perrin came back from the dead to find the boring middle-class lifestyle he escaped had become, of all things, fashionable, because of a general acceptance of Thatcherism. Everyone aspired to own a dull semi-detached house in the suburbs and go to work in a dull job in the City. A middle-class hero suddenly became something to be. The coffee morning became the 'in thing'. Everyone wanted Gold Blend coffee at these events. Indeed, a sequence of advertisements featuring the burgeoning romance of a couple whose close relationship blossoms over several cups of coffee became extraordinarily popular – so much so that the last advertisement featuring the Gold Blend Couple drew a larger audience than popular soap operas such as *EastEnders* and *Coronation Street*.

Even 1960s rebels were falling over themselves to become respectable. Roger Daltrey, the lead singer of The Who, had sung in the 1960s hit 'My Generation', 'I hope I die before I get old'. Yet in the 1980s he had got old, and was now telling middle-class people that it was a jolly good idea to get a credit card. Even Mrs Mary Whitehouse, the much derided campaigner against television sex and violence, suddenly found herself going round for regular cups of coffee with Mrs Thatcher at number 10 Downing Street. This seems to indicate that a crucial, yet ignored part of the Thatcher revolution was to elevate the coffee club brigade almost into a government think-tank. Everyone was 'tuning in and turning on' not to LSD but to *This Morning* with Richard Madeley and Judy Finnigan. This popular daytime television show featured, of course, a special interlude known as 'Coffee Time'. No doubt Reggie Perrin was wishing he had never returned from the grave.

Even so, it is difficult to neatly pigeon-hole the middle class. Much definition of the middle class still revolves around the differences in their employment situations. A common assumption these days is that the middle class is extremely fragmented. However, there is general agreement that most middle-class people fall into one of four broad categories. The first are the higher professionals – doctors, lawyers, architects, accountants and business executives. They may lack the power and wealth of the upper class but they are certainly a distinct group. Higher professionals value education, training and independence. They have all been to university and in most cases have postgraduate and professional qualifications. They have generous pensions, holidays, expenses, sick pay and considerable freedom within their own job. It is quite noticeable that family members of this group tend to follow their parents into a professional career. For example, 64 per cent of the sons of higher professionals end up in similar jobs, while only 2 per cent end up in a manual job. This low level of downward mobility suggests a high level of shared values concerning hard work and educational attainment which are passed on from generation to generation.

However, this higher professional group is not a completely closed élite. In 1972, for example, 28.3 per cent of male professionals were the sons of manual workers. One recent study showed that 34.5 per cent of top professionals had a father from a similar background. There are clearly difficulties for a working-class person finding 'room at the top', to quote the title of a well-known 1957 novel. Indeed, the novel's leading character, Joe Lampton, shows the difficulties an upwardly mobile member of the working class faces when entering the world of the upper-middle class. Joe Lampton is portrayed as a ruthless opportunist who marries upwards to a life of boredom and soul-destroying disillusionment – the underlying moral being that working-class people who wish to rise can only do so by acquiring the moral scruples of vipers. Oddly enough, this powerful image of educated working-class people 'selling out' and feeling ill at ease 'above their station' has acted as an effective weapon to prevent talented members of the working classes ever wanting to find any 'room at the top'. This may explain why only 6.5 per cent of top professionals had fathers with semi-skilled or unskilled manual backgrounds. Indeed, in many of the top professions the proportion of those whose father came from a manual background is exceptionally low. Hence, the medical profession, merchant banking and the judiciary are largely Joe Lampton-free zones.

The second major group in the middle class are salaried professionals (sometimes known as 'The Salatariat'). This group includes university and college lecturers, school teachers, local government officials, civil servants and social workers. They too have all attended university, and often have postgraduate and professional qualifications. In most cases, they have modest pensions and some freedom over their own job. Yet they have nowhere near the same level of salary autonomy enjoyed by higher professionals.

The largest group in the middle class are routine white-collar workers. A great deal of white collar work takes place at a desk and is heavily supervised. It is very much a nine-to-five job with little freedom. Clerical work is now becoming female-dominated. In 1911, for example, 21 per cent of clerks were women. Today the figure is 78 per cent. Some clerical jobs such as a secretary or a telephone operator are almost totally held by women. Many now work part time. Oddly enough, 50 per cent of clerical workers now view themselves as part of the working class. However, there is little evidence of clerical workers flocking to join old working-class bastions such as trade unions. They do not exhibit an 'Us' and 'Them' view of themselves and their employers. In general, lower-middle-class employees use their jobs to improve the quality of their lives through consumer goods, foreign holidays and entertainment.

The final group in the middle class are the self-employed. They became the 'stars' of the 1980s in cultural terms. These small businessmen and shopkeepers have more control over their working lives than clerical workers. They view themselves as middle class. Yet they work exceptionally long hours, have no career structure and must finance their own pensions. In many cases, they earn less than a routine clerical worker. The self-employed have always been the staunchest supporters of the Conservative Party. Advertising, which is really an art concerned with influencing public opinion, focused a great deal of its energy in the 1980s on popularising the self-made business person, epitomised perhaps by Harry Enfield's character 'Loadsamoney', a loud-mouthed 'Essex man' who brandished a roll of banknotes to emphasise his rising social status. This was the era when it was fashionable to 'go it alone'. A famous car advertisement featured a man who gives up a steady job to start his own business and drives a Renault car which 'takes your breath away'. Another introduced us to 'Vector Man' who did not just know his own mind, he knew his own bank account and told his bank manager so. He was not stupid either. Even at the height of the brief 1980s boom, he wanted a free overdraft facility. Many similar advertisements portrayed high-flying businesswomen who told insurance sellers and bankers where to get off. These women would give up everything except their Volkswagen and their Gold Blend. This climate in which 'greed was good' and 'lunch was for wimps' made the self-made person a hero. It clearly had benefits for the Conservative Party. Lord Young, architect of the 'enterprise culture' promoted by the Department of Trade and Industry during the 1980s, recently confessed that much of the promotion of self-employment in the 1980s was 'social engineering'. Of course, the great financial crash of 1987 brought all these dreams of 'rags to riches' down to earth. The housing market collapsed. No doubt Vector Man's bank manager is telling him what sort of repayments he wants on his bank account these days. The Gold Blend couple have doubtless switched back to ever reliable PG Tips. Never has a revolution been as dependent on the strength of public relations and coffee as the one instigated by Mrs Thatcher.

The working class

It is the working class, at the bottom of the social pile, who have been most closely examined. More ink has been spilled about them than any other group in British society. They have been portrayed in novels, plays, films and television documentaries. Endless sociological surveys on working-class life and numerous government reports have been produced. Unfortunately, most of these studies have been conducted by members of the middle class. For example, George Orwell in *The Road To Wigan Pier* (1937) views the plight of the unemployed working class of the 1930s through the eyes of a bourgeois intellectual. Many films contain the idea that 'it's grim up north' for a member of the working class. Even the recent television series *Our Friends in the North* (1996), produced as part of a 1990s 'acceleration of nostalgia' for the 1960s, repeats many of the old stereotypes about traditional working-class life in the north. Richard Hoggart, an eminent

FIGURE 5.3 Poster for the popular soap opera *Coronation Street*, which stresses its accurate depiction of northern working-class life

writer on working-class life, has been accused of being over-critical of the life his education had allowed him to escape. Hence, what we know of the working class is more often than not what the middle class think about them.

In the 1950s, there was a traditional picture of typical, usually male, members of the working class. Such people left school without any qualifications to find a job as a manual worker. They had a regional accent, a trade union membership card and lived in a close-knit community of 'two-up-two-down' terraced houses owned by a landlord or the council. They enjoyed a pint down the local pub, a bet and a trip to a football match. The chip shop was the central aspect of local cuisine and the Sunday roast dinner was a national ritual. They always voted Labour and enjoyed a shared experience. Of course, the working-class woman was depicted as a wife who always stayed at home to look after the kids with very few leisure activities, except perhaps Bingo. The working class saw themselves as 'Us' and the middle and upper classes as 'Them'.

Even in the 1950s it was already being suggested that this traditional picture of working-class life was undergoing change. The sweeping victories of the Conservatives in general elections in this period led many writers to speculate whether improved wages, living conditions, education, welfare and consumer goods had led the working class to no longer feel part of the 'lower orders'. It was even suggested that as workers became more affluent they ceased to feel a close affinity with the Labour Party. The idea that a classless – You Never Had it So Good – consumer society had emerged was widespread. It seemed as though the working classes were looking forward to their next consumer purchase and not some grand socialist revolution. Many books, novels and films reflected the idea of a new working class emerging. *Saturday Night and Sunday Morning* (1960) which examined the life of an affluent worker within a traditional working-class community in the late 1950s is a prime example. The film portrays the life of Arthur Seaton, a young lathe operator from Nottingham who, though highly paid, is dissatisfied with the parochial attitudes and restricted cultural activities of the working class. He proclaims with rugged individualism: 'I'm Me, and nobody else; and whatever people say I am, that's what I'm not, because they don't know a bloody thing about me.' This rugged individualism leads Arthur to feel contempt for his new-found affluence which is mostly spent on drink, women and fishing. Significantly, he is indifferent to politics.

A flood of studies appeared in the 1950s and 1960s which examined whether affluent workers had ceased to feel close class solidarity. The most prominent example was a detailed study of Ford car workers. This showed that affluent workers had grasped the idea of a better life through consumer goods and spent a great deal of time on 'domestic pleasures'. Yet these studies concluded that in cultural terms the majority of affluent workers did not aspire to be middle class. They still saw being a mem-ber of a trade union and voting Labour as extremely important expres-sions of their class identity. Even so, these affluent workers placed a better life for their family as a greater priority than the strug-gles of the Labour movement. This tends to indicate that the advent of a consumer society, and improved standards of living, were already leading to a more individualistic approach to poli-tics among the working class before the 1980s.

It is, however, the years since Mrs Thatcher came to power in 1979 which have reopened the debate over the 'embour-geoisement' of the working class. Previous assumptions about the working class are being discussed once again. The Thatcher years are being viewed as a period of cultural transformation which has produced an increasingly fragmented working class. There are few who would doubt that the working class has changed. The crux of the traditional picture of working-class life suggests a shared experience. In 1979 male manual workers formed a majority of the workforce and most belonged to trade unions. Today, nearly 50 per cent of the present workforce is female or a member of an ethnic minority. The membership of trade unions has fallen from thirteen million to less than eight million today (of which 35 per cent are female). In the 1970s, trade unions were seen as having the power to bring down governments. Yet this power has been all but extinguished by successive trade union reforms during

TABLE 5.1 Membership of selected major unions in 1994

Amalgamated·Engineering and Electrical Union	835,000
Banking, Insurance and Finance Union	141,000
Civil and Public Services Association	132,000
General, Municipal and Boilermakers' Union	835,000
Graphical, Paper and Media Union	224,000
Manufacturing, Science, Finance	516,000
National Association of Schoolmasters, Union of Women Teachers	138,000
National Communications Union	122,000
National Union of Civil and Public Servants	112,000
National Union of Teachers	169,000
Transport and General Workers' Union	949,000
Union of Communication Workers	167,000
Union of Construction, Allied Trades and Technicians	136,000
Union of Shop, Distributive and Allied Workers	299,000
UNISON (formed by merger of NALGO, NUPE and COHSE[a])	1,458,000

Note[a] NALGO = National and local Government Officers Association; NUPE = National Union of Public Employees; COHSE = Confederation of Health Service Employees.

Source: D. Butler and R. Rose, *Parliamentary Yearbook* (Nuffield College)

the 1980s. Trade union leaders who enjoyed national fame in the 1960s and 1970s are now unknown figures. Many former steel, coal-mining and dock areas have become industrial wastelands. Many have even been turned into industrial museums. In 1994, there were sixty-eight unions affiliated to the TUC. Membership figures for some of the largest are given in Table 5.1.

However, the greatest new division within the working class is the gap between the employed and unemployed. The living standards of those in full-time jobs have improved, but the plight of

FIGURE 5.4 *The Big Issue* magazine is sold by and for the homeless in Britain

the unemployed has worsened. For a start, unemployment has increased rapidly. From 1951 to 1979, unemployment never rose above 1.5 million. Since 1979 it has been as high as 3.5 million and rarely below 2 million. A great many male unskilled workers have fallen down a black hole of despair with no job, little hope and no future. They have become walking museum exhibits. These changes have led to talk of the development of an 'underclass' in

ISLE COLLEGE
RESOURCES CENTRE

Britain which is cut off from the consumer society, poor and politically apathetic. In 1979 only 6 per cent of the population lived at the lowest rate of social security benefit. Today, 19 per cent live at this level. Homelessness for many is the big issue – this conviction spawned a publication of that name sold largely to fund its vendors.

Alongside the growth of poverty has come riots in very poor urban areas such as Toxteth (Liverpool), Moss Side (Manchester), Handsworth (Birmingham) and Brixton (London). Street begging and the 'cardboard cities' of homeless people in London and other major cities are other symptoms of a new harsher climate. Even diseases such as diphtheria and tuberculosis are making a comeback. This 'underclass' is excluded from the 'flash' car, the Vector bank account and Gold Blend coffee. Many of the new poor go to 'car-boot sales' where people sell second-hand goods, usually from the back of a very ancient car which really does 'take your breath away'. In many areas of inner city Britain crime has risen to record levels, drug addiction resembles the American inner city and unemployment is over 60 per cent. A recent study showed that one in five households now has no adult in any sort of employment. The growth of one-parent families in Britain is higher than in any other European country. Contrary to the 1950s image, the working-class woman of the 1990s is often depicted as an unmarried single mother living on a council estate.

Social change

This out-of-work underclass is divided from those in work. Indeed, a 1992 earning survey showed that the average manual worker's full-time pay was £268 per week, compared to £248 for the average clerical worker. Nevertheless, there has been a sharp decline in male manual workers, a group always seen as the core of the traditional working class. From 1951 to 1981 the number of manual workers has fallen from 15.6 million to 13.3 million. In 1951, 70 per cent of the workforce was made up of manual workers. In 1991 they made up only 46 per cent of workers.

Few doubt that the lifestyle and cultural activities of manual workers have changed. The majority of manual workers still in work own their own homes, have a car, a fridge, a washing machine, a television, a telephone and inside toilets and bathrooms. They now go abroad on holiday and their diet no longer revolves around the fish and chip shop. The number of foreign restaurants in working-class areas has increased rapidly. Foreign foods such as naan bread, pasta and Australian wine are now sold in the majority of supermarkets.

The greatest revolution, however, has been in housing choice. In 1950, over 80 per cent of skilled and unskilled manual workers lived in private rented or council-owned properties. In 1988, 72 per cent of skilled and 55 per cent of semi-skilled manual workers owned their own home. A recent opinion survey showed that 90 per cent of manual workers who lived in council property would like to buy their own homes. Since 1981, 33 per cent of all council tenants have bought their council houses.

The modern working-class manual worker spends less time with workmates at the pub (increasingly the preserve of youth) or football match (increasingly attended by the middle class) and much more time at home. The growth of DIY superstores has led to more working-class men spending time making their homes more attractive. Industrial change has radically altered many former working-class communities which depended on heavy industries such as coal-mining, shipbuilding, dock work, railways and steel making. New industries tend to be located some distance from where workers live.

An additional change in the traditional pattern of working-class life has been in the role of women. A majority of working-class women are now going out of the home into either part-time or full-time work. Thus, female members of the working class are actually much less home-centred than ever before. Of course, much of this work is poorly paid and part time. Nevertheless, more opportunities for women in expanding service sectors such a retailing, banking and insurance exist and over 30 per cent of householders now boast a female breadwinner. Hence, working-class women are much less reliant on males. This has resulted in more all-female social activities outside the home. A recent example is the popularity of male groups of strippers, the most famous being the Chippendales, who are viewed by women as sex objects. The idea of a working-class woman accepting a traditional housewife role is declining. The novelty of the house-husband has emerged in the working class. There is also evidence that an unemployed male is increasingly being seen as a poor marriage partner – hence the sharp increase in one-parent families

It seems that the majority of working-class people aspire to higher levels of consumer spending. The power to withdraw one's labour has been eroded – and replaced by the power to buy goods. This has led to a climate in which 'we are what we buy'. Working people have become more money-centred, family-centred and individualistic. House and car ownership in working-class areas has become a symbol of rising status.

However, this cultural revolution has not completely led to the working class no longer feeling working class. When account is taken of what the working class say about class, we find they still do not feel middle class. They still believe that class has a detrimental impact on their life. They still consider class to be an important part of British life. Accordingly, the working class still see themselves as part of a particular class and few believe they live in a classless society.

The nature of politics

There are numerous organisations which agitate for political change outside the formal channels of government power. Some prominent examples include Greenpeace and Friends of the Earth which are concerned with environmental matters, the Campaign For Nuclear Disarmament (CND) which agitates for the adoption by the government of a nuclear-free British defence policy, the National Farmer's Union (NFU) which lobbies the government on behalf of the agricultural community, the Confederation of British Industry (CBI) which represents the interests of big business, the

Trades Union Congress (TUC) which lobbies on behalf of workers, and Shelter which speaks on behalf of the homeless. British pressure groups are proliferating at a rapid rate and enjoy the support of people whose ordinary lives are nowhere near as radical. Yet these groups are primarily interested in a single issue rather than a broad range of policies. They all seek to influence the government in London.

It is clear that the dominant mechanisms of power still reside with Parliament at Westminster. Many writers would suggest that the power of central government has never been stronger. Equally, the power of local government and pressure groups has never been weaker. In 1979, when Mrs Thatcher took office, she promised to end the 'enlarged role of the state'. But this bold claim never really came true. In 1979 the state was responsible for 43 per cent of the economy and in 1990 the state was *still* responsible for 43 per cent. Indeed, Britain is the most centralised state among all the major Western industrial democracies. Power has increasingly been concentrated in the hands of the Prime Minister and the Cabinet. The power of central government has been extended since 1979. Under the 1994 Police Act, the police, previously organised on a local basis, were brought under the control of the Home Secretary. In 1988 British universities came under central research and teaching regulation for the first time. British schools now have a National Curriculum. Regional health authorities have been abolished and the National Health Service is now under the control of the Health Secretary. The power of local government has been dramatically weakened between 1979 and 1995. Local authorities no longer have the right to build homes. The introduction of rate-capping (limits on the amount of money raised through local taxation) has turned local councils into little more than the agents of central government. London is the only major world capital without an integrated local government agency. Other centrally controlled agencies have appeared, including the Child Support Agency, the Student Loans Company and the National Rivers Authority. Even the National Lottery, though privately managed, is under central government control.

Oddly enough, not since the days when the monarchy once dominated Parliament has power been so centrally controlled as it is from Westminster today. Yet, since the English Civil War in the seventeenth century, the power of the monarch over Parliament has dwindled. It has always been claimed that the British monarch reigns but does not rule, whereas the American president rules but does not reign. Today, Queen Elizabeth II remains the head of state but is little more than a ceremonial figure-head. She even pays income tax. The symbolic power of the Queen over Parliament is reflected in the State Opening of Parliament, which takes place each November. At this ceremony, a messenger of the monarch (Black Rod) has the door of the House of Commons slammed in his face, to symbolise Parliament's independence from the monarchy, before MPs decide to listen to the 'Queen's speech', which outlines the legislative programme of the government for each year and is written by the Prime Minister.

The whole ceremony may seem to be one of those eccentric British rituals; yet it emphasises the way power has shifted from the monarch to Parliament which is made up of two Houses. The least important of these is the House of Lords. This is a non-elected body based on hereditary and life peers. Until 1911 the House of Lords had a veto over government legislation. These days it acts as a body which gives advice on government legislation. The dominant political forum is the House of Commons. In 1992 this was composed of 651 MPs. Each MP represents a particular part of Britain, known as a constituency, and is elected at General Elections held every four or five years. The growth of the power of the House of Commons has been accompanied by an expansion of the electorate through various parliamentary reform acts (today everyone over the age of eighteen has the right to vote) and the growth of organised political parties with leaders, national organisations and competing policies. After a General Election, the party leader who wins a majority of seats in the House of Commons forms a government from members of her or his party. The Prime Minister selects a Cabinet, which is composed of ministers individually and collectively responsible for carrying out the legislative programme of the government. The dominance of the Prime Minister and the Cabinet over the British system has led to charges that the British political system is an 'elected dictatorship' of the Party leader (and the leader's closest associates) and an Opposition leader (and Shadow Cabinet organised on a similar basis).

Party politics

The two main parties in Britain today are the Conservative Party and the Labour Party, and they have dominated elections since 1918. From 1950 to 1970, a total of 92 per cent of votes went to the two major parties. Even in 1992 the Conservative and Labour parties took 78 per cent of the available votes.

The Conservative Party emerged in the 1830s from the 'Tory' grouping in Parliament. In the later nineteenth century, under the leadership of Disraeli, the party was concerned with defending traditional institutions such as the monarchy, the aristocracy and the empire. Disraeli also popularised the idea of 'One Nation'

FIGURE 5.5 (a) a Conservative political club building representing middle England stability contrasts with (b) an anti-democratic poster advertising the Anarchist Communist Federation, the extreme fringe of extra-parliamentary activity

Conservatism. This suggested the Conservative Party was the only true national party which could rise above class and special interest groups to represent the people as a whole. After 1918, and the creation of a mass electorate, the party has constantly and successfully adapted its policies to suit prevailing trends in British society. In the 1930s the party started to shed its aristocratic image and was led by businessmen. In the 1950s the Party accepted Labour policies such as nationalisation and the Welfare State. This led many commentators to speak of Britain from 1951 to 1979 as

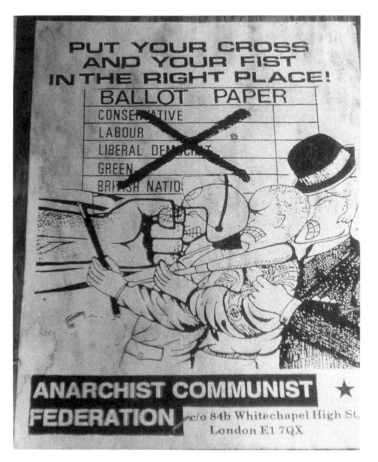

FIGURE 5.5 *(continued)* (b)

having a consensus politics in which there was very little difference between the two major parties. Under Mrs Thatcher, the
party moved away from 'One Nation' Conservatism towards a
set of policies aimed at business, the consumer and the upwardly
mobile. Thus, the Conservative Party, once the party of the
Establishment and the classic aristocratic, stiff-upper-lipped ruling
class is now associated with the business and commercial sections
of society. However, the legacy of Mrs Thatcher's conviction politics for the long-term electoral appeal of the Conservatives remains
uncertain. Since her fall from power in 1990, the party under
John Major has been greatly divided as to the way forward. No
doubt inherent pragmatism and the desire to keep power will
emerge once more. After all, the Conservative Party is the most
consistently successful British political party.

The second major party is the Labour Party. This was formed
in 1900 with the financial backing of the trade unions to represent the interests of the working class. In 1918 the party made a
firm commitment to the 'common ownership of the means of
production'. The first Labour government came to power in 1924.
By 1929 the Labour Party had replaced the Liberals as one of
the two major parties. The Labour Party gained a spectacular
victory in the 1945 General Election. This government introduced
several important social reforms, most notably the National
Health Service, the social security system, mass education and the
nationalisation of several leading industries. The party won power
again under Harold Wilson from 1964 to 1970 and was in
office again from 1974 to 1979. However, while the Labour Party
has established itself as one of the major parties, it has never
ruled for longer than five-and-a-half years. Labour has spent the
majority of time in opposition. The failure of the Labour Party
to dominate politics has been attributed to its image as a
party of the labouring working class in major industrial cities.
The close link with the trade unions has also deterred many voters.
This may explain why the party has difficulty in winning support
from non-union members and from those living in affluent middle-
class suburbs or rural areas. However, under Tony Blair, the
Labour Party has attempted to ditch its old 'cloth-cap' image. The

party constitution now gives greater powers to individual members. The former dominance of the trade unions over the party is downplayed. In 1995, the party revised Clause Four of its constitution and thus ended the historic commitment of the party to state ownership. The party is now portrayed as 'New Labour'. Yet the long-term success of this strategy with the electorate remains uncertain.

The third largest party are the Liberal Democrats. This was an amalgamation of the old Liberal Party and the Social Democratic Party, the latter being a breakaway group from the Labour Party, formed in 1981 by the 'Gang of Four' (Roy Jenkins, Shirley Williams, Bill Rogers and David Owen). The Liberal Democrats advocate policies based on freedom of the individual and support for the adoption of proportional representation at elections. However, in spite of its desire to 'break the mould of two-party politics' it remains a minority party which draws support from voters dissatisfied with the two major parties. This may explain why its most spectacular victories are in by-elections in single constituencies. Thus, the Liberal Democrats are a party of protest rather than a real alternative for government. The image of the party is moderate and appeals predominantly to middle-class people, often in rural areas.

The other parties represented in parliament are the Ulster Unionists who largely campaign on the question of Northern Ireland remaining part of the UK, the Scottish Nationalist Party which demands independence for Scotland, and Plaid Cymru which makes similar demands for Wales. There are all manner of small fringe parties who have no representation in parliament. The most prominent examples are the Socialist Workers Party (SWP) which advocates a socialist society on the principles of Marx and Trotsky, the Green Party which champions environmental policies, the British National Party which advocates 'Britain for the British', and the 'Monster Raving Loony Party' run by 'Screaming Lord Sutch' which advocates free ice-cream and, at a by-election in Bootle, Merseyside in 1990 actually gained more votes than the Conservative candidate.

Voting behaviour

The most important part of political activity for the average individual is voting at elections. The way people vote has become the subject of enormous discussion. Between 1951 and 1966 over 90 per cent of voters strongly identified with and voted for one of the two major political parties. Even at the 1992 election, 78 per cent of voters still voted for one of the two major parties. Table 5.2 gives an indication of the current two-party dominance in the House of Commons.

The 1992 election was the fourth consecutive victory for the Conservative Party. However, the Liberal Democrats who polled nearly six million votes were hampered by the 'first past the post' system. This system gives a seat to the candidate who wins the most votes in each constituency instead of giving a number of seats to each party based on their percentage of all votes, as is the practice in systems with proportional representation. Not surprisingly, the Liberal Democrats favour the adoption of a proportional representation system and the Conservatives are the strongest supporters of the present system.

It has long been claimed that in Britain class is closely related to voting choice at elections. At the 1964 General Election, for

TABLE 5.2   The 1992 General Election

	MPs	Votes (to nearest '000)	Share of vote (%)
Conservative Party	336	14,001,000	42.3
Labour Party	271	11,557,000	34.9
Liberal Democrats	20	5,998,000	18.1
Welsh and Scottish Nationalist Parties	7	786,000	2.4
Northern Ireland Parties	17	785, 000	2.3

Turnout: 77.7 per cent
Overall Majority for Conservatives: 21

example, there was a 2:1 chance in favour of a person from a manual working-class background voting Labour and a 4:1 chance in favour of a person from a non-manual middle-class background voting Conservative. The major anomaly for pollsters has been to explain why 33 per cent of the working class do not vote Labour. Indeed, most Conservative election victories have included at least 30 per cent of votes from the working class. The classic example of the working-class Tory in popular culture used to be the character of Alf Garnett in the popular comedy series *Till Death Us Do Part*. He voted Conservative because he thought they were patriotic and high-born. He wanted to be ruled by what he saw as his betters, not his equals. Even at the 1987 election, Neil Kinnock, the Labour leader, was castigated by working-class Tory voters in opinion polls for 'not sounding or looking like a prime minister'.

However, many writers have suggested that class voting is in decline. The result is a growing apathy with both major parties, accompanied by an upsurge of support for centre and fringe parties. In the six General Elections since 1970 the share of the votes of the two major parties has fallen from 92 per cent to 75 per cent. It seems that more and more people are willing to vote for the Liberal Democrats, or the Scottish, Welsh and Irish nationalist parties. At by-elections, the share of the vote for numerous fringe candidates has grown enormously. The number of 'floating' voters who switch their votes to different parties at each election has also grown. Nowadays most people are less attached to any political party than ever before. In 1964, 48 per cent of voters said they identified strongly with one party. But in 1992 this figure had fallen to 21 per cent. This growing apathy may also explain why the number of non-voters has increased. This is especially true of the 18–24 age group. In the 1992 General Election less than 40 per cent of such people bothered to vote at all.

This apathy may also be linked to the fact that the public standing of politicians has never been lower. They have become figures of ridicule. On *Spitting Image*, a comedy show which used caricatured puppets, leading politicians have been portrayed in negative and often ludicrous terms. Indeed, many politicians have complained about the images presented of them in the programme. Some of the most memorable images include Kenneth Baker (Conservative), who was depicted as a slimy, crawling snail, Norman Tebbitt (Conservative), portrayed as a leather-clad cockney 'bovver boy', Roy Hattersley (Labour) as a spluttering fool, David Steel (Liberal Democrat) as a fawning dwarf, Tony Blair (Labour) as an overgrown schoolboy, and Peter Mandelson (Labour) as a slimy half-worm, half-snake. This programme has served to hold up politicians as figures of ridicule rather than admired leaders.

Another reason for the low public standing of politicians has been the reporting of their sexual activities outside of Parliament. A long list of political sex scandals has been eagerly discussed in the tabloid press during the past few years. Indeed, coping with a daily diet of new allegations of political sleaze has become a central aspect of British political life. The popular tabloid press has a mighty appetite for such stories. All the participants in such scandals are offered enormous sums of money by newspapers to 'tell all'. For example, when it emerged that the Liberal Democrat leader Paddy Ashdown had once had an affair with his secretary, he was dubbed by the *Sun* newspaper as 'PADDY PANTSDOWN'. Similarly, the *News of The World* bought the story of an unemployed actress who had had a torrid affair with the Tory Cabinet Minister David Mellor. It was revealed that Mellor had made love to her while wearing a Chelsea Football Club shirt. Not surprisingly, he was forced to resign. The tabloid press made a scandal out of the claim that Norman Lamont, the Tory Chancellor of the Exchequer, rented out his basement flat to what they called a 'bondage-queen'. The reporting of the sad and lonely death of a Tory MP who had asphyxiated himself while engaging in an obscure sexual activity which involved a plastic bag and an orange seemed to plunge the standing of politicians to an all-time low. This climate of sleaze, heated up by the tabloid press, has no doubt contributed to the growth of political apathy among voters.

It seems that even for those who do vote, single issues are playing a vital part in voting choice. During the 1992 election campaign, voters put the Labour Party well ahead on all the 'caring' issues such as social welfare, the NHS, education and unemployment. Yet the majority did not trust Labour on taxation and keeping down inflation and so voted for the Conservatives again. This suggests the key issue at the election was the 'pound in your pocket', which indicates that the likely victor at future elections will be the party which allows the consumer greater economic stability and more opportunity to consume. In practice, this is likely to mean the party which keeps tax down and inflation low. Thus, the slump in Labour's fortunes from 1979 to 1992 can be put down to offering policies which were unattractive to the consumer's needs. Hence, a user-friendly leader who deals in 'sound bite' politics, such as Tony Blair, may prove popular with these volatile single-issue voters who have ceased to be aligned to any party.

Another factor that has been noticeable in the four election victories of the Conservatives from 1979 to 1992 has been the growth of stark regional differences. At the 1983 General Election, for instance, the Labour Party, won only three seats south of the Midlands, excluding London. Most of Labour's seats were won in big inner city areas with high proportions of working-class people. At the 1992 election, the Conservative Party held less than ten seats in Scotland and Wales put together. In fact, the Labour vote in many of its working-class heartlands has increased from 1979 to 1992. In Wales, 69 per cent of the working class voted Labour. However, Labour has lost the support of the working class in the south of England: only 30 per cent of voters there chose them in 1992. Thus, the Conservative dominance at elections since 1979 has been in the expanding working-class Tory vote in the Midlands and the south of England. This strongly suggests that Mrs Thatcher's hardcore support came from areas which were not part of industrial Britain in the first place. The yuppie lifestyle of the 1980s was also largely based in the south of England. Hence, the class composition of the south has produced a situation in which, in three-cornered fights between the Conservatives, Labour and the Liberals, it was the Tories who were able to come out on top in 1979 and 1992.

Conclusion

For the reasons cited above, pronouncing the death of class in British society does seem premature. The stark regional differences between the affluent south and the more impoverished north suggest that Thatcherism represented a rather narrow class appeal. In fact, Mrs Thatcher never won more than 44 per cent of the vote at any general election, while in 1950 the Labour Party polled 51 per cent. The link between class and politics has not been completely broken. It seems that the overwhelming majority of manual workers still vote for the Labour Party. Yet this group, due to the decline of manufacturing industry, has fallen within the workforce, especially in the south east. Class position still remains the best way of establishing long-term voting patterns. At the 1987 General Election, 48 per cent of working-class voters chose the Labour Party, while only 15 per cent of salaried professionals did so. The self-employed are still the staunchest Conservative Party voters. The Liberal Democrats are most strongly supported by salaried professional and white collar members of the middle class. What has probably happened is that the size of the classes has changed. This has resulted in the middle class growing in size in certain geographical locations in the Midlands and the south.

Finally, to trace a couple of intersections between this chapter and Chapters 3 and 6, we may ask the question: in which political party were women and members of ethnic minorities to be given the fairest chance of advancing themselves? One of the complaints made against Mrs Thatcher was that she 'never did anything for women'. This may well be so in terms of legislation, membership of her cabinets and furtherance of the interests of those traditional families where women did not work outside the home. Yet many others have argued that Thatcher certainly offered a powerful role model for women. The Labour Party under Tony Blair has tried to increase the number of its prospective parliamentary candidates who were women. However, all-women shortlists for seats at Westminster were judged to be illegal in 1995. Prospective parliamentary candidates are chosen by polit-

FIGURE 5.6 One part of Chila Kumari Burman's diptych *Convenience Not Love*, 1986–7, showing Margaret Thatcher wearing John Bull clothes

ical parties who send then for interview to local constituencies, with a view to their 'adoption'. It was judged to be against the law for Head Office to submit only women for such scrutiny. The proportion of women and ethnic minority MPs in different political parliamentary parties remains extremely low. The earlier

235

attempt to introduce 'black sections' in local constituencies was shelved after heated debate. However, individual MPs, including Diane Abbott, Bernie Grant, Paul Boateng and Keith Vaz have raised the profile of ethnic minorities in Britain. These four were all elected Labour MPs in 1987 (the first black representatives in Parliament for sixty years) but it was not until 1992 that a Conservative MP, Nirj Deva, was elected from an ethnic minority.

For the future, perhaps the most significant aspect of contemporary politics is the fact that the next generation, Britain's young people, seem to be alienated not just from allegiance to individual parties but from the whole democratic process. Hence their cultural identity is formed far more by consumer considerations and single-issue politics than by a belief in the potential for party politics to bring about change for the better.

EXERCISES

1 Offer a definition of upper, middle and working class.

2 To what extent do British people vote along class lines?

3 What is your understanding of the voting systems, 'first past the post' and 'proportional representation'? Which, in your opinion, offers the better model on which to base a system for electing a government?

4 How have British class attitudes and styles changed since the 1950s?

5 Name some well-known British people from a range of occupations. Can you place them in terms of class?

READING

Hutton, Will. *The State We're In.* Jonathan Cape, 1995
Wide-ranging, accessible review of Britain's political economy in relation to its competitors.

Jenkins, Simon. *Accountable to No-one: The Tory Nationalization of Britain.* Hamish Hamilton, 1995
Book about the privatisation and commodification of Britain, and the Conservative Party's shift to centralised control.

Marr, Andrew. *Ruling Britainnia.* Michael Joseph, 1995
Popular account of recent British government.

CULTURAL EXAMPLES

■   *Films*

Betrayal (1983) dir. David Jones
Harold Pinter's love-triangle play about British middle-class manners and infidelities.

Damage (1992) dir. Louis Malle
Cold film about a British politician's love affair and subsequent family crises (an updated fictional treatment of the theme found in *Scandal*, Michael Caton-Jones's 1989 film based on the early 1960s Profumo Affair).

Life is Sweet (1991) dir. Mike Leigh
Light, poignant comedy, typical of the director's films, about the British lower middle class and working class.

The Ploughman's Lunch (1983) dir. Richard Eyre
Concentrates on a cynical reporter attempting to give a critical analysis of British morals during the Falklands War.

■   *Books*

John Braine, *Room at the Top* (1957)
Portrays the social ascent of a young man whose education
and marriage enable his upward mobility.

David Caute, *Veronica, or the Two Nations* (1989)
Critique of Thatcherism taking its title from a novel by
Disraeli.

David Hare, *The Secret Rapture* (1988)
Allegorical play about morals, materialism and politics in
1980s Britain. Also made into a film in the early 1990s.

■   *Television programmes*

GBH
Highly acclaimed fictional drama serial about private and
public tensions behind the running of a city council.

House of Cards
Fictional series about a manipulative Conservative MP
seeking power whose skill at political evasion and double-
dealing was compelling, and whose typical hypocritical
expressions such as 'You might think that, but I couldn't
possibly comment' and 'I have no ambitions in that direction' became catchphrases.

The New Statesman
Comedy series about an obnoxious but successful ultra right-
wing Tory MP.

Spitting Image
Very influential topical programme in which prominent
public figures, from royalty to politicians to television
personalities are represented by grotesque puppets and held
up to ridicule.

Yes, Minister
Comedy series about the opposition between government and the Civil Service in which an MP, seeking change and votes, and his Private Secretary, seeking continuity and bureaucracy, try to outmanoeuvre one another. Every episode illustrates the political, and supposedly British, art of compromise.

■ *Music*

Blur, *The Great Escape* (1995)
A series of comments on British life from the opening track on 'Stereotypes', through a song on the 'Country House' to 'Top Man' (a clothes shop).

Billy Bragg, *Workers' Playtime* (1988)
Named after a postwar radio programme broadcast from a factory canteen, this, like all Bragg's albums, is a collection of love songs and political anthems such as 'Waiting for the Great Leap Forwards', 'Tender Comrade' and 'Rotting on Remand'.

The Clash, *The Clash* (1977)
Archetypal British punk featuring songs like 'White Riot', 'London's Burning', 'Career Opportunities', 'I'm So Bored with the USA' and 'Police and Thieves'.

Pulp, *Different Class* (1995)
Album of vignettes about class politics, drug culture and British social attitudes.

Ethnicity and language

■ Gerry Smyth

241

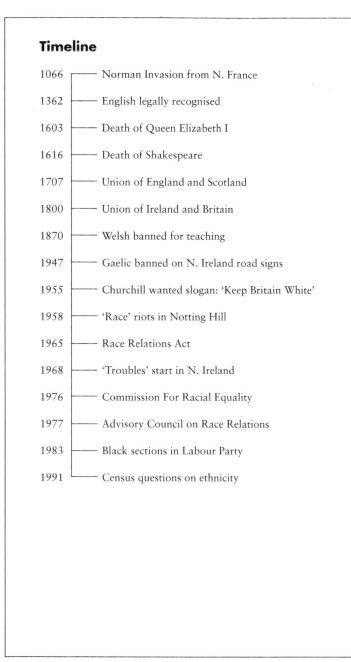

Timeline

1066	Norman Invasion from N. France
1362	English legally recognised
1603	Death of Queen Elizabeth I
1616	Death of Shakespeare
1707	Union of England and Scotland
1800	Union of Ireland and Britain
1870	Welsh banned for teaching
1947	Gaelic banned on N. Ireland road signs
1955	Churchill wanted slogan: 'Keep Britain White'
1958	'Race' riots in Notting Hill
1965	Race Relations Act
1968	'Troubles' start in N. Ireland
1976	Commission For Racial Equality
1977	Advisory Council on Race Relations
1983	Black sections in Labour Party
1991	Census questions on ethnicity

ISLE COLLEGE
RESOURCES CENTRE

Introduction

A SURVEY CARRIED OUT IN A NUMBER of London schools in 1980 found that only 15 per cent of pupils spoke what their teachers considered to be standard, or 'correct' English. The rest spoke twenty different varieties of English from the British Isles, forty-two dialects of overseas English, and fifty-eight different world languages. Another survey of the same period found that there were at least twelve languages in Britain which could claim over 100,000 speakers. To some people, such linguistic diversity might seem surprising in the homeland of arguably the world's most successful modern language. These statistics, however, are indicative of the multitude of ways used by the citizens of modern Britain to communicate.

These languages, moreover, are closely linked with the ways in which people perceive themselves and their role in British society. For, although the United Kingdom is a state, many people within this state think about themselves, their families and their local communities in quite different ways. One way of describing these individuals and the groups to which they belong is in terms of 'ethnicity'. Ethnicity is a highly complex and contentious concept. For the purposes of this chapter however, it can be defined as the patterns of behaviour, cultural values and political affiliations shared by certain individuals who come together to form a group within a larger population.

The census of 1991 was the first to include a question on ethnicity. It was discovered that 5.5 per cent of the population of Great Britain (just over three million people) identified themselves as belonging to an ethnic group. (These figures will have to be seriously revised if the children and grandchildren of people born in the Republic of Ireland are granted ethnic status before the next census in the year 2001.) The largest ethnic populations

TABLE 6.1   Comparison of ethnic populations[1]

	Inner London	Great Britain	Merseyside
Total	2,504,451	54,888,844	1,403,642
White	74.4	94.5	98.2
Black Caribbean	7.1	0.9	0.2
Black African	4.4	0.4	0.2
Black Other	2.0	0.3	0.3
Indian	3.0	1.5	0.2
Pakistani	1.2	0.9	0.1
Bangladeshi	2.8	0.3	0.1
Chinese	1.1	0.3	0.4
Other Asian	1.8	0.4	0.1
Other	2.3	0.5	0.4

Note: [1] The percentage disparities are the result of rounding

Source: 1991 *Census*

are found in Inner London (25.6 per cent) and West Midlands Metropolitan County (14.6 per cent), and the smallest in the rural areas of Scotland (1.3 per cent), Yorkshire (0.9 per cent) and Northumberland (1 per cent). Because many of the references in this chapter are drawn from Liverpool (in the metropolitan county of Merseyside), and because the area of Inner London offers an extreme example, the statistics in Table 6.1 are supplied for comparative purposes.

Additionally, the United Kingdom comprises four separate indigenous populations, one very large – English (48 million) – and three small – Scottish (5 million), Welsh (3 million) and Northern Irish (1.5 million). What all this means is that there are a large number of people in the United Kingdom – around 20 per cent (twelve million people) of the total population who do not have a straightforward relationship with the political state in which they live. In recent years, this problematic relationship between the state and its ethnic and regional minorities has become the subject of one of the most important debates in modern British life, and in this chapter I want to examine some of the practices, attitudes and strategies which have emerged around this debate.

Ethnic and regional identity can appear in many forms. Historians, sociologists and anthropologists have discovered, however, that one of the most important ways in which ethnic groups identify themselves is through language. Not only is language the principal conveyor of symbols, ideas and beliefs which are of importance to the ethnic group; very often language becomes a powerful possession in itself, something to be protected and preserved as the main badge of ethnic identity. Much of the time then, the alternative allegiances which constitute ethnic identity emerge specifically as tensions about language and the social status and cultural possibilities of different accents, dialects and vocabularies.

The recognition of ethnic status has significant legal, educational and social implications. But ethnic status, going back to our definition, also has important sociological and psychological implications for the kind of person the individual understands him/herself to be – that is, for an individual's identity. The point of departure for what follows is that a significant part of our individual identity is constituted through language – the language the world uses to communicate with us, and the language we use to communicate with the world. Putting this all together, then, these issues of ethnicity, identity and language are going to be our main areas of focus in this chapter. Specifically, I want to examine three interrelated issues – the usage and status of:

1   'standard' and 'non-standard' forms of the English language and implications for English and British identity;
2   other indigenous British languages – Welsh, Scots and Gaelic – and the challenge to the domination of English;
3   non-English languages brought to Britain by immigrants and other groups, such as Chinese and West Indian.

Varieties of English

In the nineteenth century, the notion of 'correct', 'good' or 'pure' English became something of an obsession for many literary critics, philosophers and educationalists. The result of this anxiety was the invention of an ideal form of the English language, covering aspects of grammar, vocabulary, pronunciation and so on, but also importantly linked to ways of acting, systems of belief and systems of value. Such an ideal was needed to support Britain's self-image as a great industrial and imperial power, and to measure various kinds of linguistic deviance. The fact that this ideal or 'standard' English was an invention did not appear to worry those who used it to condemn the linguistic 'errors' made by the vast majority of the British population. It must have seemed strange to a person, for example, from Northumberland or Somerset, regions with dialects evolved over a thousand years and completely immersed in local history and local geography, to be told that the way they spoke was wrong – according to the arbitrary rules invented by certain intellectuals and scholars!

The question of the correct way to speak and write English has continued to exercise a great influence in British life throughout the twentieth century. Many people in the 1990s adhere to the model of standard English (or 'received pronunciation' as it is sometimes referred to) invented in the nineteenth century, believing it to be the real or true English language, a fixed linguistic structure against which deviations and mistakes can be measured. These people remain anxious about what they consider to be falling standards in spoken and written English, feeling that this is in some way related to Britain's wider economic, cultural and political status. Letters are written to the 'quality' newspapers (such as *The Times*, the *Independent*, the *Telegraph*, and the *Guardian*) and to the British Broadcasting Company (BBC), both radio and television, about bad practices in spoken and written English. In the early days of broadcasting, the 'BBC accent' was the hallmark of correct spoken English and newscasters are still seen as 'custodians' of the language. But in recent years this 'BBC accent', like its close relation 'the Queen's English', has in itself

FIGURE 6.1 Shakespeare continues to be taught in the National Curriculum but with new and changing possibilities
Source: *Routledge*

become a minority form; one of the few people likely to be heard speaking 'the Queen's English' is the Queen herself, in her Christmas Day speeches to the Commonwealth. The clipped pronunciation and mannered voice of Prince Charles, as well as his constant use of the impersonal pronoun 'one' (as in 'one feels one's responsibilities'), is also somewhat of a throwback to an earlier stage in Britain's linguistic history. Although versions of the 'BBC accent' still exist – for example, in some sports commentary such as tennis, cricket, equestrian events or in some arts programmes – in the 1990s it is more likely to be used for satiric or ironic purposes.

Adequate command of English constitutes a major part of modern British education, even for those who do not speak the language regularly at home or outside of the classroom. One way in which the fixation with the language manifests itself is in the debates surrounding the educational significance of William Shakespeare. Of course, to anyone familiar with it, Shakespearean language can hardly be thought of as a viable means of communication in the late twentieth century. Nevertheless, Shakespearean language is felt by many to represent the pinnacle of British cultural achievement, and it is widely argued that in his poetry and plays Shakespeare captured the essence of English (though not British) identity. To those taking this line, it therefore appears obvious that young British people, of whatever ethnic origin, should become familiar with Shakespeare's works so that they can appreciate the history and the society of which they are now a part. Drawing on these opinions, a 'Shakespeare industry' has become established, linked in many significant ways with other major industries such as publishing, leisure, tourism and heritage.

On the other hand, some people claim that Shakespeare's relevance is only historical, and that modern education should be dealing more with students' contemporary practices, values and beliefs. Both in terms of theme and language, it is argued, Shakespeare has limited significance for those from different ethnic backgrounds possessing important cultural and linguistic traditions of their own. The same could also be said of certain sections of the indigenous British population which have traditionally been excluded from the high cultural institutions where 'Shakespeare' has been enshrined for so long. During the 1980s one cultural critic claimed that a television soap opera such as *Coronation Street*, set in contemporary Manchester and detailing the experiences of a community of working-class people, was of far greater interest and significance to millions of people throughout Britain than anything by or about Shakespeare. This was because the themes, language and accents of *Coronation Street* were closer to what most British people experienced in their daily lives. This is a contentious argument, as it might be seen to deny people from working-class or ethnic backgrounds access to a valuable cultural experience.

Regional variations in accent, vocabulary and pronunciation, as practised by the characters in *Coronation Street*, are of great importance in British life, as well as having an important bearing on the question of standard English. Some of the more easily distinguishable accents are those of Cornwall, the West Midlands, Tyneside, Northern Ireland and Clydeside, although to a sensitive ear, there are dozens of separate regional accents in Britain, and hundreds of minor linguistic peculiarities which set one region, one town, even one village, apart from another. The city of Liverpool, for example, has a very strong and recognisable accent known as 'scouse', deriving from a mixture of Lancashire, Irish and Welsh influences, and those speaking with this accent are referred to as 'scousers'. One version of 'scouse' was brought to national and world attention by the success of the popular music group The Beatles in the 1960s. The phrases, slang and inflections which characterised the speech of The Beatles however, were but one version of what is in fact a highly complex set of linguistic practices operating within the city of Liverpool.

One factor influencing all the varieties of English in contemporary Britain is the economic and cultural domination of the United States of America. Especially since the end of the Second World War, the issue of American influence on British life has been hotly debated. Some people fear that sharing a language with the most culturally successful nation in the world will erode

Britain's own linguistic identity, while others argue that the global dominance of English ensures Britain's continuing cultural vitality. It does seem that through exposure to popular music, cinema and computer technology, British people are becoming more and more familiar with the various speech patterns of the USA, even learning to differentiate between them (for example, Southern drawl, New York nasal, Californian rising intonation). Distinctive American rhythms, intonations and slang are becoming common throughout Britain, not only in pubs and clubs, but to an increasing extent also in more formal contexts such as education and the media. Much British popular music since the 1960s, for example, is heavily influenced by American styles. Against this, part of the attraction of groups such as the Cranberries (Ireland), the Proclaimers (Scotland) or Blur (London) is hearing the singers using their local accents. At the same time, it is clear that English, albeit American English, remains the dominant language of diplomacy and of popular culture, and it could be argued that this has given British people cultural and economic opportunities they might otherwise not have had.

All the issues raised in this section have important implications for the question of British identity. The ways in which the English language is used continue to be of great importance, for those who adhere to standard English as well as for those who accept and rejoice in the latest slang words and phrases. The possibility of a single, ideal English language was always remote, both because of its artificiality and because of the active role played in cultural life by accent and regional variation. But such an ideal is becoming less and less viable, given both the speed with which language circulates in the technological age, and the number of British people for whom the English language is deeply problematical. With regard to this latter group, what I now want to discuss are those non-English languages which are, nevertheless, indigenous to the British Isles.

Gaelic, Scots, Welsh

Before modern communications made travel and the spread of information so much quicker, it was possible for people from different parts of the British Isles never to hear the English language spoken. From the influx of European invaders and migrants who began to come to the islands around two thousand years ago, a great number of distinctive local dialects, as well as a smaller number of discrete languages, emerged. But as English evolved into the successful international language it is today, these other, mainly Celtic, languages tended to be marginalised. For many people, this predominance of the English language is a problem in that it deprives individuals and communities of the chance of having access to a distinctive local cultural inheritance. Instead, it collapses all history and all possible experience into an homogeneous yet spurious Britishness. A character of James Joyce's describes a conversation at his school in Ireland with his teacher, who is an Englishman:

> The language in which we are speaking is his before it is mine. How different are the words *home*, *Christ*, *ale*, *master*, on his lips and on mine! I cannot speak or write these words without unrest of spirit. His language, so familiar and so foreign, will always be for me an acquired speech. I have not made or accepted its words. My voice holds them at bay. My soul frets in the shadow of his language.
>
> (James Joyce, *A Portrait of the Artist as a Young Man* [1916], Penguin 1977, p. 172)

For many minority language speakers, Joyce manages to capture in this passage the social and personal frustrations of being caught between a way of speaking which is specifically attuned to local experience and local history and an all too 'familiar', too dominant language such as English, in which they are expected to perform.

Gaelic is the language of the Gaels, Celtic invaders from Europe who came to the British Isles in the second and third

FIGURE 6.2 Graffiti in Gaelic calls for the release of all prisoners of war

centuries before the beginning of the Christian Era. Gaelic rapidly became the principal language of Ireland, and later it was also widely spoken on the west coast of Scotland where many Irish Gaels emigrated in later years. (The census of 1991 showed that out of a Scottish population of 4.9 million, 1.4 per cent – about 70,000 people – spoke Gaelic in some form.) Gaelic remained the first language of Ireland until the middle of the nineteenth century, when the Great Famine (1845–1848) decimated the population. Death, mass emigration and the association of Gaelic with poverty and backwardness combined to marginalise the language, so that by the time the southern part of Ireland gained partial independence from Britain in 1922, Gaelic was only spoken in small pockets (called Gaeltachts) in the north and the west of the island.

This marginalisation did not go unopposed, however. During the 1890s a cultural movement known as the Celtic Revival became very influential throughout the British Isles, and this movement was closely linked with the idea of political independence for Ireland. An important part of its programme was the restoration of Gaelic as the first language of Ireland. This was felt to be necessary because, going back to the introduction to this chapter, language was seen as the crucial element of a distinctive identity, and it was therefore not possible for Irish people to achieve real freedom if they continued to speak English.

In 1992 the Northern Ireland Office spent £1.2 million promoting Gaelic projects, and although this is only a fraction of the amount spent on Scottish Gaelic and Welsh, it has been welcomed as official acknowledgement of the importance of Gaelic for the cultural health of the community. The city of Belfast has bilingual schools, a Gaelic newspaper (called *Lá*, meaning 'Day', which began publication in 1981), and a (very small) number of Gaelic radio and television programmes broadcast by the BBC and independent stations. While the state of the language is now declining in the south, voluntary Irish classes flourish throughout Northern Ireland. All this activity is encouraging for Gaelic supporters, although whether the language can truly escape its sectarian heritage and help resolve the political divide in Northern Ireland remains a hotly debated question.

One of the most interesting British languages, precisely because of the debate as to whether it is a distinct language or merely a dialect of English, is Scots. Scots is descended from the Northumbrian dialect of Old English, and at one time forms of the language existed in all the non-Gaelic regions of Scotland, including the remote Shetland and Orkney Islands. By the sixteenth century one particular form of Scots supported a highly developed cultural and political tradition entirely separate from England. At that point, however, a number of factors combined to force Scots into decline, the most important of which was the union of the Scottish and the English Crowns in 1603. After the abolition of the Scottish parliament in 1707, Scots, like Irish Gaelic in the nineteenth century, began to be rejected as a sign of cultural backwardness, and the ruling classes attempted to purge their speech of any remnants of the old Scots tongue. Despite interest in what came to be known as 'Lallans' (Scots for 'Lowlands', as opposed to the mostly Gaelic-speaking Highlands) amongst some poets and novelists of the eighteenth century, the language survived only among the peasantry and, after the industrialisation of Scotland during the nineteenth century, among the urban working class.

Scots has been under constant threat throughout the twentieth century because, unlike Scottish Gaelic, most people do not regard it as a separate language but as a deformed version of English, or as an artificial dialect invented by the romantic writers of the eighteenth and nineteenth centuries. Both of these misconceptions add to the stereotypical notion of Scots that tends to be reproduced in the popular imagination as the 'sign' of Scottishness – words such as 'wee' (small), 'braw' (fine, good), 'lassie' (girl), and so on, as well as a heavily inflected accent when speaking English. Mr Scott, from the original *Star Trek* series (played by an American actor James Doohan), possesses probably the most famous, and least convincing, Scots accent in popular culture. The comedian Gregor Fisher, who plays the part of working-class Glaswegian Rab C. Nesbit in a BBC Scotland television series of the same name is the nearest one will find outside Scotland to a genuine Scots speaker; part of the irony of this situation is that it would be very difficult for anyone who did not speak English as a first language to understand the language used in this programme.

Scots receives little institutional support in the 1990s. It is not recognised for census purposes, and given the success of Welsh and Scottish Gaelic in competing for what funds *are* available from central government and the BBC, this situation is unlikely to change in the near future. As with the Gaelic language in the Republic of Ireland, it is only amongst a relatively small number of historians, critics and writers that Scots is still valued; indeed, this intellectual support confers on Scots a sort of cult status, granting the language a vogue somewhat at odds with its shrinking working-class base. The familiar argument is that despite its impoverished condition, the language articulates a way of life, a way of thinking about the world, a way of being Scottish, that cannot be adequately expressed in English. This argument is rejected by many however, and not only by those 'Unionists' who maintain that Scotland's future depends on remaining an English-speaking region of the United Kingdom. The revival of Scots is also dismissed by many nationalists (seeking separate national sovereign status for Scotland) and devolutionists (seeking an autonomous Scottish parliament while remaining part of the United Kingdom) who feel that, given its history of strong cultural and political independence, Scotland does not need the support of an artificially resurrected language. This latter understanding of the relationship between language and national or ethnic identity is in marked contrast to the feelings underpinning the most successful non-English language of the British isles: Welsh.

Like Scotland, Wales has, since the nineteenth century had great difficulty in asserting its cultural independence from England. Before the Education Act of 1870, which prohibited teachers from using Welsh as a medium of education, about nine out of ten people spoke the language. As with all the minority languages mentioned so far however, Welsh became stigmatised as the language of the poor and the backward, and when the southern part of the country began to industrialise, it was only in rural areas such as the counties of Gwynedd and Dyfed in the north and west that Welsh managed to survive.

Since the 1960s, however, a new attitude towards the language has become evident. The rise of Welsh political nationalism has encouraged a pride in the Welsh language, and in recent years the ability to speak Welsh has become a highly prestigious attribute. This pride has manifested itself in many ways, but the basic impetus is towards the conversion of Wales into a fully bilingual country.

Many people began in the 1960s by abandoning anglicised names in favour of Welsh ones, while for those who had not yet mastered the language, it was possible to assert a Welsh identity simply by using the heavily inflected Welsh accent. Once over the border, all road signs are now given first in Welsh and then in English, as are most job descriptions, and the language has had great success at all levels of education. Welsh programmes represent well over 50 per cent of the country's radio and television output, and the success of the annual Eisteddfod Festival adds to the sense of an autonomous nation supporting a distinctive national culture. Although the number of Welsh-speakers as a whole dropped from 19 per cent to 18.7 per cent between 1981 and 1991, the number of speakers aged between 3 and 15 rose from 17.7 per cent to 24.4 per cent, a real rise of 21,000. This augurs well for the future of the language, and is in marked contrast to Scottish Gaelic where the highest percentage of speakers are aged 65 and over. However, some Welsh nationalists argue that the success of the language has been achieved at the cost of a coherent political programme, and that central government support for various cultural initiatives does not represent a relinquishing of power, but merely a way of redistributing it.

We should remember that Welsh is reviving, not revived, and in the industrialised south, Swansea, Cardiff, Glamorgan and the Rhondda valley, where over half the population lives, Welsh is still to all intents and purposes a foreign language. Even so, the relative success of the language has been difficult for many English people to cope with. One recurring image is that of English tourists feeling intimidated and offended by their exclusion from the Welsh conversations of local bilingual communities. Stories such as these reflect more, perhaps, on the insecurity of English people who hold an idea of Britishness specifically invented to incorporate the various identities of the British Isles under one, English-led, banner. For it hardly seems strange that Welsh people should wish to converse in their own language, nor that in the absence of political self-determination this should represent a valuable means of identification for them.

It may be that given time and the global domination of English noted in the previous section, Gaelic, Scots and Welsh will suffer the fate of other non-English languages of the British

Isles such as Cornish (from Cornwall) and Manx (from the Isle of Man), ceasing to be living languages, preserved only in the artificial confines of the library and the university. Welsh appears to be in a reasonable state of health, but Gaelic and Scots must give cause for concern to their supporters and speakers. It might be wondered why, having being so neglected for so long, Britain's non-English languages have aroused so much interest in recent years. Certainly there has been concern about the fate of Gaelic, Scots and Welsh since the beginning of the twentieth century, but one could argue that it is only since Britain's non-indigenous ethnic minorities began to work for proper recognition of their distinctive cultural heritages that the islands' Celtic minorities have begun to see their languages in a new perspective. I will now turn to those non-indigenous languages.

New languages, new identities

Since the end of the Second World War (1945), immigration has become an issue of increasing public and political concern in Britain. Not only that, but the very terms in which the question of immigration is considered are also highly charged. If you reread the previous two sentences, you will see that the words I have used at the beginning of this discussion of immigration and ethnicity are 'issue', 'concern' and 'question'; other terms invariably used when this subject is raised are 'problem', 'solution', 'answer', 'debate', etc. For many people, such language is itself part of the 'problem' in that it only allows immigration and ethnicity to be discussed as anomalies in an otherwise efficient system, anomalies that 'we' – that is, the established indigenous population of Britain – need to resolve. Being constituted a 'problem' or an 'issue' or a 'cause for concern' even before their arrival in the country has serious implications for the way in which ethnic communities perceive their relations with the state and with Britishness generally.

People have been migrating to and from Britain for centuries, and as long as this has been so, native and immigrant have been

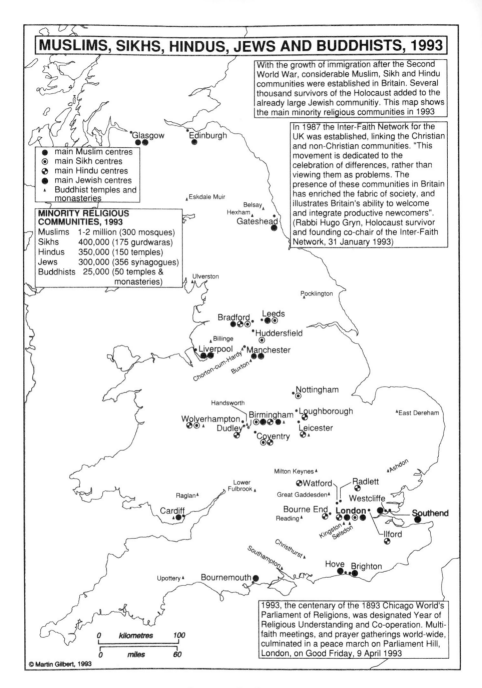

MUSLIMS, SIKHS, HINDUS, JEWS AND BUDDHISTS, 1993

With the growth of immigration after the Second World War, considerable Muslim, Sikh and Hindu communities were established in Britain. Several thousand survivors of the Holocaust added to the already large Jewish communitiy. This map shows the main minority religious communities in 1993

In 1987 the Inter-Faith Network for the UK was established, linking the Christian and non-Christian communities. "This movement is dedicated to the celebration of differences, rather than viewing them as problems. The presence of these communities in Britain has enriched the fabric of society, and illustrates Britain's ability to welcome and integrate productive newcomers". (Rabbi Hugo Gryn, Holocaust survivor and founding co-chair of the Inter-Faith Network, 31 January 1993)

- ● main Muslim centres
- ◉ main Sikh centres
- ◎ main Hindu centres
- ● main Jewish centres
- ▲ Buddhist temples and monasteries

MINORITY RELIGIOUS COMMUNITIES, 1993

Muslims	1-2 million (300 mosques)
Sikhs	400,000 (175 gurdwaras)
Hindus	350,000 (150 temples)
Jews	300,000 (356 synagogues)
Buddhists	25,000 (50 temples & monasteries)

Glasgow Edinburgh

Eskdale Muir

Belsay
Hexham
Gateshead

Ulverston

Pocklington

Bradford Leeds
Billinge Huddersfield
Liverpool Manchester
Chorton-cum-Hardy Buxton

Nottingham

Handsworth
Wolverhampton Birmingham Loughborough ▲East Dereham
Dudley Leicester
Coventry

Milton Keynes ▲Ashdon
Lower Fulbrook Watford Radlett
Raglan Great Gaddesden Westcliffe
Cardiff Bourne End London Southend
Reading Kingston Ilford
Selsdon

Christhurst
Southampton Hove Brighton
Upottery Bournemouth

1993, the centenary of the 1893 Chicago World's Parliament of Religions, was designated Year of Religious Understanding and Co-operation. Multi-faith meetings, and prayer gatherings world-wide, culminated in a peace march on Parliament Hill, London, on Good Friday, 9 April 1993

0 kilometres 100
0 miles 60

© Martin Gilbert, 1993

FIGURE 6.3 Distribution of ethnic groups in Britain, 1993
Source: Martin Gilbert, *Atlas of British History* (Routledge, 1993)

constantly reviewing their mutual relations. In 1596 the Parliament of Queen Elizabeth I issued an edict limiting the number of black people entering England. This may be seen as the first of a large number of measures taken by British governments in an effort to define exactly what kinds of people had the right to enter Britain and claim citizenship. The years since 1945 have seen numerous immigration and citizenship and race relations Acts, all in an effort to supply British identity with a legal and constitutional basis. Over this more recent period, two opposing attitudes appear to be at work. If, as some commentators suggest, increased population mobility is becoming a characteristic experience of the late twentieth century, then cultural and political systems which used to construe immigration and ethnicity as 'problems' may no longer be applicable. Such systems indeed, it is argued, were never acceptable in the first place. On the other hand, with the breakup of the Soviet Union, the reunification of East and West Germany and the growth of Europeanism, the issue of borders, national and ethnic identity has become very important throughout Europe. Britain, as we have already seen, has its own internal borders and identities, a situation which has led to its unique political constitution. The exact nature of Britishness however, has become even more complex in the decades since 1945 with the influx of a new range of ethnic identities, and the subsequent emergence of new ways of being British.

There have been well-established Black, Chinese and Indian communities in Britain since the nineteenth century, especially in London and some of the bigger seaports such as Liverpool and Cardiff. The postwar period has seen the arrival of people from many geographical backgrounds – West Africa, the Caribbean, Hong Kong, India, Pakistan and so on, countries and regions known as the 'New Commonwealth' (as opposed to the 'Old Commonwealth' of Canada, Australia and New Zealand). Traditionally, the most positive response in Britain to immigration from the New Commonwealth has been mild interest in the possibility of viewing exotic cultures at close hand. Asians from the Indian subcontinent and Pakistan, for example, have been 'contained' by mainstream British culture in terms of the 'colourful' or 'alternative' practices – food, clothes, music, religion and philosophy – brought from their homelands.

The multitude of identities brought by immigrants from that part of Asia are frequently collapsed into one exotic 'brown' identity which can then be more easily accommodated by modern 'multicultural' Britain. The Indian restaurant and the Pakistani newsagent or corner shop are established parts of British life, and certain other stereotypical traits and practices – Yoga, the Sikh and Muslim turban, the raga (the distinctive pattern of Indian music), arranged marriages, as well as of course the 'strange' way of speaking English – have become representative of what to most people seems a tolerable degree of difference within a larger British identity.

The identity of Indian and other people in Britain is complicated by a history of colonial relations, and this in its turn is linked with the other major form of response to modern immigration. Since the nineteenth century, certain theories regarding the relations between race, nation and culture have led to the development of ideas which cast immigration and ethnicity in a very negative light. Influenced by these ideas, much of the modern British response to immigration has been characterised by xenophobia and racism. Racism in modern Britain can take two forms. An older, biological racism tends to be linked with violence and aggression, as, for example, during the 1960s and 1970s when extreme right-wing elements went on 'Paki-bashing' sprees, and, even developed political organisations based on repatriation of immigrants. This form of racism is increasingly rare, although it would be a mistake to underestimate the capacity of certain outmoded 'scientific' discourses of race to feed the cycle of racial hatred inherited from earlier times.

The newer, cultural form of racism is more subtle. It claims that it is unfair to ask people from a particular background to accept the kind of changes in lifestyle necessary for them to become proper British citizens. For example, one former politician caused a controversy in the 1990s with his 'cricket test'; Lord Norman Tebbit argued that if people living permanently in Britain support other nations in sporting or other cultural events, then they have not sufficiently adapted themselves to British life, and cannot therefore legitimately be called British. Tebbit used the example of the way in which many black Britons support the West Indies cricket team, but the point was intended to apply to any instance of cultural 'treason'. Indeed, the issue of sporting affiliation has become even more heated since the publication of an article in a prestigious cricketing journal in 1995 which suggested that it would be a mistake to expect any 'ethnic' sportsperson selected to represent Britain, even if born here, to be as committed as a 'real' (that is, white) Briton.

It does seem clear however that Britain's ethnic minorities do not have a straightforward relationship with the state. People from the Commonwealth coming to live in Britain have as a rule identified with it as the 'mother country', and most have sought to become good citizens. Yet, the uncertainty of status, the forms of racism invariably experienced, as well as the very act of displacement from familiar places and practices, means that the individual may wish to preserve, and indeed emphasise, his/her ethnic identity. Of course, not all ethnic minorities will understand their relationship with the host country and the English language in the same way. Each community brings its own assumptions and aspirations, its own cultural values and beliefs, to the relationship with British identity. When one considers that there are many such ethnic communities in Britain, all experiencing different levels of assimilation and alienation; and when one further considers that different generations will not engage with the available identities in the same ways, then one may begin to appreciate that the question of what is and is not 'British' has become extremely complex in recent years. It now appears, in fact, that the practices, attitudes, beliefs and values that come together to form any identity are enmeshed in an intricate web of similarities and differences, and this web covers every area of modern British life – religion, politics, work, leisure, culture and education. Nowhere can this complicated situation be seen more clearly than through the subject upon which we have been focusing throughout this chapter – language.

Many British people do not use English as a first language, but speak instead the language of their home country, or of their parents' home country. Chinese people living in Britain, for example, have not traditionally placed a high priority on integration into the host community. In a city such as Liverpool, which has one of the largest Chinese populations in the country (0.4 per cent as against the 0.3 per cent national figure), it is clear that Chinese people make less use of the English language than the city's other ethnic minorities. There are a number of reasons why this might be so: the extreme difference between the Chinese and English languages; the hope of many Chinese people eventually to move back to their native country; the wish to preserve a valued cultural heritage; the unwillingness to 'lose face' by speaking English badly. Whatever the reasons, the older Chinese population of Liverpool have maintained a low profile in the social and economic life of the city and as a consequence a high proportion of the community still speak very little English. Chinese children on the other hand, whether immigrants or born in the city, learn to speak the language of their parents (usually Mandarin or Cantonese) at home, but have to learn English for school and for their other interests outside the community. This bilingualism can influence the ways in which the younger Chinese population understand their status in the contemporary life of Liverpool. Familiar both with the traditions of their parents and with the facts of modern British life, the younger Chinese people appear to possess greater confidence than their parents and grandparents, and are not afraid of raising the profile of their community. The Chinese New Year has become a major event in the social and cultural life of Liverpool and street names in the area known as 'Chinatown' are given in English and Chinese. At the same time, these young Chinese people have problems which are different from the ones faced by their parents and different again from those faced by the city's other ethnic minorities. Bilingualism is just as likely to bring a sense of being marooned between identities as it is confidence. Third generation Chinese, having different familial, religious and cultural values, will accept (or deny) their British identity differently to third generation West Indians,

FIGURE 6.4   Chinatown in Liverpool

Indians or Irish. In fact, generalising about such relatively small populations can be a dangerous business. So we see again the complexity of the whole issue of ethnicity and language.

One of the most interesting examples of the complexity of modern British ethnicity is illustrated in the language brought by immigrants from the Caribbean. People from the West Indies – mainly Jamaica, but also Trinidad, Guyana, Barbados, the Windward and Leeward Islands – were actively recruited for the British labour market in the years after the war when business was beginning to recover and unemployment was low. When these people came to Britain they brought with them their cultural traditions, the most obvious and important one being their language. But what was this language?

Standard English is the official language of Jamaica and many of the other West Indian islands. But most West Indians speak a version of 'Jamaican Creole', a language developed from the slave culture of the eighteenth and nineteenth centuries. Members of many West African tribes were brought over to the West Indies, and they spoke different languages, so in order to communicate amongst themselves they developed a form of language known as 'pidgin'. Pidgin drew on the language of the slave-masters – English – but reworked it using the linguistic forms of the numerous West African languages. And this language is basically the same one that has become known as Jamaican Creole (a 'creole' is a 'pidgin' dialect that has become a standard language for a particular community).

Many people would not consider Jamaican Creole to be a distinct language in itself, but merely an exotic form of standard English. This is certainly true at one level, yet according to linguists and anthropologists, it is possible for a West Indian person to derive 90 per cent of her/his vocabulary from English and still speak a language that is not English. This is because language involves much more than words. Language involves complex physical and mental strategies, verbal styles and techniques, narrative genres and traditions, tones of voice, turn-taking protocols, speech rhythms, and a hundred other things, some of them immensely subtle. As a gesture towards this subtlety, consider this short passage from a poem called 'I trod', written by the Black British writer Benjamin Zephaniah and published in 1985:

I trod over de mountain
I trod over de sea
one ting I would like to see is
up pressed people free
I trod wid I eye peeled . . .

(Benjamin Zephaniah *The Dread Affair*
(Arena 1985), p. 86. Reproduced courtesy of
The Hutchinson Publishing Group)

This example is interesting in a number of ways. First, the theme is very significant in Caribbean history and one that emerges in much black British culture – the search for freedom. The poet uses the device of a physical journey over the landscape to represent the quest for a means to remove the spiritual and political scars of slavery. This theme is supported by the language of the poem, in which there is an attempt to reproduce the accents and pronunciations of Jamaican Creole – 'the' becomes 'de', 'thing' becomes 'ting', 'with' becomes 'wid'. Instead of being 'oppressed', these people are 'up pressed', a neologism (a new word invented by the writer) that suggests both the pressure coming down on the people from above, and the people's determination to resist that pressure. This reworking of the language is also a way of linking past and present, as the refusal of standard English is part of the process whereby black British people resist their 'enslavement' in contemporary Britain. In danger of becoming part of a permanent black British underclass and thereby repeating the cycle of slavery and mastery, Zephaniah celebrates his West Indian identity by emphasising his distinctive speech patterns and rhythms in the face of Anglo-Saxon cultural domination.

The analysis should not stop here however. The phrase 'I eye' is not typical of Jamaican Creole (in which it would be 'me eye'), but derives from the discourse of Rastafarianism. This religion, which encompasses both a spiritual and a socio-political outlook and which is associated with certain cultural practices

FIGURE 6.5   Black youths in American-style clothing

such as reggae music, marijuana and dreadlocks (a hair-style), originated in Jamaica and has in recent years become one of the dominant images of West Indian identity. Rastafarians reject words such as 'me', 'my' and 'we' in favour of a single word ('I') which celebrates the unique identity of the individual speaker and his/her unique relationship with Jah (the Rastafarian notion of God). At the same time, Rastafarianism is far from dominant amongst Britain's West Indian population which, typically of the wider British situation with regard to religion, encompasses a wide range of Christian, Islamic and atheistic positions. In these few lines, therefore, the poet can be seen as identifying with a very specific group. Analysis of the poem also shows the complex connections between contemporary British society, Caribbean history and a particular religious system.

Two points should be noted. The first is that even from the fairly sketchy reading provided here, it is possible to appreciate that Zephaniah's position is not *typical* of black Britishness, but shows instead the diversity of language and identity available to a British person of West Indian ethnicity. The second point is that Jamaican Creole, if not an *actual* separate language, certainly operates as a separate language for those members of the West Indian community who speak it to signal their lack of identity with dominant British culture. If Jamaican Creole is at one end of the spectrum and standard English at the other, then a person born in Britain of West Indian parents has potential access to all the variations and nuances of language in between. How the individual from an ethnic community speaks will depend upon that highly complex cultural web mentioned earlier – different backgrounds, different generations, different levels of assimilation, different desires.

Like all the other languages and dialects mentioned in this chapter, Jamaican Creole has attracted a number of stereotypical images in modern British culture. The West Indian cricket team is the Caribbean cultural image with the highest profile in Britain. Their extended superiority over the 'English' team (which over the years has included 'naturalised' players from all over the Commonwealth, as well as from Scotland and Wales) is, as previously mentioned, a source of pleasure to many black Britons and of much resentment to many 'real' Britons.

In recent years, other images and role models have helped to reveal the complexities involved in ethnic identity. The Notting Hill street carnival in London, which began as a local celebration of West Indian culture, is now the biggest event of its kind in Europe. This cultural festival has in the past seen clashes between Black Britons, organised racists and the metropolitan police, but more recently it has been peaceful and hugely successful, attracting up to two million people from all over the country and indeed the world. Likewise, the television programme *Desmond's*, about a barber shop owned by a West Indian family, relies for much of its comic effect on the differences in perception between the older generation, born in the Caribbean and speaking variations of Jamaican Creole, and the children, born in London and speaking English with a typical London accent. Both the street carnival and the television programme confront the confusion which arises from the wide range of identities available; both attempt to offer positive, enabling options rather than insisting on a final decision for or against Britishness.

Conclusion

In this chapter we have looked at how regional accent, as well as dialects and languages such as Gaelic, Scots and Welsh, challenge the apparent homogeneity of the English language (and the British identity which it supports) from well-established positions within the state. Further, we have seen that although sharing some of the same concerns and strategies, ethnic groups from Asia, the Caribbean and other parts of the world pose a different kind of challenge to British identity. All the issues examined in this chapter have important implications for British identity, and they impact in significant ways throughout the cultural and political life of the country. By way of conclusion, I want to demonstrate this by looking briefly at three areas which are of great importance to British people of whatever background or allegiance – popular music, work and sport. These areas are examined in greater detail in other parts of this book, but here I wish to focus upon them specifically in relation to the issues of ethnicity and language which have been our concern in this chapter.

Music is one of the principal ways in which ethnic identity is manifested. For example, Ireland has a vibrant folk music culture, encompassing strong traditional elements as well as an avant-garde interested in experiment and innovation. For Irish people living in Britain, or for British people wishing to identify with what they consider to be an 'Irish' way of life, folk music offers a readily accessible means of ethnic identification. In the absence of a Gaelic language, certain distinctive sounds and rhythms come to be associated with Ireland and Irishness, and these effects are invariably reproduced whenever Irish identity is invoked. This close link between identity and cultural practice is always liable to stereotyping, however, as we have noted with much of the material mentioned so far; the same sounds and rhythms that produce a positive identification for some will suggest a whole range of negative, comic, racist images for others. It is difficult to know why this, or indeed any other instance of stereotyping, should be so, and work in modern British universities is given over to analysing the reproduction of these processes in contemporary British life.

Folk music is also very popular and active in Scotland and Wales, where it fulfils slightly different functions while nevertheless continuing to serve as a badge of cultural heritage. The English folk scene, on the other hand, although widespread and successful, tends to attract a more specialist audience, and the music does not play the part in national life that it does in the Celtic countries. One reason for this is perhaps that during the period of the rejuvenation of Celtic folk music – since about the 1960s – English folk music has had to compete with another kind of music in which England has been consistently successful – 'rock'n'roll'. This form of popular music developed in the United States of America in the 1950s, and once again, the fact that the vast majority of songs were in the English language meant that young British people had an advantage when it came to producing rock'n'roll music of their own. There is in fact a widespread belief amongst both English and non-English speakers that effective rock'n'roll music can only be produced through the medium of the English/American language. For example, many of the entries for the Eurovision Song Contest – an annual event attracting huge television audiences across Europe but nevertheless evoking much derision and amusement amongst 'genuine' rock musicians – are now in English, a trend started by the Swedish group Abba in the 1970s. It is certainly true to say that since the 1960s, British rock musicians have been responsible for some of the most interesting and successful innovations in the genre.

Despite legal and voluntary moves towards 'equal opportunities' for all, certain kinds of employment in modern Britain tend to attract certain kinds of people speaking in particular ways. At one level, this is explicable with reference to social class and gender. At another level however, the way one speaks and the ethnic background with which one identifies have always played a major part in the kinds of work one can expect to find (or not find) in Britain. Certain associations between ethnicity and employment – the Chinese laundry or take-away (food), the Indian restaurant, the Irish 'navvy' (i.e., building labourer), etc. – have in some cases become so established in popular culture that it can be difficult for individuals from these ethnic communities either to imagine or to be accepted in different employment contexts. Much contemporary popular culture turns on the comic exploitation, or (more subtly) the dramatic refutation of these stereotypes.' The very currency of these images however, or the desired 'surprise' effect when they are shown to be untrue, points to the fact that most British people still accept them as having some basis in reality.

A typical example of ethnic employment stereotyping is the association of West Indians with the rail system. Many of the Caribbean people who came to Britain in the 1950s and 1960s were invited specifically to work for organisations such as British Rail, and this remains an option for second and third generation West Indians. At the same time, Black Britons are under-represented in almost every other area of employment and especially in the professional sector – medicine, higher education, law, the media, and so on. Those who have made the breakthrough into higher-paid, more prestigious jobs tend to be haunted by the ambiguities of 'tokenism' and 'positive discrimination' – that is, the racist accusation that they have been selected especially to give the impression of equality of opportunity rather than on personal merit.

Whereas Welsh, Scottish and Irish accents appear to be acceptable as indicators of certain kinds of 'natural' ethnic qualities, it is very rare to hear a lawyer, politician or media broadcaster speaking Jamaican Creole. This is certainly a result, as already indicated, of institutional pressure, but also, it would seem, of personal choice. Black British professionals, that is, tend as a rule to speak a version of standard English, apparently because they (or their parents, if it is the language of the home and family) have decided that this is more suited to their professional status.

One area in which Black Britons have made a major contribution to British life in recent years is sport. Indeed, in some sports, such as athletics, boxing and soccer, people of Afro-Caribbean ethnicity far outstrip their level as a percentage of the population. The success of people of West Indian origin in representing Britain in sport has generally not been equalled by other ethnic communities – Indian, Chinese, etc. – and the reasons for this are not clear. However, while some regard the success of black athletes as a positive thing – the full identification of people of Afro-Caribbean origin with Britain – others see it as a sign of the lack of opportunity for Black Britons in other areas of society, as a way of diverting dangerous social and political tensions into harmless leisure activity and as a way of consolidating racist myths about the physical prowess of black people, as opposed to the supposed mental superiority of Caucasians.

While sport still does much to concentrate national and ethnic identity, the cultural ambiguities upon which ethnicity rely can help to expose the narrowness of traditional sporting affiliation. Again, Ireland is an interesting case in point. The soccer team representing the Republic of Ireland has had great success in recent years under the management of a famous Englishman, Jack Charlton. Many of the players representing the country at international level were in fact born in Britain, but claim Irish citizenship through their immigrant parents or grandparents. A high percentage of these sportsmen, in fact, are of mixed race origin, possessing English, Scottish and Caribbean ties as well as Irish. This phenomenon has extended, in a highly popular and accessible way, the possible range of Irish identity, no longer restricted to the 3.5 million who live in the Republic itself, but incorporating the huge number of people throughout the world – more than 70 million according to some estimates – who identify to some degree with Irishness.

Concluding a chapter on British identity with an example from a non-British country nicely captures the complexity of the issues we have been discussing here. The ethnic, racial and linguistic factors operating in modern British society make for a highly sensitive, highly nuanced set of possibilities, in which identity is under constant pressure, not only from the society in which one lives, but also from the person one believes oneself to be.

EXERCISES

1 Choose a particular regional accent and try to identify some of the stereotypical characteristics that are associated with it. What are the principal differences between British English and American English – vocabulary, grammar, intonation? List some examples.

2 Why do some British people insist on speaking minor languages and dialects, even when they are bilingual? Try to identify some words or phrases from Scots, Welsh and Gaelic that have entered into the English language and are used regularly in Britain today.

3 What special 'problems' are faced by ethnic communities in Britain? What other factors influence *young* British people from ethnic backgrounds?

4   Try to obtain a current listing of the British pop music Top Forty. How many of the singers/groups are British? How many are American, or some other nationality? How many are black?

5   Compose a sentence defining exactly what you understand by the phrase 'equal opportunity'.

6   What is cockney rhyming slang and do you know any examples? Can you think of any other similar cases of communities constituted through language, speech or word-play?

READING

Foster, Roy. *Paddy and Mr Punch: Connections in Irish and English History*. Allen Lane, 1993.
Series of essays exploring the historical relations between Ireland and England in a scholarly yet readable way.

Gilroy, Paul. *There Ain't No Black in the Union Jack: The Cultural Politics of Race and Nation*. Hutchinson, 1987
Influential analysis of race relations in contemporary Britain.

Nairn, Tom. *The Break-up of Britain: Crisis and Neo-nationalism*. Verso, 1981.
Somewhat dated, but still a forceful investigation from the left of the unique and precarious condition of modern Britain.

Solomos, John. *Race and Racism in Britain*, 2nd edn. Macmillan, 1993
A wide ranging introduction to the politics of race in Britain.

Sutcliffe, David. *British Black English*. Blackwell, 1982
Very accessible account of the varieties of language spoken by Britain's West Indian population. Includes examples and glossaries.

Watson, James L. (ed.). *Between Two Cultures: Migrants and Minorities in Britain.* Blackwell, 1977
Somewhat dated, but none the less a useful series of essays about different communities in Britain.

CULTURAL EXAMPLES

■ *Films*

A Clockwork Orange (1971) dir. Stanley Kubrick
Pre-punk alienation of white British youth, manifested in violence and a specialised group language. Kubrick refuses to allow the film to be shown in Britain because it allegedly provoked 'copycat' violence on its first release.

Letter to Brezhnev (1985) dir. Chris Barnard
Exploration of regional and national identity during the course of a story in which a Liverpool woman falls in love with a Russian sailor.

My Beautiful Laundrette (1985) dir. Stephen Frears
Sexual and racial tensions between Asian and white Britons in 1980s London.

■ *Books*

Amit Chaudhuri, *Afternoon Raag* (1993)
A highly praised poetic and evocative novel recounting the life and thoughts of an Indian student at Oxford.

James Joyce, *A Portrait of the Artist as a Young Man* (1916)
Classic exploration of the tensions between family, nation, religion and art.

Hugh MacDiarmid, *A Drunk Man Looks at the Thistle* (1926)

A poetic plea for a modern Scots language to support a modern Scottish identity.

Colin MacInnes, *Absolute Beginners* (1959)
Race relations and riots in 1950s London, as seen through the eyes of a jazz-loving teenager.

Caryl Phillips, *The Final Passage* (1985)
Novel about the great emigration in the 1950s from the Caribbean to England, and the life that a young woman, Leila, finds there. Subsequently made into a television drama by Channel 4.

■　*Television programmes*

Bandung File
Channel 4 discussion forum for issues of ethnicity in Britain and beyond.

The Buddha of Suburbia
Very successful version of Hanif Kureishi's novel about an Anglo-Asian boy growing up in South London in the 1970s.

Desmonds
Comedy about a West Indian barber shop in London.

Rab C. Nesbitt
Sharp edged comedy about the adventures and opinions of a working-class Glaswegian.

■　*Music*

Apache Indian
Indian singer whose name puns on the native North American tribe of 'Indians'.

Bob Marley
West Indian musician who brought reggae to a worldwide audience.

RunRig
Scottish folk-rock group including many songs in Gaelic.

Clannad
Irish group crossing folk and popular divide, singing many songs in Gaelic and Breton, the Celtic language of Brittany in Northern France.

Religion and heritage

■ Edmund Cusick

Timeline

1532	Church of England formed
1580	Congregationalists formed
1620s	Quakers formed
1650	George Fox: 'Quake at the sight of God'
1739	Methodists formed
1760	Board of Deputies of British Jews
1774	1st Unitarian Chapel in London
1833	John Keble: Oxford Movement
1843	Free Church splits from Church of Scotland
1850s	Broad Church formed
1880s	Christian Socialism
1942	British Council of Churches (all non-R. C.)
1948	World Council of Churches
1972	United Reformed (Congregational and Presbyterians)
1978	London Mosque, Regent's Park
1980	Modern English C of E service
1994	1st C of E woman priest
1995	Hindu Temple, Neasden
	Sheffield rave services condemned

Introduction

T HE TIMELINE OPPOSITE PROVIDES a brief resumé of key religious movements, milestones and changes in the UK over the last five hundred years. Most will be touched upon in this chapter, which will be looking at the importance of public and private religion in the lives of British people and considering the role that notions of 'heritage' have come to play in ideas of national identity in recent years.

A peculiarly British phenomenon is the presence of *established* churches such as the Church of England. These churches have an official constitutional status within the legal and political framework of Britain and the Christian religion is to some degree woven into every level of British life: government, education, architecture, the arts, broadcasting and many other areas. In Northern Ireland, religion has the extra political significance of marking the line between Catholic and Protestant paramilitary factions. At a personal level, Christianity may have been encountered in the form of prayers or hymns that were taught at school, or personal acquaintance with a local vicar or a chaplain at a hospital. Most British people feel in some way reassured by the background presence of this religion, even if they do not wish to become actively involved with it.

Yet, despite the official uniformity provided by an established church, and the shared heritage of, for example, religious music and the Lord's Prayer ('Our Father, Which art in Heaven'), the religious experiences available in contemporary Britain form a complex and remarkably varied picture. The fact that Britain is commonly assumed to be a Christian country (and a majority of people feel themselves to be 'Christian' in terms of their general principles) is undermined by a number of factors: the rapidly declining levels of people's involvement with the churches to which

FIGURE 7.1   A redundant church is put to other uses

they nominally belong; the sharp decline in the value which young people attach to Christianity; the growth of a range of New Age religious practices, and the presence of large Hindu, Sikh and Muslim communities as a result of postwar immigration. All these changes result in considerable variations between the religious identity of ethnic groups and of different generations.

One way in which this 'ingrained' religious identity of British people is communicated is through the physical landscape. The historical evolution of British religion is visible to any visitor. In the countryside, every village will have one or more churches and even quite small English towns usually have a range of different churches representing Protestant and Catholic belief, most of which have been present in Britain for two centuries or more, though in larger towns and cities new churches such as those of the Church of Jesus Christ of Latter Day Saints (the Mormons), Jehovah's Witnesses, or Christian Science and Friends'

Meeting Houses (Quakers) may also be seen. The visitor will also notice a large number of church buildings which are no longer in use as places of worship. Some lie derelict, while others have been converted to new uses as apartments, restaurants, warehouses or even night-clubs.

Alongside this decline in Christian practice over the last fifty years, particularly in the big cities, there has been a rise in other faiths (see Table 7.1). In addition, in every town high street, book-shops have extensive sections devoted to mythology, witchcraft, palmistry, spiritualism and related subjects. Off the high street, particularly in seaside, market or university towns, there are small shops selling incense, crystals, relaxing music, jewellery and books on magic and meditation. In gross terms, the people who attend the churches are few, elderly and overwhelmingly female. The people in the New Age shops are young, enquiring and unbound by any sense of religious duty, motivated rather by their generation's belief in personal freedom. These all indicate Britain's changing religious environment.

Another aspect of this change is the way in which religious buildings have become a part of what is called 'British heritage'. One obvious example is the *marketing* of a number of great cathedrals which are to be found across the UK, though this is particularly noticeable in medieval cities such as Chester, York, Winchester and Durham. These buildings are now both religious centres and centres of tourism. A new meaning to the term 'heritage' has arisen – heritage now reflects the intervention of the tourist industry to re-create images and artefacts from Britain's past. The 'heritage industry' has grown rapidly to become one of the fastest developing, and most visible, of Britain's areas of employment and enterprise. It is also one that promotes a partic-ular version of Britain which celebrates continuity, tradition and conservative values.

Partly for this reason, Christianity in Britain is in many ways more of a cultural force than a spiritual one. Table 7.1 indicates that the number of practising Christians is in fact much more in balance with, rather than exceeding, that of other faiths. In the early 1990s there were, nominally, twenty-seven million Anglicans

FIGURE 7.2 In the medieval city of Chester, a church is marketed as a heritage site

in Britain; that is, almost two-thirds of the population claimed to belong to the Church of England. However, at the same time the Anglican Church had fewer than two million registered members. Membership signifies active involvement with the Church, for example, in attending services and offering financial contributions. Between 1960 and 1985 the Church of England's registered membership halved, while the number who think of themselves as belonging to the Church, in comparison, barely changed. This apparent contradiction between those who choose to think of themselves as Anglicans and those who are actively committed to Anglicanism is perhaps the single most important

TABLE 7.1   Religious observance in Britain (1992)

	Members ('000s)
Christian denominations	
Registered Anglicans	1,808
Practising Roman Catholics	2,049
Presbyterian	1,242
Methodists	458
United Reformed Church	148
Baptists	170
Quakers	18
Other faiths	
Muslims	1,200
Hindus	400
Sikhs	500
Jews	410

Source: Adopted from P. Brierley and V. Hiscock (eds) *UK Christian Handbook 1994/5* (London, Christian Research Association, 1993)

feature of British Christian life, and is discussed in more detail below.

There are five million Catholics in Britain. However, on any given Sunday more Catholics than Anglicans will attend a church service – it has been estimated that in Britain 40 per cent of Catholics registered as church members actually attend regularly, as against only 11 per cent of non-Catholics. The north-west of England and the west of Scotland (particularly Liverpool and Glasgow) have had historically, and retain today, a distinctively Roman Catholic heritage. Liverpool is Britain's only Catholic city.

From the 1960s to the mid-1990s, religious issues in Northern Ireland were overshadowed by 'the troubles' – the continuing violence generated by the unresolved political issue of whether Northern Ireland should form part of the UK or of a united Ireland. The religious differences between Protestants and

TABLE 7.2   Church members by country (% of adult population)

	1985	1992
England	11.6	10.1
Wales	17.0	15.0
Scotland	32.4	29.4
Northern Ireland	81.6	82.7
Total	15.6	14.4

Source: C. Carpenter, *The Guinness UK Data Book* (London, Guinness Publishing, 1992)

Catholics have thus been exacerbated, as Nationalists want Northern Ireland to be part of a Catholic country (with the South) while Unionists want the province to belong to a Protestant country – that is, the UK. It is often implied by British people that 'the troubles' are based on religion, but it is probably more accurate to see the conflict as political at root, a stand-off in which the communities have both looked to their differing churches for support. At no time has either church condoned the use of violence in the dispute. As Table 7.2 shows, church membership in Northern Ireland, like attendance, far exceeds that in evidence on the mainland of the UK, and this is the case in both Catholic and Protestant communities. This is probably largely for political and cultural reasons, as church-going is an important way both of establishing solidarity within a community and of defining its differences with other communities.

Wales has a separate religious tradition in which Methodism and the Congregational Church have traditionally played an important part, both churches laying an emphasis on individual devotion and strict adherence to puritanical rules of abstention from worldly behaviour, such as drinking and fornication (sex outside of marriage). 'Chapel' (the word means a small, simple church) has come, in Wales, to represent the ordinary people who embraced non-conformism (a form of Protestantism comparatively extreme in comparison to the Church of England). Welsh chapels are plain and unadorned, and Welsh non-conformist Christianity has traditionally had no concept of the minister as priest (one with unique spiritual powers and authority to administer sacraments such as the Eucharist, or Holy Communion) but has a strong sense of the prophetic tradition (preachers inspired directly by God). There has been no established church in Wales since 1920 – the Anglican Church in Wales is known as 'the Church in Wales'. Nearly all Welsh denominations hold at least some of their services in Welsh, particularly in Welsh-speaking areas. The past devotion of the Welsh (as well as changing population patterns) is evident in the appearance of Chapels – many of which are now neglected – in the most remote areas, and the smallest of settlements.

The established Church

The Church of England occupies both a political and a spiritual role. The organisation is referred to as 'the Church of England' when considering its place in the constitution or life of the nation, and as 'the Anglican Church' when its spiritual or theological identity is at issue. Because it is the body chosen by, and connected to, the British political system of government, the Church of England is the established church (it differs, however, from the Church of Scotland). It is thus formally tied to both parliament and to the monarchy.

Partly because of this link, the relation between religious principles and the personal morality of members of the Royal Family is closely observed and, as noted in the introductory chapter to this volume, is of continuous interest to the British people and the tabloid press. Though the monarchy's religious role no longer includes the 'divine right of Kings' (the idea that the monarch's rule is endorsed by God), people now expect the royals to set personal standards in social and religious institutions such as matrimony. Revelations in the mid-1990s about the adulterous liaisons of both Prince Charles and Diana, Princess of

Wales, compounded by speculation about possible future marriages, matter to many people because the reigning monarch is still the head of the Church, the institution which above all others is supposed to offer moral guidance to the country. Likewise, prominent politicians in the UK are still expected to endorse religious belief and to attend church occasionally, while the Church is expected not to get involved in party politics.

The fact that the Church of England has also been known as 'The Tory Party at Prayer' has less to do with any identification with the political policies of Conservative governments in the 1980s and the 1990s than with its role as a guardian of the past, and of established views. It is, as British people will say, conservative with a small 'c'. On rare occasions the spiritual and the perceived political function of the Church may come into conflict – the memorial service held after the Falklands War aroused anger amongst many Conservative politicians because of its emphasis on the Christian values of forgiveness and compassion for all in the war, including the relatives of Argentinian forces killed: an attitude not shared by those who felt that the national church should identify itself only with the victorious British forces. The Church of England is, in fact, also represented within the armed forces – every regiment has its chaplain and barracks have their own chapels. It is not unusual to see stained glass windows commemorating British armed forces (through the flags or insignia of local regiments) or of Royal Air Force squadrons within English churches, and particularly in cathedrals.

The presence of the established Church is evident in numerous ways in British life. British coins bear the head of the monarch plus the Latin initials 'F. D.' signifying that the monarch is defender of the faith – that is, of the Anglican version of Christianity. In 1995, Prince Charles caused some controversy among traditionalists by suggesting that at his coronation he would like to be known as Defender of the Faiths (plural) in recognition that Britain was no longer an exclusively Christian country. He again caused controversy in 1996 when he suggested that money from the 'Millennium Fund' (money from the National Lottery which is intended to finance projects to enhance Britain's cultural life and National Prestige) should in part be spent on mosques. Despite many moves towards multiculturalism in Britain, sections of the tabloid press reacted with hostility to this suggestion, seeing mosques as a symbol of a foreign and minority religion despite the fact that British Muslims now outnumber adherents of most British Protestant denominations.

At all levels of society, Britain's churches are involved in its cultural life. Church halls are used for whist drives, jumble sales, play groups, badminton, barn dances, sales of jam by the Women's Institute, and an array of other events for charity and local causes which may be entirely secular. Most of the Church's cathedrals hold concerts of classical music, both secular and religious, and may also hold exhibitions of paintings. Nearly all British cathedrals have a gift shop, selling cards, tapes, ornaments and books, and many also have a coffee shop or café which visitors are encouraged to patronise. It is perhaps because of this greater flexibility in their use, as well as the aesthetic or historical appeal of beautiful buildings and stained glass that, while church-going is in marked decline, attendance at cathedrals (both by tourists and by worshippers) is on the increase. In 1992, St Paul's Cathedral had 1.4 million visitors – more than Blackpool Tower.

Religious tourism for recreation is also very popular, taking the place that pilgrimage for a spiritual purpose held for previous ages, and converging on the same sites. Holy Island (Lindisfarne), for example, which is situated off the Northumbrian coast near Berwick, and which combines a peaceful atmosphere and dramatic setting with the sites of some of the earliest Christian settlements in Britain, receives more than 300,000 visitors a year, most of whom are British. Such spiritual tourism is not always welcome however – such is the demand for property for retreat houses and meditation centres that local people complain of not being able to afford houses on the island, which cost twice as much as they do on the mainland.

Throughout the period between the 1960s and the 1990s the Church was in a state of change. Conscious of its rapidly diminishing appeal to the population at large, it attempted to change traditions, in some cases hundreds of years old, in order

to be more modern and hence attract more worshippers. The decision in 1992 to admit women as priests, in particular, proved controversial and divisive, resulting in many priests leaving the faith to take up holy orders in the Roman Catholic Church. Those Church of England priests who were most opposed to women priests may feel at home there but, ironically, many Catholics do not welcome what they see as their male chauvinism, and themselves see the advent of Catholic women priests as both desirable and inevitable.

Background religion

The English capacity for compromise can be seen to have emerged in what we could call 'half belief' or 'passive belief'. While membership of all Christian churches in Britain, and church-going, are in steep, long-term decline, active Christianity in Britain is not, in general, being replaced by atheism, but rather by a less taxing and harder to define 'passive Christianity' (a vague belief in a God, and a vaguer belief in Christ, but a strong adherence to the idea of being Christian). As suggested earlier, the contradiction at the heart of Christianity in Britain is that while most of the population believe themselves to be in some sense Christian, they have no commitment to, little knowledge of or belief in, things that the Church regards as central to Christianity. There is in many quarters of the non-church-going population an assumption that being English automatically qualifies one for membership of the Church of England and hence confers the right to be considered a Christian. This position is made easier to hold by the Church of England's status as the established Church. As the Church's rituals of baptism, marriage and funeral have traditionally been extended to anyone who lives within the parish of a particular church, it has been easy to assume that membership of the Church, too, is a right which everyone shares. Thus the English choose the Church of England, but choose to stay away from it – preferring a loose sense of association with it to actually attending its services. Surveys of religious attitudes in

Britain regularly reveal a higher percentage of people who claim to be Christian than of people who claim to believe in God, implying a ' cultural Christianity' in which no orthodox spiritual faith in a divine Being is necessary, however strange such a concept may be to a traditional believer.

Most British people, it can be said, live in a state of 'popular religion', which, while loosely based on Christianity, would not be recognised as faith by most priests. In moments of crisis, it is the Christian God in some form to whom they will turn in private prayer. Such religion requires no active participation, but may be satisfied, for example, by listening to radio or television broadcasts. A Sunday service is broadcast nationally every week while morning radio programmes have 'Thought for the Day' or ' Prayer for the Day' slots – uplifting spiritual thoughts offered to the nation. (For example, the foremost news and current affairs radio programme, *Today*, early mornings on Radio 4, not only has a daily interview with a prominent politician but a message from a prominent spiritual leader.) Similarly, *Songs of Praise*, a weekly televised Christian act of worship which focuses on hymn-singing, regularly attracts a greater audience than does *Match of the Day* – the most popular weekly showcase for Britain's national sport, football. The same enjoyment of passive religion is evidenced by the local and national newspapers which carry a weekly column on spiritual matters written by a pastor. In Scotland, some local papers carry a daily sermon. Across the UK, religious broadcasting, which produces thoughtful programmes of high quality, is surprisingly popular. On an average Sunday in Britain, six hours of religious programming will be broadcast by the BBC and independent television companies, and four hours by BBC radio. In general, it is the older generations who watch and listen to such programmes. In keeping with British reticence on the subject, religion only occasionally features in television drama. One exception is *Brookside*, a popular soap opera set in Liverpool, whose story lines have included a Catholic priest who leaves the church after an affair with one of his parishioners and one which dealt with a cult of extreme evangelical Christians. On BBC television, *The Vicar of Dibley* is a comedy drama series based around the life of a woman priest in the Church of England, and derives much of its humour from the clash of expectations between the traditional role of a clergyman and the new clergywoman.

Other world religions in Britain

Britain has approximately 1,200,000 Muslims, the majority of whom were born in the UK. Others have arrived from the Indian subcontinent or from African countries. The larger Muslim communities are concentrated in the industrial cities of the Midlands, in London, Bradford and Strathclyde, and in the textile towns of Yorkshire and Lancashire where in the 1960s the clothing industry attracted workers from overseas. In addition, immigrant communities which arrived in Britain from colonies and ex-colonies in Asia, West Africa and the Caribbean in the 1950s and 1960s tended to concentrate in particular areas – notably London,

FIGURE 7.3 (a) Bolton's Muslim mosque

Birmingham, Glasgow and the big industrial towns of Northern England, and this has led to large communities of Muslims, Hindus and Sikhs in these areas. Glasgow, Newcastle and Leeds have sizeable Muslim populations. Britain's Muslim population is predominantly Sunni, with only around 25,000 Shias. For the first generation of Asian settlers, the practice of Islam and the heritage of Asian culture are inextricably intertwined. For their children, who have grown up in Britain however, Islam is a cultural and religious force in its own right, so that many young Britons of Asian origin may think of themselves as British Muslims, rather than as Asians or as black Britons. Whereas in the 1980s only one-fifth of the Muslims in Britain claimed to actively practise their religion, in the 1990s that figure rose to half.

For this generation the challenge is to continue to find ways to integrate the religious traditions of Islam into contemporary British life and to create a new British Islamic identity. It is a process which involves some difficulty, exacerbated by the fact

FIGURE 7.3 *(continued)* (b) Hindu temple in Liverpool

that although Britain has laws of blasphemy which could be invoked when Christians were offended by Martin Scorsese's film *The Last Temptation of Christ*, Muslims who objected to Salman Rushdie's *The Satanic Verses* had no legal recourse. The Rushdie Affair, as it came to be known, in many ways started abroad. Objections to Rushdie's blasphemy against the Prophet in his book were first voiced in India, and later in Pakistan and, of course, Iran, from where the Ayatollah Khomeini issued his *fatwa*, which Rushdie heard on Valentine's Day 1989. In Britain, the famous organised book burnings had only begun the month before. The Affair raised awareness of Islam in Britain and several groups emerged into the public eye. For example, the Bradford Council of Mosques attacked Rushdie while trying to create a political Muslim collective, and the Women Against Fundamentalism group defended him while trying to dislodge stereotypical views of Muslim women.

British law recognised that no blasphemy had even occurred however. In 1996, moreover, there was a widespread boycott by Muslims of religious education classes in schools (which, by law, may teach about other religions but must be predominantly Christian). Despite there being state-funded schools offering an education which is distinctively Anglican, Catholic or Jewish, no state money has been awarded to assist in creating a Muslim school. This anomaly may arise because Islam is still seen as intolerant, or even as a threat, by many conservative Britons, whose folk-memory of Islam is in terms of the Crusades (a word used with a positive emphasis in many British circles but which must have adverse connotations for Muslims). Young British Muslims, however, represent an important strand in British identity, feeling themselves to be in the forefront of the development of Islam in Europe. Positive cultural public images have been supplied by the cricketer Imran Khan, and Yusuf Islam, the pop singer formerly known as Cat Stevens.

The history of the presence of other faiths and peoples, and their role in public life in Britain, is little known. For example, Asian performers are recorded in London in the seventeenth century, and Indian sailors, called Lascars, were living in London at the end of the eighteenth century. England had several Indian professors in the 1800s and a British India Society was established in 1839 (under the influence of the first widely known Indian nationalist Rajah Rammohun Roy) followed by a London Indian Society in 1872. Already, by the middle of the nineteenth century there were significant Indian communities in London, Southampton and Liverpool, and these were in fact smaller than other black communities in Britain. As an indication of this level of cultural presence, it is worth noting that Queen Victoria – who never visited India – asked a Muslim servant, Abdul Karim, to teach her Hindustani. The founding President of the London Indian Society, Dadabhai Naoroji, also one of the early presidents of the Indian National Congress, was the first Indian elected to the British Parliament, in 1892, when he stood as a Liberal candidate in East Finchley, while another Parsi, Mancherjee Merwanjee Bhownaggree, a merchant from Bombay, was elected Conservative MP for Bethnal Green Northeast in 1895.

There is therefore a long cultural heritage of Asian people and faiths in the UK. This was well demonstrated in 1995, by the opening of the largest Hindu temple outside India, in Neasden in London. This event attracted much media interest since it was the only such structure to be built outside India for a thousand years. It used largely volunteer labour and was paid for entirely by donations from the Hindu community. In the 1990s, the majority of Hindus live in Greater London although Birmingham, in the Midlands, has also become a centre of the community. Many British Hindu families came from India and Sri Lanka but considerable numbers also arrived from Uganda and Kenya, when they were expelled by the authorities there in the early 1970s. There are now Hindu temples across the UK in major cities and towns. The Sikh community is also well represented in Britain and is concentrated in particular areas – for example, in Southall, Greater London, and Gravesend in Kent. Most early postwar migrants, in the 1950s, came from the Jat caste, and were predominantly men. At first they would hold a *diwan* or religious meetings at home, often in all-male households, but they subsequently set up *Gurdwaras* (Sikh Temples) for Sunday services. Their families followed from the Punjab in the 1960s and stronger domestic and religious ties were established.

Britain also has the second largest Jewish community in Europe. The majority live in London, but there are Jewish communities in most large cities. There are several hundred Jewish congregations in the UK, many Jewish schools, and synagogues serving both the Orthodox faith and the minority Reform group. Fears have been voiced that in the mid-1990s half of Jewish men are marrying non-Jewish women and that this will lead to a decline in faith and religious observance.

Finally, the Rastafarian religion has had a sizeable cultural influence in Britain. Rastafarians' philosophy of life was originally based on their adaptation of the Christianity they experienced in the colonial West Indies. They see themselves as Israelites displaced from their homeland, and Babylon is the collective name for all countries of exile outside Africa. Rastafarians have been influential in many cultural ways in Britain. Their 'dreadlocks' hair-style is shared by some New Age travellers or Crusties and they were probably influential in promoting a climate of tolerance towards soft drugs, a major aspect to their religion, in the 1980s. For example they staked out their territory in urban areas of such cities as Liverpool with graffiti claiming: 'Toxteth Not Croxteth', meaning that marijuana was welcome in Toxteth, but not the heroin which was available in another district of the city.

Though the religious group is small, millions of others appreciate the characteristic Rastafarian music, reggae, and particularly that of Bob Marley and the Wailers. Marley's music has been enormously influential, even with many British white punk bands (such as The Clash, Stiff Little Fingers and The Ruts), and more mainstream groups like Culture Club and UB40. Among other black British groups displaying Rasta influence are Aswad, Misty in Roots and Steel Pulse. In addition the critically acclaimed Rastafarian poets Benjamin Zephaniah and Levi Tafari have published widely and speak for large numbers of people in expressing a spirit of black resistance.

Religious festivals

One of the most obvious examples of religion in contemporary British life is the progression of the year through festivals and significant dates. The Anglican Church has traditionally divided the year according to a liturgical calendar – basing the year around a number of key religious feasts and thus creating holidays such as Whitsun, named after the feast of the Pentecost which is celebrated on the seventh Sunday after Easter, when the Holy Spirit appeared to the Apostles. British life is punctuated by such national holidays, some of which still have a religious meaning, but many are now largely secular festivals. An example of the latter is Mother's Day which is based on Lady's Day (25 March), a celebration of the annunciation to Mary that she was pregnant with Christ, who was to be born nine months later on 25 December. Some public festivals have roots in the pagan religions that held sway in Britain before the arrival of Christianity, lost religions whose customs are being re-created and celebrated by a new generation of 'pagans', who observe seasonal events such as the winter and summer solstices (mid-points), by meeting out of doors at ancient sites of worship, most famously at Stonehenge.

The name Easter is derived from the name of the Saxon goddess of spring, Eostre, (related to a Mediterranean pagan goddess mentioned in the Bible, Astarte). In some areas, Easter rituals, as well as celebrating the resurrection of Christ, include ceremonies which were once probably part of pagan fertility rites, though they are now performed in a spirit of secular fun, for example, the rolling of eggs down hills or the eating of pancakes on Shrove Tuesday at the beginning of Lent, the period of fasting before Easter (observed by few Christians in Britain, while the month of Ramadan is observed by Muslims). For most non-religious British people Easter is an occasion for the exchange of chocolate, though this chocolate is usually in the shape of an egg or a rabbit (the Easter Bunny), both symbols of fertility. The day after Easter Day, Easter Monday, is also a public holiday. Many British people who never normally go to church will attend a service on Easter morning.

1 May or May Day is a public holiday introduced by a Labour government. It is a socialist revival of a much more ancient pagan festival of Beltane which is still celebrated by Morris dancers, who dance traditional dances, clad in straw hats and with bells on their ankles, around a Maypole. In places such as Oxford (where there is a tradition of greeting the dawn on May Day morning), morris dancers are likely to be joined by neo-pagans – young people dressed in the fashions of youth counter-culture – ex-army coats, trousers and boots, dreadlocks, strings of coloured beads or leather thongs worn as bracelets or necklaces, and pierced noses and ears. That such people will share the same celebration as well-heeled middle-class students and conservative middle-aged people points to the deeper rhythms of British life which unite people who otherwise feel themselves to be profoundly different, politically and culturally.

Hallowe'en, on 31 October, is a British festival which now shows many traces of American influence. For example, children are now beginning to play 'trick or treat' – that is, to call at houses on Hallowe'en dressed in macabre fancy-dress costumes and ask for sweets. This new and growing fashion, pagan in origin, can be contrasted with the Christian tradition of groups of carol singers going from door to door at Christmas, singing in exchange for coins or refreshments. Carol singing is in marked decline. Some people feel uneasy about Hallowe'en. It was originally a pagan festival of remembrance for the end of the old year (according to the pagan calendar) and of communion with the dead (it falls on All Souls' Eve). It is celebrated principally by children, who enjoy the frightening atmosphere created by make-up, masks and costumes on the theme of ghosts, witches, spectres and skeletons. While in the 1960s and 1970s schools would enthusiastically participate in Hallowe'en, in the 1980s and 1990s many schools, particularly in Scotland, which had a particularly strong Hallowe'en tradition, banned the celebration, because of pressure from Christian parents who believed the festival was connected with black magic and witchcraft, or because it encouraged children to go out at night unsupervised.

Guy Fawkes Night (5 November) also known as 'Bonfire night' or 'Fireworks night' is another example of how a festival which is now seen as entirely secular can grow from religious origins. While, again, its origins lie in pre-Christian pagan customs (a fire festival to welcome the winter), this custom of gathering to light outdoor bonfires and to burn effigies symbolically representing the old year, was adapted by the Christian state in the seventeenth century to commemorate the defeat of a Catholic plot (the Gunpowder Plot) to blow up the Houses of Parliament. Like Christmas, Bonfire night is remarkable in being one of the few customs which actively unite British people. All across the UK, everyone is acutely aware of, if not participating in, festivities typically consisting of a display of fireworks around a bonfire, on which a human effigy of Guy Fawkes (discussed in the introductory chapter to this volume) is burned.

The role of the traditional churches as part of the British state is most obvious on Armistice Day (the Sunday nearest to 11 November). This day is also known as 'Poppy Day', as many British people, particularly of the older generations, will wear a red paper poppy to show that they remember those who have died fighting for their country. (In the First World War many British soldiers were killed in battle in the wheat fields of Flanders, which had poppies growing in them.) All over the country, ceremonies which combine military drill and Christian ritual are held to remember the war dead, especially those killed in the 1939–1945 war. This is principally a time of mourning and of celebration for the generations who have lived through the Second World War, and those who died. However, even many young people, who feel uncomfortable about the solemnity and emphasis on the past of Poppy Day, also feel that some of their sense of identity as British subjects is defined by this day. Even if the themes of patriotism and military service are not those with which they personally identify, the commemoration ceremonies held in schools, churches and town centres provide an annual reminder of another history of British identity – one which now needs to be negotiated alongside strengthening links with the EU.

For those without significant religious festivals, Christmas (25 December) is without question the single most important event in the British social, religious and cultural calendar (though it should be noted that in Scotland, where it was not until the 1950s that Christmas day became a public holiday, the alternative celebration of 'Hogmanay' or New Year has historically been of much greater importance and, in the Highlands of Scotland particularly, remains so). Christmas Day is the one time when people feel the need to re-enact the importance of the family, and most young people who otherwise live elsewhere will still spend that day with their parents. For most British families the Christmas period is the only time, apart from weddings and funerals, when the 'extended family' – including different generations and the children of different branches of the family – are gathered together. It is the time when, as John Betjeman put it in his poem 'Christmas': 'girls in slacks remember Dad/ And oafish louts remember Mum.' This can prove to be something of a strain for many people, as the British are not used to sharing their lives so closely with so many other relatives for several days and this is reflected in statistics for violent domestic crime.

While the Christmas festival, celebrating the birth of Jesus, is of course a religious one, it could be argued that for most British people any religious meaning is very slight, and the celebration consists chiefly of drinking and eating (especially the traditional Christmas dinner of turkey, roast potatoes, Christmas pudding (a very rich fruitcake), mince pies (sweet fruit pies of mixed dried fruit and brandy), exchanging presents and watching special Christmas programmes on television. Passive religion, however, is more popular at Christmas than at any other time, with many people listening to carol services on the radio, such as that broadcast by the BBC from King's College in Cambridge. For many British people, the Christmas story has sentimental appeal, if only because it reminds them of when they first heard it as children, and it is this, rather than religious faith, which makes the Church seem more attractive at Christmas. Generally speaking, public performances of the nativity story of Jesus's birth, which is primarily reserved for children's school plays, take second

FIGURE 7.4 An 'integrated' festival (Protestant and Catholic) in 1995 at Bellygawley, County Tyrone: the first for twenty-five years

place to pantomimes and productions of Dickens's *A Christmas Carol* across the country.

Some Christmas traditions are of fairly recent manufacture. Prince Albert, Queen Victoria's consort, introduced the Christmas tree to Britain from his native Germany. 'Father Christmas' or Santa Claus's red uniform and white beard is said to have been inspired by a Coca Cola advertising campaign in the 1920s. Despite the widespread commercialism however, most British people do derive some religious meaning from Christmas and, for this one time in the year, will participate in Christian ceremony. They will also listen to the monarch's only annual talk to the nation, which has an ostensibly religious purpose. It is broadcast on both radio and television and the Queen or King asks for God's blessing on the British people. For most of the nation this is a dated occasion devoid of any religious meaning, and indeed, of any meaning at all. While in the 1970s up to 27 million people, more than half the population, watched this broadcast, in 1994 this number had fallen to around 15 million, and in 1995 to 13 million. One may only speculate on why 13 million British people watched the broadcast, and what they got out of it. For many it is simply 'a tradition' – part of the Christmas ritual.

The New Age

'New Age' is a broad term devised to describe the renewal of interest in a range of approaches to the spiritual dimension which promote individuals' ability to discover and develop their own spirituality. Whereas Christianity is seen by many as emphasising adherence to a strict moral code (for example, through the Ten Commandments, the Bible, confession or sermons), New Age religions concentrate on developing the spiritual awareness which they believe is present in each person. Their practices have a huge variety in their origin – some being revivals of the pagan magical and religious systems that Christianity replaced in Britain, some being extensions of Eastern meditative and religious practices, and some, such as yoga and t'ai chi, being concerned with physical exercises. It may be that the presence of an increasingly diverse multi-ethnic community in Britain has boosted the popularity of some practices. For example, interest has grown in vegetarianism and veganism (large Hindu and other communities have added a considerable market for vegetarian food, which has in turn stimulated British caterers and retailers, and thus aided their popularity) and while ten years ago vegetarian options on a pub menu were rare, they are now standard. The practice of Chinese medicine, meditation and yoga are also rapidly increasing in Britain.

The belief in reincarnation, which many young people who have been influenced by paganism adhere to, is one which, while alien to older generations brought up under Christianity, is fundamental for example, to Hinduism. Similarly, it is not unusual for young British people involved in the New Age to talk about 'karma'. Other New Age practices have a distinctly European origin, stemming from a revival of interest in Celtic myth and culture, or from a new publicity given to old systems of occult knowledge through for example the Kabbalah or palmistry. Hundreds of thousands of people are directly involved in activities such as meditation or astrology (the belief system where people's personalities and destinies are determined by the star signs under which they are born). But more significant is the effect of these beliefs on the overall sense of how British people see themselves and their world. For example, a quarter of British people, claimed in a survey in the 1990s to regularly read their horoscope as published in a magazine. Many more will read their horoscope as a form of light-hearted entertainment, but will still hope for good news. Television programmes such as *The Para-Normal World of Paul McKenna* which explores 'inexplicable' phenomena, are also extremely popular, as is Mystic Meg, a television seer on the BBC's weekly National Lottery show who predicts the type of person destined to win the jackpot each week. Furthermore, business people have adopted many alternative spiritual practices as a cure for stress and as a source of inspiration or energy, while a small but growing number of people among the professional classes are turning to Buddhism.

The term 'New Age' is used to link all of the above activities, and this grouping has some justification, not least because those who have an interest in one of these practices often also have an interest in others. The term itself is derived from astrology, which holds that every two thousand years the solar system enters a new age. The Piscean age (from the sign of the fish) which started approximately at the birth of Christ was the Christian age (Pisces is seen by astrologers as the sign of self-sacrifice and mass movements), while the new astrological era will be that of Aquarius. (Aquarius is the sign of individualism, and hence of any religion which allows individuals freedom.)

Some of the increasingly popular practices which have been placed by the media in the New Age category are distinctively religious. For example, Wicca (witchcraft, or worship of British forms of the Mother Goddess, often associated with the practice of magic) and Buddhism are religious preoccupations. Interest in oriental medicine, health food and yoga, however, does not require or imply faith. Many facets of the New Age, such as the interest in astrology or in Eastern meditation, are religious in the sense that they involve establishing a link between individuals and a spiritual realm. However, in other ways these activities seem more like hobbies than parts of organised religions as they involve individual study or meditation rather than a formal structure with its own hierarchy and moral code. New Age groups are thus the antithesis of the highly controlled, brainwashed 'cults' which fascinate newspaper editors in Great Britain (such as followers of the Unification Church, known as 'Moonies').

New Age practices, in the widest sense, are the most important and most rapidly developing area of religious change across Britain and must be considered seriously. Aspects of the New Age have permeated very different sections of British society: from business people turning to meditation as a release from the stress of pressurised, urban, executive life, to the Donga tribe – young pagans who have abandoned normal British society and who live largely out of doors, and who came to national prominence for their role in actively protesting against the government's appropriation of sites of rare natural value to build new motorways.

In many ways, currents of New Age religion have enabled changes which have occurred in British life between the 1980s and the 1990s to find a religious expression. The rising tide of concern for the environment, for animal welfare and rights (a subject the British are uniquely concerned with, though they have fewer domestic animals per capita than, for example, the Dutch), for conservation and for green or ecological politics, has helped to create a climate in which religions such as paganism, which celebrate the earth and its wildlife, fulfil a need for many people. A powerful element within the identity of young British people is a sense of identification with the countryside, and a resentment of the loss of countryside to modern building, and in particular, to the road-building programme, which the Conservative Government pursued from the 1980s and early 1990s.

Famously, while statistically very few young people seek active involvement in any of the national political parties, and there is generally much cynicism about politics in British life, one area in where there is genuine idealism is in the concern for the landscape, with many environmental protesters enduring poverty and great physical hardship to fight new road-building. Such activity earns considerable sympathy from many Britons of all generations. Far more young people are involved in such 'single issue' protests than in party politics, as referred to elsewhere in this book (see Chapter 5). Whereas for previous generations the sense of belonging to a nation may have been expressed through such institutions as the Church, the armed forces, or in some cases, a university or a public school, many of the young generation find their ideals and their sense of belonging in nature and in the land itself.

While Christianity is identified politically with authority, the Establishment and the older generation, many New Age beliefs, and paganism in particular, are identified with the young and the disaffected. The most visible adherents are 'New Age travellers', who, in the hot summers of the 1980s, fought annual battles against the police to reach Stonehenge, Britain's most important ancient site, because they believed that they had both the right and the duty to celebrate the summer solstice, and, in particular, to name their children there. The latter idea offers an example of how quickly an idea essential to identity – the ritual of naming – can become part of British subculture, and how the New Age generates its own 'instant' mythology through which people define themselves.

The British appetite for passive religion and the commercial forces of tourism show their influence on pagan sites as well as Christian ones. Stonehenge is one of Britain's most popular attractions, receiving 672,000 visitors a year, many of whom are drawn by a vague, but powerful, sense of communion with some other world, or mystic power, which lives on in the imagination of the visitors, if not in the stones themselves. The young New Age pagans who worship at the stones are in a sense a natural extension of British instincts rather than a violation of them, despite their anti-Establishment posture.

Religious differences: age and sex

The decline of Christianity in Britain is not due to individuals losing their religion, but rather to a process of generational change.
A generation which was very religious, at least in terms of church
attendance and social attitudes, and which has been the main-
stay of church life in England over the last thirty years, is literally
dying out and being replaced by a generation which cares far less
for church observance and for Christianity in general. Christianity
is associated for young people with the unfashionable and unnecessary code of restrictive, negative morality of the value systems of
their parents or grandparents. Many associate a figure such as
the Pope with an authoritarian patriarchal Jehovah and tend to see
Christianity, and Catholicism in particular, as a series of prohibi-
tions – 'don't take drugs', 'don't have sex', 'don't get drunk' and
'don't swear'. As such it has very little appeal and has also been
seen as male-centred, dictating women's lives: under Catholicism,
women cannot be priests, use contraception or have an abortion.
Attempts by some within the church to integrate elements of
1990s youth culture into worship, including some ideas borrowed
from New Age spirituality and others from the 'rave' music scene,
have caused problems and controversy. They have been backed by
many bishops as an attempt to bridge the enormous cultural
gap between the Church and young people, yet resisted by many
ordinary worshippers who cannot reconcile flashing lights, ampli-
fied electronic music and cinema screens as part of recognisable
Christian worship. A visitor to a church service in Britain will be
struck by the advanced age of the worshippers: many congregations are largely made up of women in their sixties or seventies, or
still older. The chief exceptions to this are evangelical congregations, both within the Church of England and outside it in churches
such as the House churches, Baptists or Pentecostals, which place
a strong emphasis on a dramatically emotional conversion experience, and conservative moral values and family structures (for
example, no sex except in marriage).

One example of the gulf between the Church and society
was the Church's disapproval of the National Lottery. The Church

FIGURE 7.5 A Christian bookshop with the ancient symbol of the fish in its sign

has once again been seen as basically prohibitive. While some serious commentators on national life agreed with its reservations about the damaging effects particularly on poor people of the compulsion to gamble, and of extreme wealth on the winners, the week when the Church raised its strongest objections was also one in which nine out of ten British people bought a lottery ticket for a £40 million jackpot. The Church may still try to exercise its role as moral guardian of the nation, but few people take this seriously enough to be guided by it in their own lives. This is even more the case with the young. For them, Christianity is profoundly unfashionable. It is significant that, almost in imitation of the subcultural pagan practice of wearing occult jewellery whose meaning is known only to another 'initiate' of the subculture, Christians have, in Britain, increasingly embraced the symbol of the fish (an ancient secret sign used when Christianity was itself a minor religion, a cult) rather than the cross, as a badge to identify themselves only to other believers.

Church weddings, despite the aesthetic attraction of historic church buildings and music, are in decline. The comment of one future bride, 'We're not religious at all, we don't believe in God but we want to get married in a church' sums up the confused motives behind many such weddings – the fact that the wedding is a Christian ritual, involving religious vows, is somehow invisible to those used to passive religion. The hit film *Four Weddings and a Funeral* offered an illustration of the lack of religious interest in the Church at English and Scottish weddings, which is paradoxically matched by the cultural importance to the upper classes of having a church wedding. Christenings – the Christian rite of baptism – are now becoming rare.

It should be noted that, while the Church is dominated by men, surveys reveal that in groups of every age women are more likely to acknowledge the importance of religious experience than are men. In both New Age groups and in Christian churches, it is women who predominate. It may be that British women are more open to spiritual practice and belief than men (a survey conducted for Channel 4 in 1987 found that roughly half of all British women believed in astrology, while only a quarter of all men shared that belief). It may be that men are simply more reluctant to show religious feeling outwardly. No men's magazines have astrology columns, but almost every woman's magazine has its own named astrologer. Two-thirds of the private clients of leading astrologers are reported to be women.

The heritage industry

A major cultural change in British life from the 1970s through to the 1990s was that Britons spent more leisure time and money on visiting historical sites and exhibits. It has been argued that the growth in the heritage industry has in some ways filled a gap left in people's lives by the loss of a religious dimension. Reverence for the past could be seen as replacing the religious reverence of previous generations. Britons who, a generation before, might have gone to church, now spend their Sundays visiting a stately home

FIGURE 7.6 A Roman soldier in the town of Chester. Time spent in visiting historical sites, some argue, is filling the gap left by religion

or exhibition of local 'heritage' – a modern pilgrimage. The Jorvik Centre in York (the town's modern name is derived from Jorvik, its Viking name) was the first purpose-built centre for heritage tourism. The life-size plastic Vikings of Jorvik have been followed by other exhibition centres showing everything from Oxford scholars to highland Scottish crofters. Such exhibitions use mannequins dressed up in historic costume, in restored or imitation historic houses, shops, castles or factories. They may even be staffed by actors dressed in historic costume. Paradoxically, the increasing secularisation of British life has led to less leisure time on Sundays for many, as in the 1990s shops began to routinely open on Sundays, giving the traditionally quiet Sabbath day more a feel of 'business as usual'.

The attraction of a 'museum culture' does not just extend to the remote past, but applies even to the twentieth century, and to areas of life that have only recently been part of normal life rather than historical curiosities. For example, in South Wales (where coal-mining was the dominant industry until the 1980s, but has now almost disappeared) it is possible to be guided around a redundant coal-mine by men who used to work there, but who are now dressed as miners only to show tourists around. While much of this repackaging, particularly in metropolitan areas, might seem to be arranged or created for foreign tourists, in fact most of the visitors to many such attractions are British, being reintroduced to their own past through the professional presentation of a host of corners of its geography and commerce. As justifications for the 'greatness' of Great Britain fall away, it could be said that its people turn to the past to find symbols of their identity, and indeed, their importance. Of these, the stately home is perhaps the most enduring as well as the most successfully marketed to the public.

In some ways the Church has benefited from this – the great cathedrals which combine Christian heritage and monuments from the past have never been so popular. In other ways, too, the British could be accused of living in their past. Many films lovingly recreate Edwardian England, particularly those of Merchant and Ivory, who have specialised in finely detailed costume dramas and adaptations of literary classics such as *A Room with a View* and *Howards End*. Other films of the 1980s and 1990s, such as *The Remains of the Day* or *A Month in the Country*, and television series such as *Brideshead Revisited* are profitably sold around the world as an image of an ideal Britain, and eagerly consumed by Britons themselves as a kind of national myth. The common elements of the aristocracy, venerable buildings and English eccentrics occur over and over in such films, offering a picture of a quaint, gentle England.

Fantasies of the Britain of previous generations, particularly of rural Britain, predominate in television drama series such as *Heartbeat, All Creatures Great and Small, The Darling Buds of May* and *Brideshead Revisited,* and in advertising – notably for various brands of bread, biscuits and cakes. Historical settings are also used in some of the numerous situation comedies which British people watch. *Dad's Army* and *'Allo 'Allo* for example, are set during the Second World War, a time which many in the older generations look back with nostalgia and pride. The celebrations in 1995 to commemorate the fiftieth Anniversary of VE (Victory in Europe) day were the occasion of a collective nostalgia for the comradeship and certainties of wartime. It should be stressed, however, that children and young people in general know very little about 'the [1939–1945] war' – the defining moment in twentieth-century British history, and the flooding of print and broadcast media with images of the war in 1995 made very little impression on them. For example, a popular television series, *Goodnight Sweetheart,* with a hero who, by means of time travel, has a double life – one part lived in the wartime 1940s, and one lived in contemporary Britain – appealed particularly to the old, who have a hunger for nostalgia.

Another feature of the British fascination with the past is the re-creation of the world – particularly in rural areas far from London – as a series of places defined by some cultural product. Thus one is able to go on an excursion not just to another place, but, at least imaginatively, to another time. For example, the Lake District is advertised as Wordsworth's home, the Yorkshire Moors as 'Brontë Country', and even towns used for recent television productions – parts of Yorkshire for the televisions series *Heartbeat* (now known as 'Heartbeat Country') – have become marketed in this way, and there is a steady demand from the public for such attractions. Alongside Britain's real geography, through which one is guided by blue motorway signs, and green trunk road signs, there is an alternative network of reddish-brown road signs – indicating the presence of 'heritage' Britain. This may be formed of real places – castles, stately homes, preserved factories – or of invented attractions. For example, in North Wales it is possible to journey through the tunnels of an abandoned mine now converted into 'King Arthur's Labyrinth' – a site with no connections to Arthurian legend, but one where an underground heritage display has been erected. For a country declining economically, there is an added commercial incentive to turn to the past – not just for nostalgia but for a product which, for example, is unavailable in the US yet which is also linked to many of the people, the tourists, from that country.

Conclusion

The question of the role played by religion in establishing British identity is a complex one, and one that reveals great differences between people of different ages in Britain. For a large number of British people over 50, religion is a quiet and distant but important presence in their lives. It is a touchstone of shared British identity at great national or public occasions and a continuing link with the past. It is also a source of comfort available at times of private or personal tragedy and celebration, such as weddings and funerals, when religion becomes temporarily of far greater importance for all generations.

In England, even many of those who do not believe in Christianity feel a sense of attachment to the Church of England. While they may never attend a church service, they like to know that they are there and would feel robbed if they were taken from them. For a number of people, the Church of England encapsulates in its rituals, liturgies, hymns and music a distinct cultural expression of Englishness. For that minority of the population who adhere actively and strongly to Christianity, this element of religion as an expression of national identity is also there but is probably less important.

For young British people whose parents were born elsewhere in the world, religion – such as Hinduism or Islam – is one important strand of their identity: a key element in the culture that marks their own contribution to Britishness as distinctive and creates a link with another heritage elsewhere. For most people under 30, Christianity is associated with a past to which they feel they have little connection. Some will describe themselves as atheists, and many as agnostics, but for those who are interested in spiritual things, the New Age is more likely to attract them. While not part of a formal or organised system, such practices offer people freedom and individuality as well the possibility of exploring spiritual paths for themselves.

EXERCISES

1   Do you recognise the following phrases? To hide one's light under a bushel; to go the extra mile; to turn the other cheek. What do they mean? How do you feel Christian ideas might be at odds with people's lives in Britain today?

2   Many British commentators try to link a decline in religious practice with a perceived deterioration in morals. Do you think this is a fair connection to make, and what signs or changes in Britain do you think lead people to argue that there has been a worsening of moral standards?

3   What are hot cross buns, Shrove Tuesday pancakes, and chocolate Yule logs? When would they be eaten? Remembering that dates such as Valentine's Day (14 February) have a religious background, how would you

311

map out the British calendar in terms of firstly, Christian festivals, and secondly, significant dates for all faiths?

4   Where would you locate the following ten World Heritage sites (established by UNESCO) on the map in Chapter 1 (see p. 42): the City of Bath; Blenheim Palace; Canterbury Cathedral; Stonehenge; Westminster Palace; the island of St Kilda; the Giant's Causeway; Hadrian's wall; Ironbridge; and the castles and town walls of Caernarfon, Conwy, Beaumaris and Harlech. Do you know, or can you find out, the natural or cultural significance of each site?

READING

Cashmore, Ernest. *Rastaman: The Rastafarian Movement in England*. Allen & Unwin, 1979
A slightly dated but definitive and widely available review of British Rastafarianism.

Fowler, Peter. *The Past in Contemporary Society: Then, Now*. Routledge, 1992
Examines the extent to which our heritage is still with us in the present.

Parsons, Gerald. *The Growth of Religious Diversity: Britain from 1945*, 2 vols. Open University/Routledge, 1993
Careful and thorough analysis of Britain and religion since the Second World War.

Visram, Rozina. *Ayahs, Lascars, and Princes: The Story of Indians in Britain, 1700–1947*. Pluto, 1986
Reveals the largely unknown heritage and history of Hindus, Muslims, Sikhs, and Parsis from India in the UK.

■ *Films*

Excalibur (1981) dir. John Boorman
New Age philosophy and Celtic magic projected on to the myth of Arthur's England.

Leon the Pig Farmer (1992) dirs. Jean Vadim and Gary Snydor
Young Jewish Londoner moves to rural Yorkshire.

No Surrender (1985) dir. Peter Smith
Rival Catholic and Protestant Irish factions collide in a Liverpool club.

Priest (1993) dir. Antonia Bird
A social drama exploring the conflicts between Catholicism and homosexuality in an impoverished Liverpool parish.

Truly, Madly, Deeply (1991) dir. Anthony Minghella
One woman's private trauma of grief after bereavement.

The Wicker Man (1973) dir. Robin Hardy
A cult movie with a horrifying ending in which a mainland policeman discovers that pagan fertility rituals, including human sacrifice, still dominate the society of a small northern island.

■ *Books*

Asian Women Writers' Collective, *Flaming Spirit* (1994), ed. Rukshana Ahmad and Rahila Gupta
Religion, identity and nostalgia for home are common themes in this collection of stories from Asian women across Britain.

David Hare, *Racing Demon* (1990)
David Hare's intelligent and questioning play about two Church of England priests engaging in theological debate and sociological comment in contemporary South London.

Hanif Kureishi, *The Black Album* (1995)
Novel of Anglo-Pakistani youth growing up in London against the backdrop of the Rushdie Affair.

David Lodge, *How Far Can You Go?* (1980)
Analysis of modern Catholic faith and responsibility in Britain.

Jenny Newman, *Going In* (1995)
A British account of entering a French convent and the relationships between the religious and secular worlds.

Salman Rushdie, *The Satanic Verses* (1988)
The novel whose portrayal of Islam sparked a major controversy over blasphemy and free speech.

■   *Television programmes*

Father Ted
Comedy series about three Irish priests and their sometimes less than spiritual lifestyle.

Songs of Praise
Perennial Sunday evening favourite in which a congregation and community are visited by the BBC for a weekly service.

The Vicar of Dibley
Sitcom about a woman vicar written by the author of *Four Weddings and a Funeral*.

Conclusion: present and future Britain

■ Ross Dawson

Introduction

T HE CULTURAL IDENTITIES THAT HAVE been outlined
in this book point to what one recent British magazine has
called 'New Times'. In these times, certain old stereotypes have
been eroded by new developments outside, as well as inside,
Britain: international social and environmental movements, the
end of Soviet Communism, new technologies, Europeanisation,
and the spread of American culture. This shift has been acknowl-
edged in the previous chapters as a relatively recent process,
punctuated by dramatic events in the last fifteen years. Internally,
identities have been transformed within a cultural climate that
has been named Thatcherism by commentators of all political
stripes. Yet this tends to neglect the fact that cultural identities
are being changed by momentous forces occurring without as
well as within the nation. The 'external' world has come to
stay in the UK now in the shape of the second generation
of British-born sons and daughters of postwar immigrants, the
consolidation of the European Community with the removal of
trade barriers in 1992 and the plan for a single European
Currency, the rise of fundamentalist Islam around the world, the
decreased relevance of the Commonwealth and the intensification
of Americanisation, and the role of multinational corporations.
All of these formations have complicated the 'Britishness' of any
new identities.

By way of conclusion there are three aspects of shifting identities that may help us to think about the future. First, the
Americanisation of British culture will as elsewhere, disrupt the
sense of coherent national identities. Second, flourishing multi-
ethnic identities within the UK continue to challenge notions of
a traditional British culture. Third, identities in Britain are increasingly expressed through new technologies, through the computers,

faxes, mobile phones and camcorders which require different kinds of communication and interaction.

American and British

A report presented recently to the National Heritage Committee on Broadcasting predicted that by the year 2000 only 13 per cent of all programmes on British screens would be made in the UK. (In 1993 63 per cent of BBC programmes and 53 per cent of programmes on Channel 4 were British.) This was reported as part of a mounting crisis of national identity, compounded by the inevitable multiplication of channels due to the introduction of cable and satellite television. These two technologies invite the globalisation of television and more probably a significant increase in the appearance of American programmes on our screens. This Americanisation of British culture has been a long-term trend but recent years have shown a marked increase in the presence of America 'over here'. For example, the most popular films in Britain year after year are American (90 per cent of all box-office takings in Britain in 1990 were for American films and in 1994 nine out of the top ten films were American). US television shows have brought their worlds into British living rooms to the extent that they are no longer thought of as 'American' and even sometimes as a part of something essentially 'British': this is illustrated in the ritualistic showing of Hollywood musicals such as *The Wizard of Oz* and *The Sound of Music* every Christmas in Britain. If identity is defined by cultural activities, we in Britain are necessarily part-American.

The US is seen as a world which reflects back on the inadequacies – for example, austerity, repression, complacency – as well as the virtues – for example, reservation, asceticism, scepticism – of the British people. Not surprisingly, when an advertising agency conducted a survey of how the rest of the world views Britain, the list of adjectives that were said to most sum up the British were 'proud', 'civilised', 'cultured', 'arrogant' and 'cold'. These stereotypes are of course significant and conform to a range of images of British identity that has sometimes been called 'UK plc' and is marketed world-wide (through the Royal Family, old British films and history books). The National Heritage industry has focused on this version of Britain, one constructed around images appealing to the key tourist countries, especially Japan and America (there were nearly twenty million visitors to the UK in 1993). This marketable version of Britishness may be far from most of the identities that we have discussed in this book, but it remains the most common way that our culture is represented to the rest of the world – and the most profitable. The British monarchy is now often justified in terms of the tourist income that it brings in, and not because it is vital to national cultural identity. British people's identities are necessarily influenced by such national images, not least when the British venture off the island and are presented with these dated stereotypes by others. It should be mentioned that the British are not only occupiers of the theme park 'Britain' but increasingly tourists themselves – there were over thirty-five million visits made abroad by UK citizens in 1993. Indeed, the roles of traveller and tourist have contributed to more complex identities, which may account for the erosion of nationalism in Britain: in 1993 a crisis was announced in the press when a poll showed that over 50 per cent of all Britons would rather live in another country, even if the majority would preserve their British citizenship. This shift is illustrated by the popularity of the round-the-world trip, the new middle class movement to places in Europe such as the Dordogne in France, and the attraction of the American entry visa, or 'green card', as a way out from Britain's economic predicament.

The Americanisation of cultural identities is a global phenomenon and now, in the words of one writer, 'the world dreams itself to be American'. The spread of American culture has been most clear in its corporate signs, such as Coca-Cola, Levi Strauss, Budweiser, Disney, Nike and McDonald's. McDonald's stands for fast, friendly service, hygienic food preparation, and a clean, limited, inexpensive menu. This $26 billion company has come to dominate the take-away food industry over the past twenty years. The first British restaurant was established in Woolwich in 1974 and by December 1995 there were 620 McDonald's restaurants in the UK. Mrs Thatcher's old constituency of East Finchley is the location of McDonald's Hamburger University, a training centre for the 'McJobs' that characterise the new service industries. Perhaps one of the most significant elements of what might be called the McDonaldisation of Britain has been the increased importance of standardisation and quantity. The bestselling 'Big Mac' is prepared in exactly the same way with the same ingredients throughout the world; it is also not principally 'delicious' or 'tasty' or anything other than 'Big', as is Burger King's 'Whopper'. Many other representations of America appear to dwarf England's 'quaintness' and appeal to the desire for 'more' that fuels a consumer-driven culture. In fast-food restaurants today it is impossible to buy a 'small' anything – even bags of fries only come in 'regular' and 'large' sizes.

As was suggested in Chapter 6, the preference for an American future over a European one is coupled with the issue of language (British people often take some pride in the fact that most of the world's population is coming to speak their language but of course it is really 'American' that people are learning). It is also due to the 'special' political relationship between America and Britain, and the continuing scepticism about Britain's commitment to the European Community. While the 'vulgarising' of British culture is resisted by new and traditional cultures alike, the process of Americanisation in industry and the new service economy underlies many shifts, particularly regarding work identities. Alongside purchasing habits, work and mass culture are also becoming largely American. British cultural and political rhetoric became Americanised in the 1980s as stockbrokers and financial managers embraced a much more established view in American that 'greed is good', a phrase taken from the American film *Wall Street*. Terms such as 'wealth creation', 'total quality management', 'go for it', 'the bottom line' and 'achievable goals' have entered the common speech of British work life, as certain traditional scepticisms about the power of money and business language have been eroded for a 'brave new world'. The changes in the new economic climate have also helped to break down some of the 'old boy networks' that have traditionally occupied the institutions of power in Britain. None the less, as described in Chapter 2, the institutions of official culture have in some cases been more resistant than others, in particular, Whitehall, the BBC, Law, Oxford and Cambridge Universities as compared to the City – most private City institutions are now foreign-owned and London is home to over five hundred overseas banks. Businesses have relinquished some of the British 'traditions' orientated around being 'one of us', 'fair play', 'security', 'seniority', 'loyalty', for the priorities of the global market: 'profit', 'risk', 'meritocracy' and 'individual goals'. These new identities have undoubtedly been bolstered if not created by the powerful presence of American culture: the increasing availability of US self-help books for business and personal success are indications of these trends. Further, the image and 'sound bite' (short but powerful media-friendly phrase) manipulation of Tony Blair by 'spin doctors' (public relations experts employed to present bad news in the best light) show the tendencies of an American version of politics. For example, one commentator suggests that when Bill Clinton campaigned his way to the Presidency, the political stylists of New Labour were studying Clinton's techniques 'with all the rapture of Elvis look-alikes lip synching "Love Me Tender"'.

It could be said that this Americanisation is a process not necessarily understood by many of the British people as 'American' but as part of a more general narrative of 'change' or 'progress'. At the same time in other quarters of popular culture there is a recognition of American images as both desirable identifications and ones to be challenged by indigenous national culture. The marketing of Britpop around bands like Oasis and Blur has been a recent overt form of popular cultural resistance to the Americanisation of music. America as an inevitable future has made for an uneasy combination of influence and resistance for youths who see this choice as no choice. In Britain, as suggested in Chapter 4, the importance of the Ecstasy-fuelled rave scene has expressed some of this disaffection, while America's guitar-orientated 'grunge' scene has inspired a new wave of 'indy-rock' in pubs and clubs in the UK. Since rock music was considered by Richard Hoggart in the 1950s to be one of the negative influences of American culture, it has generally been accepted that the British music industry has been one of the most significant of popular cultural exports to the world, beginning with the 'British invasion' of the 1960s led by the Beatles. Some critics have drawn attention to the cross-fertilisation of Anglo-American-Caribbean black culture and the need to understand it as a new kind of cross-national identity. Transatlantic culture is probably most apparent in popular music since rhythm and blues, jazz, soul and reggae are rooted in the music of black American and Caribbean culture. The recent popularity of hip-hop culture and rap music from the black American urban ghetto has influenced and been inflected by black British culture such as Soul II Soul's fusion of hip-hop, soul and jazz music and 'jungle' music's recombination of dark raps, the rhythms of techno-dance music and the Caribbean influence of Ragga. More generally speaking, the national identities variously asserted in the preceding chapters all show the influence of American cultures. T.S. Eliot's description of British culture at the beginning of this book may have been recalled by Prime Minister John Major, but it seems an increasingly inadequate description of collective identity in Britain today. While some look across the channel and others across the Atlantic, there is often no further to look than the British Isles to see cultural examples of 'Europe', 'America', 'Asia' and 'Africa'.

Multiculturalism and racism

The 'Little England' described at the beginning of this book presents a version of the nation based around cultural or ethnic purity as well as a version of the past as essentially rural and aristocratic. This vision is based on the idea of 'Great' Britain, a country with a glorious imperialist past that was in fact built on slave-trading and colonising the 'dark' continents. This nostalgic appeal to history is premised on narrow ethnic stereotypes, a Britain that is WASP (white, Anglo-Saxon and Protestant).

The survival of this tradition, if only as a silent assumption of the mass media and official institutions, has meant the persistence of institutional racism that alters the cultural identity of all British citizens. Britain is still predominantly 'white', but the designation of 'black' to refer to most immigrants from the Asian subcontinent as well as from Africa and the Caribbean, shows that it is race and not ethnicity that still dominates both social and individual understandings of distinctions between the 'white' British 'indigenous' identity and black 'Third World' immigrants. In the Introduction to the book, it was noted how linguistically negative the English word 'foreigner' is. This term is used to racialise all non-British people, including other Europeans, and is particularly evident in the following extract from a lyric by the cabaret duo Flanders and Swann and which Lord Tebbitt, of the Conservative Party, used in 1995 to describe his version of 'Englishness':

> And crossing the channel one cannot say much
> For the French or the Spanish, the Danish or Dutch;
> The Germans are Germans, The Russians are red
> And the Greeks and Italians eat garlic in bed
> The English are moral, the English are good
> And clever and modest and misunderstood . . .

These national stereotypes may still reside in the 'Little England' that attempts to bring the 'ghost of Britain past' back to life and this is supplemented by the persisting British fear of immigration. In 1986, one tabloid headline read '3,000 Asians Flood Britain' just before new restrictions for visa applications were imposed. Margaret Thatcher appealed to this fear when she promised that she would not let Britain be 'swamped' by a different culture. The perception of a Third World tide of immigrants waiting to engulf Britain encourages a fortress understanding of Britain and the need to preserve its 'culture'. Meanwhile in 1997 John Major has given 50,000 wealthy Hong Kong citizens the right to settle in Britain when their country is handed over to Chinese rule. It is not surprising that blacks within

Britain have pointed to such policies as designed to limit the number of Asian and Afro-Caribbean immigrants to Britain.

The urban 'race riots' in the UK in 1981 and 1985 seemed to confirm many old-established fears. 'Why? Why? Why?' asked one tabloid headline, while another announced 'Black War On Police' after the riots that spread through the black neighbourhoods of Britain's major cities. However, these political actions were accompanied by a great deal of cultural innovation in music, film, photography, art and even sport. New black film (Isaac Julien), art (Chila Kumari Burman), photography (David A. Bailey), music (Soul II Soul) has celebrated cultural diversity and challenged the narrow ethnocentrism that characterised much of British cultural and intellectual life (see Figure 5.6, p. 235).

If we take up the example of sport, the Liverpool player John Barnes was the first black footballer to establish himself as an England star, and, despite the dominating presence of black players in Premier League football, remains the only regular black player in the national team. It is perhaps notable that he has maintained a complicated relationship to his 'Englishness' by maintaining his Jamaican passport despite his success. Frank Bruno, the heavyweight black boxer has in contrast remained closely connected to an idea of national representation in which his physical strength and modest, self-deprecating personality have caused him to be accepted as 'British'. Sport has in this sense been a way of reinforcing black stereotypes while at the same time providing more visibility for black people and hence a recognition of the 'multicultural' nature of modern Britain. However, the racial make-up of professional football, for example, is perhaps notable for its absence of representation from the largest 'black' group in Britain: the south Asians. A recent study shows that the most popular sport among young Asians is football even though there is only one Asian professional in the leagues. The survey further reveals that a significant majority of the professional football officials questioned believed that Asian footballers are physically inferior to other footballers. The generational rifts within these communities were shown when over half of the Asian footballers said that their parents actively discouraged them from playing. None the less, sport is an important field of visibility for black athletes and the presence of those like Ian Wright (football), Devon Malcolm (cricket), Jeremy Guscott (rugby) and Linford Christie, the 1992 Olympic 100 metres champion, does mean that sport does not equate England or Britain with a homogeneous 'white' culture.

Unsurprisingly, sport has also been a key cultural practice involving the Europeanising, Americanising or globalising processes that have further encouraged or complicated crises of British national identities. British teenagers can be seen wearing Italian football jerseys, as well as American baseball caps, while Italian soccer can be viewed three times a week on network television as can American football and, most recently, the National Basketball Association. The American magazine *Newsweek* recently claimed that Michael Jordan, the American basketball player, was the most popular athlete in Britain.

Official British culture has been slow to acknowledge multicultural identities, but as we have seen in this book, contemporary British people do not understand their identities in simple and singular ways. We must remember that while older collective identities have been eroded, new, perhaps more fluid identities form, and both British culture and British identities are today forged by mixtures of people and ethnic practices which only forty years ago would have been regarded as, in both senses, 'foreign'. The term 'British' will only survive as a worthwhile label of identity if it can be used to embrace all of these multicultural identities, while recognising and valuing the differences between them.

Technology and the future

The most certain thing to say about the future is that life will speed up. The pace of technological change is such that the young will be better equipped to deal with many aspects of the world of the twenty-first century than the middle-aged. Culture will change just as fast – films and CDs come and go in weeks, posters in days, sports events in afternoons, television programmes in hours, advertisements in minutes. Throughout this book, the contributors have offered some up-to-date suggestions for television programmes, videos, books and films which you should consider carefully in order to form your own understanding of Britain today – but with the rider that new images and practices, and consequently new cultural identities, will appear tomorrow. We have looked at two of the reasons for this – the spread of American culture and the growth of multicultural societies – but a third is the irresistible rise of the microchip.

The culture of the 1990s is increasingly delivered by new technologies. CD Rom, the internet, virtual reality, faxes, pagers and mobile phones have contributed to the increased access to knowledge and the simultaneous location of culture in the home. Of course, this technocultural literacy is not equally available to everyone and the 'active' techno identities of the superhighway are more to do with access to education and hardware than egalitarian opportunities. In fact, the most significant machine interventions in everyday lives remain the television, with its development of video plus 'interactive' game technology, and the car, which has not only contributed to the decline of British public transport but emits large amounts of pollution. Many thinkers anticipate that our future will be in the hands of a new technocracy with control over key communications technology. What is certain is that the speed of British culture will continue to accelerate, leading to more and increasingly shifting identities.

Currently about 300,000 British people log into the internet, but with marketing ploys by British Telecom and others, by the year 2000 there will be an estimated 2.5 million people with e-mail addresses in Britain. These cyberspace identities have been celebrated as network communities across the world proliferate and contribute to the speed and volume of information flow across unchecked national borders. While hackers and 'techno-nerds' have worked to open the network to individuals, new legislation and commercial initiatives will limit access to those who have 'paid', and the censorship of certain information on the internet seems likely.

Unfortunately, machines have not in recent decades reduced work hours, as predicted, but have contributed to unemployment, to the standardisation and privatisation of British culture, and to greater surveillance (a recent survey has suggested that the average British person appears on seven video surveillance cameras each day and recent legislation will mean that there are over two million surveillance cameras in place by the year 2000). On the one hand, individuals now have encyclopedias on CD Rom, huge libraries of information available to them over the internet, telephone banking, 'hole-in-the-wall' cash machines, faxes and mobile phones, computerised toys and appliances. But, on the other hand, private ownership and privatisation do not mean privacy and the technologies of surveillance through the internet and video camera systems developed by the Ministry of Defence, plus credit card information banks, mean that certain commercial and state centres of control are able to construct identity profiles that may be used to undermine individual and collective freedoms. These new possibilities of 'big brother' intrusions into private life mean that identities or 'i.d.s' are known and regulated in advance. Ironically, while the British will mock bureaucracy and administration, a poll in 1996 suggests that 70 per cent of the public support the new authoritarian measures, many of which include new technologies such as surveillance cameras, police use of CS gas and mandatory i.d. cards.

Significantly, most communication today is made via machines and the consequent decrease in direct human contact may contribute to new ideas of cultural identities generally and not just to the disappearance of traditional collective cultures. As this book's Introduction suggests, television is the main source of what can be called a common culture in Britain today. The 'box' dominates the living room of most British households and the onslaught of satellite and cable has meant that television culture can be accessed twenty-four hours every day. The use of new technologies by counter-cultures, like the videorecording of various injustices by 'eco-warriors', is currently overwhelmed by official technologies. Contemporary visions of the future by British people, from Ridley Scott's film *Bladerunner* to Jeff Noon's popular novel *Vurt* aim to reveal the abuses of technology by those in power. In these futures the division between nature and technology is even breaking up in the face of the possibility of cyborgs (part human, part machine). Many suggest that, alongside a global culture and a multicultural local community, it is within the boundaries of this techno-power that most cultural identities in the next millennium will be formed.

Conclusion

Recently, Dr Nick Tate, the Chief Executive of the School Curriculum and Assessment Authority, called for schools to teach 'British Cultural identity'. His claim was that 'true British culture' or 'majority culture' should be the fundamental aim of education rather than 'watered-down multiculturalism'. Central to his proposals were the English language, English history and literary heritage, the study of Christianity and the classical world, all of which he suggests is at the heart of our common culture and national identity. As we have seen, the proliferation of identities makes the assumption of such an identifiable stable culture impossible and not necessarily desirable. This rearguard action by the state is characterised by the persistent myth of a British past that is increasingly unhelpful as people recognise and experience the variety of the present. What is also important, however, is that the reconstruction of Britishness, while denying the 'new' cultural identities, recognises the significance of education in all cultural understanding.

In the title of this book, the plural term 'identities' has been used to indicate that Britain today is a very complex society made up of people from numerous backgrounds and traditions with hugely diverse interests, and this has been illustrated in most of the preceding chapters. In the Introduction were listed some attempts to define Britishness by choosing characteristics which people have traditionally thought of as typical – the kinds of things that films make use of: bowler hats, umbrellas and pinstripe suits (think of Steed in *The Avengers*), twin-sets and pearls (as worn by Vivienne Leigh), Scottish kilts (as in *Four Weddings and a Funeral*). These may be parts of a 'Britain that never was', but which some people like to think did exist.

In Britain today, partly because of the clash between the new diversity and a more traditional view of what it means to be British, there is division and dissent. But there is also creative tension. There is hope in the rapid accommodations that people have had to make towards one another and towards new ethnicities. Culture is probably both the most revolutionary and the most democratic arena in which expression and change can take place. So, particularly in areas of youth culture, people look to their peers, from diverse backgrounds, to help them produce cultural change.

It does seem that there are a number of conclusions that one can draw from this. Many things do not seem to have changed. Experienced market research pollsters can 'place' most people in the street by their physical appearance in age or occupation categories. Accent reveals more – people's regional and class origins, but also their present cultural allegiances. Telephone clerks for theatre ticket agencies claim that, before tickets are specified, they can tell from an accent which of twenty shows any particular caller will choose. There has also been a perceptible shift from a collective social ethic to an individualistic ethic in the 1980s. In modern Britain there is less emphasis on community than previously and people more often fight local and national issues for personal political reasons, than campaign along party lines. Although authority is under attack, it is responding by hardening its position in terms of both legislation and the treatment of, for example, road protesters. Many people are also disillusioned with such Establishment institutions as the monarchy, the Church and Parliament. Finally, while the work ethic is still in evidence, the rapid change in the types of skills that people must possess has made it more pressing than ever that they be adaptable and that they depend on forces other than work to establish their identities.

Alternatively, the most profound changes in Britain are to do with multiculturalism and the gradual, contested relaxing of boundaries in mainstream culture as a result, in areas as far apart as diet and sexuality. Avant-garde films like *The Crying Game* concentrate on 'race' and gender boundaries, but so do routine aspects of the fashion industry. Throughout Britain, culture is constantly changing and new identities are being formed by shifts in the accepted ways that roles have been assigned to people in terms of their gender, ethnicity, sexuality, age and class.

The Britain that contributors to this book have described is contemporary, post-industrial, multicultural and made up of many conflicting elements: stately homes and homeless youths; settled suburban people and New Age travellers; young evangelicals and old conservatives in religion; young radicals and Manor House Tories in politics – in other words, a Britain which is most of all diverse: composed of 'identities in Britain' as much as 'British identities'. Each of these alternative views supplies us with a 'version' of Britain which can masquerade as a 'whole' or inclusive portrayal. But, as we have seen, any of these single views is inflected with other considerations such as region, religion, education and profession. More than ever, it is misleading to suggest that there is, if there ever was, such a thing as a single British character or personality, rather than a variety of welcomingly different and potentially collaborative cultural identities.

READING

Bryson, Bill. *Notes from a Small Island*. Secker & Warburg, 1995
Successful American writer takes a journey around Britain and offers succinct, humorous accounts.

Chambers, Iain. *Popular Culture: The Metropolitan Experience*. Routledge, 1986
Academic's account of contemporary styles and urban practices, with particular attention paid to American influences.

Marling, Susan. *American Affair: The Americanisation of Britain.* Boxtree, 1993
Looks at the way people in Britain adopt American culture and towns like Milton Keynes imitate American lifestyles.

CULTURAL EXAMPLES

■ *Films*

Bladerunner (1982) dir. Ridley Scott
Dystopian sci-fi thriller by British director envisioning an overcrowded, post-industrial, multicultural, cyborg future with dialects that combine English, Spanish and Japanese (spanglish).

Chariots of Fire (1981) dir. Hugh Hudson
Nationalistic film about British athletes preparing for victory in the 1924 Olympic Games. It was hailed at the time as the flowering of a 'new' British cinema.

The Long Day Closes (1992) dir. Terence Davies
Poetic film about postwar British youth and the magic of American film and music as an escape from the brutalities of working-class existence in Liverpool.

Trainspotting (1996) dir. Danny Boyle
Shocking and funny tale of heroin addicts in Edinburgh based on the novel by Irvine Welsh.

Yanks (1979) dir. John Schlesinger
Reconstruction of desires and fears of the English about Americans stationed in England during the Second World War: its popularity shows how vivid this memory remains for some.

■ *Television programmes*

The Brittas Empire
Contemporary British pretensions are analysed through the situation of a small leisure centre and its eccentric manager, Gordon Brittas, in this successful comedy series.

East
BBC2 programme which covers important topics and events outside of EuroAmerica, usually from Asia.

Eurotrash
Self-consciously titillating look at the Continent by two French stars, one of them Jean-Paul Gaultier. Plays on stereotypes of national identity such as British prudery.

Gladiators
Copied from an American style, this blend of wrestling and showbiz presentation has been a staple of Saturday evening viewing for several years.

■ *Books*

Martin Amis, *Money* (1989)
Novel dealing with excesses of 1980s culture in Britain and America with a protagonist appropriately named John Self.

Victor Headley, *Yardie* (1992)
Jamaican gangster pulp fiction set in 1990s Hackney, London. The novel looks at the postwar Afro-Caribbean immigrant experience in conjunction with the transnational drugs economy.

Jeff Noon, *Vurt* (1993)
Novel set in a grim, comic Manchester of the future. In a world peopled by vurt, robo and dog beings, gangs escape cops through the use of cyber-technology.

Will Self, *My Idea of Fun* (1993)
Influenced by American beat writers, this first novel looks at the dark, funny and fantastic side of British suburban life.

■ *Music*

Blur, *Parklife* (1994)
Pastiche of British pop rock tradition.

Goldie, *Timeless* (1995)
Key album in the rise of 'Jungle' music.

Linton Kwesi Johnson – *Linton Kwesi Johnson* (1985)
The original and best of the dub-poets: black Caribbean creole dialect with powerful radical politics.

M-People, *Bizarre Fruit* (1994)
British Northern soul dance music.

Neneh Cherry, *Neneh Cherry* (1988)
'Black' Anglo-American-Swedish hip-hop feminism.

Soul II Soul, *1990 (A New Decade)*
Fusion of many diasporic styles particularly hip-hop, dub and dance soul.

Tricky, *Maxinquaye* (1994)
Part of new haunting hip-hop informed synthesised Bristol sound.

FIGURE 8.1 A McDonald's restaurant in Lancashire

FIGURE 8.2 Young Asian people shopping in Bolton

FIGURE 8.3 A cybercafé

Glossary

Instead of a set of exercises and questions for the Conclusion, we have noted down the following outlines of twenty keywords that have been used throughout the book. We would like you to use these as starting points for thinking about each of the terms, but also as comprising an elementary glossary to which you may want, perhaps with the aid of a dictionary and other books, to add your own terms and short definitions.

Accent is the inflection given to, and modulation of, speech. It mainly indicates social class and should be distinguished from both *dialect* which is a combination of accent intonation and local vocabulary and indicates region, and *slang* which is the use of ungrammatical English among people in the same generational/gender groupings.

Acronyms are examples of compression in an accelerating culture. Adopted widely in the 1980s to describe new social and cultural phenomena included: YUPPIEs (Young Urban Professionals); DINKIEs (Dual Income No Kiddies); NIMBYs (people in favour of, say, gypsy sites but: Not In My Back Yard). Mrs Thatcher was nicknamed

TINA (There Is No Alternative). BOHECA (Bend Over Here Comes Another) was common in the National Health Service, referring to non-stop initiatives and reforms imposed on people. The word WRINKLY, applied to an old person, is not an acronym.

Consumerism is the idea that consumption, not production is the basis of capitalist society. Hence 'market forces' and 'value for money' can be brought into all aspects of public life. There are three stages of consumerism: goods, services (television entertainment/pizza delivery), and experience (aerobics programmes/travel).

Diaspora means literally a 'dispersal' of people and originally referred to the Jews. So it denotes, for example, Irish/West Indian/Asian communities, with common roots yet living in different parts of the world.

Drug culture is an alternative way of life which has produced a range of terminology for drugs. Heroin is 'smack'; cocaine is 'crack'; marijuana/cannabis is 'grass', 'hash'[ish], 'shit', 'slate'. Addicts are 'smack-heads', etc.

The Establishment is a neutral term for the people who are traditionally believed to run Britain – the landed aristocracy, hereditary peers, long-established business interests ('The Beerage'). Alan Clark uses it to distinguish those members of the Conservative Party who represent an old guard, as distinguished from those who currently hold political power.

Estuary English is a form of speech distinguished from 'received pronunciation' or 'proper English'. For example, 'regimental' is pronounced 'regimen'au'. 'It'll' becomes 'i'uw'. Identified in 1984 by David Rosewarne, Estuary English supplies speakers from different social backgrounds with a means of camouflaging their origins, whether cockney or public school. For example, it is commonly used by traders in London's money markets.

Gender is a division into masculine/feminine which is socially constructed – as opposed to the male/female distinction of sex, which is biologically determined.

Generation X is from Douglas Coupland's novel *Generation X Tales for an Accelerated Culture*. It identifies and defines a group of consumers born between 1964 and 1969. They appear alienated from the values of their affluent parents (Baby Boomers) by their own uncertain prospects, but the difference may be to do with style. They are also known as Busters or Slackers. They welcome the internet, quirky advertising, grunge fashion and the idea of defining themselves.

Grunge was a term used by mid-1980s rock journalists to describe a confrontational form of hard rock music. Despite its overtones of squalor and dirt it has come to describe a particular fashion look – one which is deliberately not smart.

Hegemony, from the Greek word for leadership, refers to a cluster of ideas, practices and connections which enable a small group of people to retain dominance. Formulation of the concept is associated with Antonio Gramsci.

Heritage has overtones of 'inheritance' and is about the transmission of traditional values. It is intended to be a dynamic outgrowth of static 'museum' culture and to indicate concern for the physical and historical environment. Since the 1980s Britain has had a Heritage Secretary. Some see it as just another contender in the struggle between ideologically opposed versions to 'officially' fix British cultural identity. It is thus an aspect of theme-park Britain.

Hybridity is mixing different styles of fashion, music or anything else in order to come up with a better synthesis. Within this fusion the originals (with their conflicting messages) can sometimes still be detected. Thus BBC television's 1990s Jane Austen series might place a more feminist overlay on the original texts.

Laddism is a male culture which may be seen as a reaction to the idea of the caring, sensitive 'new man' produced by the feminist movement. So laddism is characterised by a climate of rough behaviour, excessive drinking ('lager louts') and all-male attendance at soccer matches.

Moral panics are periodic bouts of hysteria, where the media (particularly the tabloid press) whip up national feeling about issues which have existed all along but have lacked the 'oxygen of publicity'. Recent examples would be: chaining of pregnant prisoners; teenage use of the drug Ecstasy, 'social security scrounging'.

New Age is a broad term devised to describe the renewal of interest from the mid-1980s onwards in a range of approaches to the spiritual dimension which emphasise the individual's ability to discover and develop their own spirituality. The term comes from astrology: every 2000 years the solar system enters a new age, the next one being the age of Aquarius (the sign of individualism). Influences are yoga and t'ai chi. It is associated with alternative culture: the occult, tarot, astrology and hippy lifestyles. Most visible elements are New Age travellers and the Donga Tribe.

Outing is the practice of publicly declaring someone to be homosexual. It has been used in particular to identify the sexual orientation of, for example, an Anglican bishop who opposes the ordination of homosexual clergy. Its use is controversial within the gay community.

Pagan was originally someone who doesn't believe in a God, but is now a New Age movement which aims to re-create links with nature. Its adherents may practise tree-sniffing and ritual drumming and believe in the mind-expanding potential of drug use.

Protestant work ethic is the idea that people must take responsibility for their own destinies and therefore not rely on others to support them but must work for themselves to 'justify their existence'. Robinson Crusoe exemplifies a robust self-sufficient practitioner.

Steaming is the practice by gangs of urban youths, mostly aged 13 to 17, of staging mass lightning-speed robberies, for example, in underground trains or building societies.

Subculture refers to both alternative culture and to individual groups operating separately from mainstream society. It often refers to rival gangs, for example, Mods and Rockers, Skinheads and Bovver Boys or Punks, but it also refers to groupings of (mainly young) people with gentler outlooks: New Romantics (from Spandau Ballet); Goths (based on Gothic Rock) and Crusties.

Theme park is an American concept, popularised by Disney and based on re-creations of fantasy worlds. It replaces the previous generation's seaside piers and amusement arcades. Popular British examples are Alton Towers, Madame Tussaud's and Camelot. The expression 'theme-park' Britain has been applied to attempts to package a slick, plastic, idealised and sanitised version of Britain's past. It is sold to foreign and domestic tourists and sustains various hegemonic interests. Traditional versions of Britain have been seen as engaged in this process. Castle banquets at Ruthin (Wales) and Bunratty (Ireland) are part of it, as are stately homes and such industrial archaeology sites as Styal Woollen Mill or Llechwedd Slate Mines.

Upstairs/Downstairs represents the idea of Britain as 'two nations': masters and servants. Particularly in Edwardian Britain, servants lived in the basements of houses and owners on the upper floors. This division was reflected in respective power relations. The concept was revived by a popular TV series of that name.

Wicca is modern witchcraft as practised by New Age. Its practices include herbalism, divination and psychic healing. Partly because of its worship of a 'Great Goddess' it has attracted many feminists looking for alternatives to Christianity and Judaism.

NOTES

Index